American Silence

Amer

S

UNIVERSITY OF NEBRASKA PRESS • LINCOLN AND LONDON

Zeese Papanikolas

ican

ilence

© 2007 by the Board of Regents of the
University of Nebraska ¶ All rights re-
served ¶ Manufactured in the United States
of America ¶ ⊗ ¶ Library of Congress
Cataloging-in-Publication Data ¶
Papanikolas, Zeese.
American silence / Zeese Papanikolas.
p. cm.
Includes bibliographical references and
index.
ISBN-13: 978-0-8032-3756-8 (cloth : alk. paper)
ISBN-10: 0-8032-3756-1 (cloth : alk. paper)
1. United States—Civilization. 2. West
(U.S.)—Civilization. 3. National char-
acteristics, American. 4. United States—
Intellectual life. 5. Silence in literature.
6. Silence in art. 7. Failure (Psychology)—
Case studies. 8. United States—Biography—
Anecdotes. 9. Authors, American—
Biography—Anecdotes. 10. Artists—United
States—Biography—Anecdotes. I. Title.
E169.1P215 2007
973.902—dc22
2006027323

¶ Set in Minion. ¶ Designed by R. W.
Boeche.

For Demetrios, Cleo, Eleni, and Tony

Table of Contents

Illustrations

George Caleb Bingham (American, 1811–79), *Fur Traders Descending the Missouri* (1845). Oil on canvas, 29 in. x 36 ½ in. Metropolitan Museum of Art, Morris K. Jesup Fund, 1933 (33.61). Photograph © 1992 The Metropolitan Museum of Art.

Few people even know the true definition of the term "West"; and where is its location?—phantom-like it flies before us as we travel.

George Catlin

Overture
The Unpaintable West

What do these figures mean? An old man, a boy, a bear cub chained to the prow of a pirogue floating downstream on a calm river in some golden morning of a past that no longer has a history.

They gaze at us. The boy leans on a skin-covered box that holds what we think is the cache of furs, his chin rests on his hand, a gun is under one arm, a mallard he has shot beside him. His face is dreamy, sweet. The old man glares at us. The smoke from his short pipe drifts behind him. The bear looks at us with the dumb stare of animals that we can neither enter nor interpret. The reflections extend themselves from the bottom of the boat, lose their outlines in the smooth water.

Because of the reflections we don't know if the painter George Caleb Bingham saw them or simply imagined them.

STILLNESS

The report from the boy's gun has stopped reverberating. The hole it has made in the morning has closed. Everything is still. Mist blurs the lines between sky and tree-lined shore and water. Or maybe sky and shore and water are only now forming themselves in that gold of a morning, composing themselves out of this stillness.

The river will run beyond the frame the canvas has made of this moment.[1] Flow on down to the shanties along the wharves of St. Louis, to the cheap hotels and eating houses, the dives and the river women. For now we have only the stillness.

Yet a tension remains underneath the painting's resolution. The snags, the chained animal, the disturbing glare of the old man evoke an unpainted presence at the edges of the canvas. Rivers come from somewhere, too. And so, in order to tell one story, I will begin with another.

THE GREAT UNKNOWN

In the fall of 1804, where the Knife River flows into the Missouri in the present state of North Dakota, the American explorers Meriwether Lewis and William Clark reached the earth lodges of the Mandan Indians. It was here, among these friendly farmers and buffalo hunters, that they would stay through the winter, preparing for the expedition into the great unknown, to the Missouri headwaters and across the divide into the waters of the Columbia and, they hoped, as far as the Pacific Coast. They had reached the edge of an imaginary landscape. Beyond the Mandans there were only things they had heard tell of. The Stony Mountains. The river they called, after the French, the Rochejhone. Another river called the Oregon or River of the West that mapmakers thought would provide the long-sought Inland Passage to India. For everything was conjecture.

That spring, with a complement of picked men, a store of medicines and trade goods for the Indians, a collapsible boat, Clark's slave York, a French-Canadian translator named Toussaint Charbonneau, Charbonneau's young Shoshone wife, and the son that had been born to her that winter, Lewis and Clark set out from the Mandan lodges. They would see the rivers feeding into the Missouri, the Little Missouri, the Rochejhone, the River That Scolds All Others. The Rocky Mountains. Finally, the Columbia itself. And then the Pacific Ocean.

Their project was to make the imaginary landscape real. So at every opportunity they measured, they observed, they drew. And they wrote. Always they wrote. In sandstorms, attacked by mosquitoes, weakened from dysentery, bitten by fleas, cold, hungry, they wrote. They wrote when the ink froze in their pens. And when the expedition ended in St. Louis two and a third years after it set out, after the balls and the dinners and the speeches, they were still writing.[2]

Constantly running through the journals, with their careful descriptions of new animal and plant life, of the Indians and their habits, of the geography of new plains and mountains and the rivers that fed the great Missouri, is the theme of wonder.

It was the essential purpose of the expedition to describe this wonder. Sitting in skin or earth lodges or under the open sky, the whites and the Indians interrogated each other through the medium of maps, a kind of language beyond words. Maps smudged with charcoal from the fire on elk skins or on reed mats or traced with sticks in the sand, embedded with the Indians' memories of cold and heat, of hungry bivouacs and plains plentiful with meat, of sights seen at eye level and canoe level and from the backs of their ponies. Then William Clark dipped his quill in ink, and drew the symbols on a page of his journal, coordinating what he had seen with his observations of the planets and the stars. Thus the American captains knew where they were, and whence they had come.

Or did they? For they were entering a world of such strangeness that once, Meriwether Lewis, hunting on the Medicine River, pursued by bear and buffalo, missing shots at a bobcat, thought it might be a dream. (The spines of prickly pear, jabbing into the soles of his feet through his moccasins, reminded him it wasn't.)[3] Always they matched what they had faintly heard, told by Indians to other Indians, then translated through the French Canadians, with what they saw. And always what they saw was new.

Meriwether Lewis at the Great Falls of the Missouri:

> *After wrighting this imperfect discription I again viewed the falls and was so much disgusted with the imperfect idea which it conveyed of the scene that I determined to draw my pen across it and begin agin, but then reflected that I could not perhaps succeed better than pening the first impressions of the mind; I wished for the pencil of Salvator Rosa or the pen of Thompson, that I might be enabled to give to the enlightened world some just idea of this truly magnifficent and sublimely grand object, which has from*

the commencement of time been concealed from the view of civilized man; but this was fruitless and vain. I most sincerely regretted that I had not brought a crimee [camera] obscura with me by the assistance of which even I could have hoped to have done better but alas this was also out of my reach.[4]

Butifull. Grand. Sublime. Specticle. Confronting the magnitude of this new landscape, the language of observation gives way to the poetics of the late eighteenth century. Even Clark, the less literary of the two captains, called one scene of river and ravines *romantick*.[5]

There is always, for the reader, a special poignancy in these journals. For if we see these scenes through the eyes of Meriwether Lewis and William Clark, we see them as well with our own: the poignancy of these first views of wonder, of the first meetings with tribes who had never seen a white man before, is that they are doomed at the moment of their telling. It will never be new again.

THE BEAUTIFUL AND THE SUBLIME

To name something means to have it in your power. Meditating on his recent discoveries at the Great Falls of the Missouri, Lewis compares two scenes:

Nor could I for some time determine on which of those two great cataracts [Colter Falls and Rainbow Falls] to bestoe the palm, on this [Colter Falls] or that which I had discovered yesterday; at length I determined between these two great rivals for glory that this was pleasingly beautifull, while the other was sublimely grand.[6]

In adopting the categories of eighteenth-century aesthetics to describe this landscape, Lewis sets up a dialectic that has, implicit in its terms, a meditation on power.

The sublime, that reminder of the awesome grandeur of God, of the littleness and contingency of man, cannot be possessed. Indeed, the sublime possesses you. The author of the sublime is the virile god who engraves the words of the laws with his finger on the tables of stone: to gaze on the terrible infinite without the mediation of a prophet or the veil of aesthetic distance is to perish. It is only beauty that can be gazed upon without such distanc-

4

ing. And beauty, for Edmund Burke, who fixed these terms for his generation, is above all things feminine.

> *Observe that part of a beautiful woman where she is perhaps the most beautiful, about the neck and breasts; the smoothness; the softness; the easy and insensible swell; the variety of the surface, which is never for the smallest space the same; the deceitful maze, through which the unsteady eye slides giddily, without knowing where to fix, or whither it is carried.*[7]

To gaze on the beautiful is to possess it. But, says Burke—and the statement is surprising—it is not commonly imagined how near love approaches to contempt.[8]

Meriwether Lewis and William Clark came to the great unknown to map, to describe, to name. Because they came as men of science, and, when they were overcome by splendor, as poets, they did not defile what they saw, but the very naming of that wonder, in its innocence and joy, began the process of its destruction. After an arduous trek across the divide, and in the midst of the dangerous descent of the rapids of the Columbia, a few miles below The Dalles, the captains saw an Indian wearing a sailor hat and jacket with his hair tied up in a queue. In a village a few miles farther on, they found a British musket, a cutlass and several brass tea kettles.[9] Beyond the falls of the Columbia they met an inscription in their own language. It was the name *J. Bowmon* tattooed on the arm of an Indian woman.[10] Already they had begun to hear a few words of English from the Indians. When they reached the coast they would hear more: *musquit, powder, shot, nife, file, damned rascal, sun of a bitch.*[11] Lewis, the soldier, knew very well what Burke had meant about love and contempt. When the Wahkiakum women of the lower Columbia knelt, their cedar bark aprons parted, and what the Americans called the "battery of Venus" was "not altogether impervious to the penetrating eye of the amorite."[12] In his stores of medical supplies Meriwether Lewis carried four pewter penis syringes.[13]

THE PHILOSOPHE

In the mind of Thomas Jefferson were stately rooms: busts of Newton, Bacon and Locke, fiddles, gadgets, cabinets of curiosities, labor-saving devices, libraries of books, porches opening to graceful gardens, and well-ordered fields. Around this rural hive of elegance and learning were the farms tilled by free white yeomen, the independent farmers who were the foundation of democracy, a bulwark against the polyglot rabble of the city. The farms fell off into a contested frontier of rough pioneers, distillers of whiskey, breakers of raw land, and then, beyond the Mississippi, into a vast unknown. Because he was a man of the Enlightenment, Reason shone its ray into the unknown. And so from his vast reading Jefferson filled this emptiness beyond the Mississippi with smoking volcanoes and mountains of pure salt, with the lumbering forms of Mammoths and Giant Sloths (in the great chain of being there were no links missing, no final extinctions). And somewhere there was a passage that would open the new republic to its destiny on the shores of the Pacific, and that little strip of coast, just beginning to be known to English and American sea captains, where the Columbia emptied into the Pacific.

But always, in the imaginary landscapes of Jefferson's mind, were the Indians, the aboriginal peoples of the land. Unlike the slaves who lurked about the margins of his ideal landscape (some of whom were his secret children), a troubling cloud passing across the sunny clarity of Jefferson's thought, complicating its moral scheme, the Indians were interesting. Eloquent, capable of intellectual motion. Like other Virginia planters there was a twig for Pocahontas on his family tree. For the Indians, too, he had a place.

So, like white sachems before him, Jefferson sent out medals and certificates and gifts—glass beads and kettles and fishhooks and blankets—and men in blue coats and brass buttons to announce that the Indian peoples of the new land had a new father. A loving and kindly father, indeed, whose other face was coercion, displacement, threat. Settled on their neat farms in that American pastoral that was Jefferson's dream, blending and perhaps intermarrying with whites whose habits they had adopted and whose religion they now shared, these settled Indians (they would be in debt to the white traders) would have much land to sell. And if the red men would not civilize themselves and would not sell, well, as Jefferson pointed out to William Henry Harrison, on the Indiana frontier, the other side of love was fear.

We presume that our strength and their weakness is now so visible that they must see we have only to shut our hand to crush them, and that all our liberalities to them proceed from motives of pure humanity only. Should any tribe be fool-hardy enough to take up the hatchet at any time, the seizing the whole country of that tribe, and driving them across the Mississippi, as the only condition of peace, would be an example to others, and a furtherance to our final consolidation.[14]

Having ripped ourselves from the terrible grasp of Mother England, it remained to conquer Mother Nature and her red children.

The light of Reason that emanated from Jefferson's study made its way across the far reaches of the Missouri watershed, sought an opening through the Stony Mountains, pushed on to the Western Sea: there, at the edge of the continent, in November of 1805 a handful of American soldiers, a few French-Canadian and French-Indian hunters, a Shoshone Indian woman, and a slave voted on where to make their winter quarters.

COMING HOME

O! how horriable is the day   waves brakeing with great violence against the Shore throwing the Water into our Camp &c. all wet and Confined to our Shelters.

William Clark, November 22, 1805[15]

The rain Contines, with Tremendious gusts of wind, which is Tremds ... The winds violent   Trees falling in every derection, whorl winds, with gusts of rain Hail & Thunder, this kind of weather lasted all day, Certainly one of the worst days that ever was!

William Clark, December 16, 1805[16]

It rained all winter long. Rain and more rain in the huddle of shelters they built inside a stockade on the banks of the Lewis and Clark, and the horrible roaring of the waves on the seacoast and the fleas and the poor elk and the miserable Indians with their flattened heads squatting like frogs around them, smoking and farting and clucking their untranslatable language and the smoke stinging their eyes and the clothes rotting and the blankets rot-

7

ting and the damp and the eternal rain. The captains' store of trinkets had shrunk to a few handfuls and the Indians were unimpressed with the merchandise. They higgled for days over a handful of roots.[17]

Since the expedition's start Sacagawea had been feeding the men, finding stores of wild artichokes the mice had hidden in the earth, probing for roots with a digging stick, discovering wild licorice, white apples, wild currants. Medicinal plants for the men who were constantly sick with malnourishment and bad water and spoiled food.

When the vote was taken about the expedition's winter quarters, Clark noted in his tally "Janey in favour of a place where there is plenty of Potas."[18] Somewhere along the route he had taken to calling Sacagawea Janey. The "Potas"—potatoes—were the wapato roots that would become the expedition's staple. Later that November Sacagawea gave Clark a piece of bread made from flour she had been saving for her child. It was the first bread he had had for months. The flour had gotten wet and the bread was sour. Clark found it delicious.

At Christmas the captains distributed meager gifts: tobacco for the men who smoked, a handkerchief for those who didn't. Lewis gave Clark a shirt, drawers, socks. Another of the men gave him a small basket. Sacagawea gave him two dozen weasel tails. That spring she had fallen deathly ill and the captains had doctored her, and once, when Charbonneau had struck her, Clark had intervened. She had not forgotten him.

On the sixth of January, Clark set out with a party in two canoes to see a whale that had been reported washed up at the seashore and perhaps take some of its flesh. About the time Clark was making his way to the sea coast, on the other side of the continent, Thomas Jefferson, the president of the United States, composed a letter to his children the Cherokees, who had lately visited him, about the virtues of the settled life that they had begun to take up. Already the Cherokees had made much progress. They would need corn mills (Jefferson insisted on these); then they would need laws. Then they would need judges . . . Jefferson sat in his study thinking of virtuous Cherokees: at Fort Clatsop one of the expedition's men came near having his throat cut by an Indian who wanted to rob him. On the same day Lewis reported that Clark had reached the great beached whale and found that the Indians had stripped it of every edible part and left nothing but a vast skeleton.[19] On the twenty-third of March, the corps of volunteers for North Western Discovery started for home.

8

Near the end of their journey, after more than two years of hardship in the wilderness, of near starvation, of clothes that rotted on their backs in the endless rain, and forced marches and broken pirogues and back-breaking portages, they met, west of the Mandan villages where they spent their first winter, two trappers from Illinois who talked John Colter, who would become (perhaps) the first white man to see the Yellowstone geysers, into turning back up the river from whence he'd come on a trapping expedition.[20] Henceforth, known, the Wilderness was ready to be exploited.

JOURNEY'S END

By the fourteenth of August 1806, the Lewis and Clark expedition had returned to the Mandan villages. Six days later, while floating down the Missouri, Clark took the time to write Charbonneau. There is a poignant urgency in the letter. Clark was urgent for Sacagawea's security, and for the future of her boy. Clark goes on to offer Charbonneau a piece of land, horses, cows, and hogs if he wishes to live with white people, a horse if he wants to visit his friends in Montreal. He offers much more. He concludes the letter:

> Wishing you and your family great suckcess & with anxious expectations of seeing my little danceing boy Baptiest I shall remain your Friend
> WILLIAM CLARK[21]

On the shores of the Pacific, Sacagawea had taken bread from her child and given it to Clark. Now, floating back to the civilization of St. Louis, he remembered her and the boy. Clark was no longer a child in the wilderness, but its conqueror.

What Clark so urgently wished came to pass. In 1808 Sacagawea and Charbonneau brought the boy to Clark in St. Louis.[22] There Charbonneau tried and failed to settle. We see the last of Sacagawea in the summer of 1811. A journalist on his way up the Missouri to Fort Manuel found himself on the fur company steamer with her and Charbonneau.

> The woman, a good creature, of a mild and gentle disposition, was greatly attached to the whites, whose manners and airs she tries to imitate; but she had become sickly and longed to revisit her native

country; her husband also, who had spent many years amongst the Indians, was become weary of a civilized life.[23]

As it happened she was going upriver to die. On December 20, 1812, a Missouri Fur Company clerk at Fort Manuel noted in his journal the death from putrid fever of Charbonneau's Snake squaw. "She was a good and the best Women in the fort, aged about 25 years she left a fine infant girl."[24] Once, importunate, she had demanded to go with the canoes to the Great Water that she had traveled so long to see, and a great fish washed up on its shore. Six years later, dressed in a white woman's clothes, she had died between the world she had been born into and the one she helped create.

Toussaint Charbonneau accompanied a few expeditions, and translated for Maximilian of Wied on the upper Missouri in 1833–34. One story has him going off with the notorious Edward Rose and trading with the Shoshones for a group of captive Arapaho women with the idea of selling them as wives to the *engagés* of the trading posts along the Missouri.[25] In 1838, at the age of seventy-one, Charbonneau married once more. The girl was a captive Assiniboin of fourteen. There is an account of the magnificent chivaree the men of Fort Clark gave him, with drums, pans, kettles all beating and guns firing. The old man went to bed with his young wife, the fort's clerk wrote, "with the intention of doing his best."[26]

What he was, he remained: profane, half-savage, a lover of women, a good hand with boudin. He could live no other way. Charbonneau died penniless sometime between that final marriage and 1843. It is he or his ghost that stares out at us in Bingham's canvas, brutal, tough, smoking his short pipe, having seen things upriver and in St. Louis perhaps better left unsaid.

And what of the boy, his son? Baptiste, or Pomp as Clark would call him, was taken in by Clark and educated in St. Louis at Catholic schools. Then he turned to the life of the hunter. He might have been a figure out of a romance: the free-spirited child of nature who turns his back on civilization and its charms and returns to the forest. At the age of eighteen, he met young Duke Paul of Württemberg in a traders' village at the mouth of the Kansas. He went to Europe with the duke for six years, learning a smattering of languages and fathering with the daughter of a soldier a child who died in infancy. By 1829 he was back in the West. He was at the famous rendezvous of 1833 on the Green River. In 1846, with the coming of the Mexican war, he became a guide for the Mormon Battalion. With the war's end he became alcalde of the Mission San Luis Rey, where he was, according to some reports, a harsh judge of the Indians. But his portion of white blood could not insulate him from suspicion of that portion that was Indian, and he resigned. And the frontier shrank around him. He went north with the gold fever of '48. The Placer County, California, Directory of 1861 lists him as a clerk in an Auburn hotel, another bit of humanity left beached with the end of the gold rush. In the spring of 1866, he went gold hunting again, and died of pneumonia in eastern Oregon after crossing a swollen stream on the way to Montana.[27]

Meriwether Lewis had long been dead, killed, probably by his own hand, in a tavern on the Natchez Trace in 1809. William Clark, more successful in his life and in his death, died in 1838. Jefferson, who had sent them to map the great unknown, had died in 1826. He had not lived to see his children the industrious Cherokees driven from their farms and settlements down the Trail of Tears, and could not guess the hard terms the exploitation of the wilderness he had helped open to white settlement would impose on the future of the land.

DESTINY

Forty years after Lewis and Clark arrived at the Pacific, when Bingham painted *Fur Traders Descending the Missouri*, the land that the Corps of Discovery had mapped had been crisscrossed by white trappers and empire builders. The Osage warrior who lurked above the river Bingham had painted as *Fur Trader*'s pendant had become a nostalgic reminder of a savage past. It is as if, in the rush of commerce, Osage warriors had simply become irrelevant. The fur trade had entered its long decline. The streams that flowed down from the Rockies had been trapped out and much of the game had been driven off. In Europe the fashion in gentlemen's hats had changed from beaver to silk. The last rendezvous of the fur trappers had been held in 1840.[28] Smallpox, introduced by the fur company steamer, had made of the lodges of the friendly Mandan, where Lewis and Clark had spent the winter of 1804–5, one vast desolation. "The scene was horrible," an eyewitness wrote Albert Gallatin in about 1837, "the large level prairie surrounding the Village had been converted into one great grave yard, whilst hundreds of (loathsome) carcasses ...

lay mouldering on the surface of the earth, emitting fetid exhalations which poisoned the surrounding atmosphere—and made it quite sickening even at a distance of several miles. . . . Thirty one Mandans only were living at the time I passed their villages."[29] Soon the buffalo on which the plains tribes' way of life depended would be virtually gone as well, killed by hide hunters and contract hunters for the railroads and by U.S. policy and by the Indians themselves. George Catlin, who had traveled through the West and painted its native peoples, heard of a large band of Sioux who arrived at a fur company fort with the tongues of 1,400 freshly slaughtered buffalo. They traded the tongues for a few gallons of whisky.[30]

THE USES OF NOSTALGIA

The friendly and flowing savage, who is he?
Is he waiting for civilization, or past it and mastering it?

Walt Whitman, *Song of Myself*

Perhaps, we think, it is something like this the old man in Bingham's painting has seen; for he stares out at us with a look of suspicion, bitterness. He looks out of a past and into our future, into Bingham's future as well, for by the time the painting was made such pirogues were a rarity on the Missouri, and even the great rafts that Bingham was to paint, ornamented with dancing raftsmen and raffish idlers, were already being supplanted by steamboats with their churning paddle wheels and fire-belching boilers.

Yet Bingham, the Whig who painted campaign banners for the Indian fighter William Henry Harrison (if the stories are true, at the Battle of the Thames Harrison's army inscribed his victory over Tecumseh on a different sort of canvas—the flayed skin of the Indian leader) and who had campaigned for steamboats and railroads and Henry Clay, painted this sour old man, this chained bear. Painted them, but placed between them, as if to link them and to pacify the terrible aggressions that they stood for, a boy.

Did such a boy belong there at all? He is of a different order than the man and the bear. He wears the same gaudy cloth shirt as his father, but the fringed leather pants of the savage world. The chained bear cub at the other end of the pirogue stands for a part of nature that has been subjugated, bounded, named. The boy is both the chained bear cub and the white man's son. Posed between two gazes, the numb gaze of nature that only exists, only suffers and the gaze of his father, the gaze of history and consciousness, he dreams. The gun loosens in his grasp. He is a figure from the pastoral, from the historyless world of myth, where time is stilled.

Remove the boy from the painting. It becomes a different thing. Paradoxical. Disturbing. The old man's glare becomes a question (look more closely and the glare itself is only the line of the mustache, the mouth beneath is sorrowful). Silhouetted against that soft, golden sky the bear becomes ominous, his shadow doubles him, hangs darkly from the waterline of the heavily laden boat. Everything is a dissonance, the figures at either end of the boat pull away from each other. A chained animal and a bitter old man.

Bingham's original title for the painting, *French Trader and His Half-Breed Son*, confirms what we have known about the old man and the boy from our first view of the painting. But there is something unpainted here, an absence. If we see a father and son in the pirogue, where is the boy's mother?

Bingham might have painted her. She might have been another version of the coy and sentimental Indian maiden of Alfred Jacob Miller's *Trapper's Bride*.[31] ("I saw the marriage of the trapper in the open air in the far / west," Walt Whitman wrote, in the same vein; "the bride was a red girl . . . / She had long eyelashes, her head was bare, her coarse straight / locks descended upon her voluptuous limbs and reach'd / to her feet.")[32] But Bingham does not paint her. Her absence calls up a deeper resonance, more complicated, and more disturbing.[33]

"I believe," wrote Alexis de Tocqueville in 1835, "that the Indian nations of North America are doomed to perish, and that whenever the Europeans shall be established on the shores of the Pacific Ocean, that race of men will have ceased to exist. The Indians had only the alternative of war or civilization; in other words, they must either destroy the Europeans or become their equals."[34]

But, of course, the Indians, as Tocqueville could well foresee, could neither destroy the Europeans nor become their equals. Thus the Indian woman, who makes the missing third of this family, is necessarily unpaintable. To give that missing Indian mother in the Bingham painting the presence she demands calls up all too well her claim to this wilderness out of which the trappers have come, and the furs they have ransacked from it; calls up the bloodshed of war for the land, the forced removals, the endless lies of treaties. But, perhaps more disturbing, the presence of the Indian woman would call up the longing for her, the joining of two races and the annihilation, in this act, of the boundary between civilized man and savage. Longing for that lost maternal world of nature that the Indian woman represented could turn into the nightmare fear of being devoured by it. Tocqueville quotes Louis XIV's governor of Canada:

> It has long been believed that in order to civilize the savages we ought to draw them nearer to us. But there is every reason to suppose we have been mistaken. Those that have been brought into contact with us have not become French, and the French who have lived among them are changed into savages, affecting to dress and live like them.[35]

Woe to them that have trespassed against God and taken strange wives of the people of the land.[36] That way lay the savage white Indian loitering on the margins of civilization, bearing within his drink-sodden form a wilderness of panic, disorder, and the linguistic chaos of a desperate pidgin.[37] "It is to be feared," wrote Washington Irving in *Astoria*, "that a great part of [the West] will form a lawless interval between the abodes of civilized men."

> Here may spring up new and mongrel races, like new formations in geology, the amalgamation of the "debris" and "abrasions" of former races, civilized and savage, the remains of broken and almost extinguished tribes; the descendants of wandering hunters and trappers; of fugitives from the Spanish and American frontiers; of adventurers and desperadoes of every class and country, yearly ejected from the bosom of society into the wilderness.[38]

We might have held up to the world the figures of eminent mixed-race leaders such as John Ross of the Cherokees, but instead we showed it Walt Whitman's Half-Breed and Poe's bestial Dirk Peters.

"Child of the two races," Tocqueville wrote, "brought up in the use of two languages, nourished in diverse beliefs and cradled in contrary prejudices, the half-breed forms a composite as inexplicable to others as to himself."

The images of the world, when they come to reflect themselves in his rude brain, appear to him only a tangled chaos from which his spirit could not extricate itself. Proud of his European origin, he despises the wilderness, and yet he loves the savage freedom which reigns there; he admires civilization and is unable to submit himself completely to its empire. His tastes are in contradiction with his ideas, his opinions with his ways. Not knowing how to guide himself by the doubtful light which illumines him, his soul struggles painfully in the web of universal doubt: he adopts contrary usages, he prays at two altars, he believes in the Redeemer of the world and the amulettes of the charlatan, and he reaches the end of his career without having been able to untangle the obscure problem of his existence.[39]

So that sexual and romantic longing for unspoiled nature must remain as it always is in the pastoral, but must remain unspecified. Generalized. A longing for connection with a feminine landscape that was, in fact, being ravaged, whose innocence, the theme of Bingham's painting, had been destroyed.

This missing, maternal nature is the world of the river and its source that Bingham has chosen to suggest by the misty outlines of the few trees, the soft lights and shades and golden colors of his landscape. It is the world of Claude Lorrain, a landscape suggesting a mythologized past beyond history. But the myth of the pastoral always has in it the seeds of its own destruction. To call up its maternal presence is always to call up the pain of its loss. The other side of our longing is our fear, and our contempt for the fragility of the very things we have destroyed. Thus the pastoral must exist in that timeless world of a suppressed history, like a locked chest; its nostalgic longings must be expressed, but not fulfilled. Once all that is missing is glimpsed, is even imagined, the pastoral enters the world of history and time. And is thus no longer functional. Its method is the perpetual delay of reverie. In a sense, then, the old man, the boy, paddling out of the Great Unknown, might be seen to have triumphed over their dependence on this maternal nature, which they have left forever behind them.

"America is the country of the Future," Ralph Waldo Emerson declaimed to the Mercantile Library Association in Boston in 1844. "It is a country of beginnings, of projects, of vast designs, and expectations. It has no past: all has an onward and prospective look."[40] But the future Emerson imagined the Young American racing toward on the railroads and steamboats that were stretching out across the continent with such rapidity and annihilating distance was in fact a continuation of the troubled conquests that had begun on the edge of the Atlantic before this country was a nation. With the triumph of the Mexican War, the republic Jefferson had helped to found stood poised to become an Empire. Yet a strain of melancholy underlay the victories over Mexicans, nature, and nature's Indian peoples. "All de world am sad and dreary, ebry where I roam," Stephen Foster wrote in minstrel-show dialect, and that melancholy note, Bernard De Voto observed half a century ago, as much as the blare of military bands and the plinking banjo of "Oh! Susanna," represented the western push of white America, and the sense of loss and sorrow under the triumphs of a restless, unstable population.[41] Hiking toward the diggings in the midst of the California gold fever with scarcely more to his name than a faded morocco dressing case, an incongruous silver-handled riding whip, a coarse blanket, a tin coffeepot, and the ever-present revolver, Bret Harte had been kept in a state of fevered excitement by the outcroppings of telltale quartz along the trail. About sunset he came upon "a mile-long slope of pines still baking in the western glare, and beyond it, across an unfathomable abyss, a shelf in the opposite mountain side, covered with white tents, looking not unlike the quartz outcrop." Now, in sight of his goal, a strange melancholy overcame him.

> *I do not know what I had expected, but I was conscious of some bitter disappointment. As I gazed, the sun sank below the serried summit of the slope on which I stood; a great shadow seemed to steal up rather than down the mountain, the tented shelf faded away, and a score of tiny diamond points of light, like stars, took its place. A cold wind rushed down the mountain side, and I shivered in my thin clothes, drenched with the sweat of my day long tramp.*[42]

That anticipatory shiver of disappointment, as much as the optimism of Emerson's historyless future, is embedded in the American inheritance.

On April 2, 1870, an old soldier named Patrick Gass was buried in Wellsburg, West Virginia. He had come out of that Scotch-Irish stock that had been the bloody edge of the white conquest of the frontier. As an infant he had come over the hills from Western Pennsylvania with his family, probably carried in a pannier on the side of a horse. He had been a carpenter, a boat builder, a woodsman, and an Indian fighter. He had taken a load of lumber in a broadhorn down the Ohio and then the Mississippi to New Orleans, had met Daniel Boone, and claimed to have caught a glimpse of George Washington. During the War of 1812 he had fought in the awful battle of Lundy's Lane and at Fort Erie had gone out to spike the British guns with a handful of rat-tail files. Chopping wood at Fort Independence he had lost an eye. Peacetime had not been kind to Pat Gass, and the succeeding forty years of his life contained, in the words of his biographer, "many chapters over which we gladly draw the veil of charity." "I am now nearly sixty years of age," he claimed in an appeal in 1829, "having no real or personal property, except wearing appearl, and not able to procure, entirely, my subsistance by manual labor, being severly afflicted by rheumatic pains, the effect of severe and continued exertions in the service of my country, since I was capable of carrying arms until the close of the late war."[43] Two years after he dictated his appeal, he married a twenty-year-old girl and had soon fathered seven children. He had been an indefatigable walker, a racist, a storyteller whose talk, according to one editor, was "better fitted for the camp than the parlor." At the age of ninety he tried to enlist in the Union Army. Toward the end of his life Gass joined the Campbellites and had himself baptized in the Ohio. It was the river he had ascended with Lewis and Clark on their way across the continent in 1804. He was almost ninety-nine when he died. He was the last survivor of the Corps of Discovery.[44]

By the time Pat Gass was buried the vast forests of oaks and softwoods had been logged off in a large part of what was now the middle of the nation. The Indian tribes had left only their names on the rivers and something of their physiognomy in the faces of the white settlers who had replaced them. The violence and freedom of the contested lands had been constricted by surveyors' chains, mortgages, and bills of sale. The settlements themselves were no longer outposts, but villages and towns and even cities. Game laws, constables, and courthouses hemmed in the hunters and trappers and their rough justice. The patches of corn and cotton and tobacco had begun to be turned into coal fields and railroads, the farmers more and more had become tenants on the land they once owned, or miners, or railroad workers, or hands in the mills. The fratricidal war that Jefferson feared and had predicted had left the white South a legacy of shame, hatred, and defeat and the black South a perilous freedom that drew the murderous rage of the lynch mob and the night rider. Two years before Pat Gass died, the dream of opening a gateway to the Pacific had finally been accomplished, not on the waters of some mythical river, but on the backs of the Chinese and Irish workers who laid the tracks of the transcontinental railroad. In 1903, scarcely two generations after his burial, the continent had been crossed by an automobile.[45]

The dream of a pastoral land beyond the settlements lived only in paintings. The beautiful image of an old trapper, a boy, and a chained bear is one of those, a relic of a time when the pastoral vision and all it hoped and all it obscured could be painted in the guise of a boy, musing in a pirogue headed downstream to a civilization we want him never to reach. Best leave this boy to dream, the gun loose in the crook of his arm, the duck he has killed forgotten, in the reverie of an eternal adolescence. Behind him, beyond the frame of the picture, a wilderness lies stripped of its cub.

* * *

I don't know when I began to be haunted by that old man in the pirogue and the half-Indian boy and that strange, chained animal and the closed chest and the reflections spreading out beneath them in the silent river. For a long time before I started this book, I had been thinking about this painting, as I had been thinking about many of the voices that populate it. I had read Hemingway early, of course. Later came Henry Adams and then Clarence King and somewhere between King and Hemingway I read Raymond Chandler's dark comedies. Then there was the problematic figure of Gertrude Stein, whose girlhood was lived out a few miles from where I now write, in houses that no longer, but for one exception, exist. She had left behind a phrase describing Oakland that had made it the butt of humorists: "There's no there there." But the phrase that captured her baffled attempt to return to the scene of her girlhood had seemed, even before I had read the book in which it appears, to have had something deeper and more poignant than a simple joke behind it. And long before any of these voices was a voice coming out of my own childhood, that half-sobbing, half-chuckling, seductive and secretly repellent voice of a singer moaning over a whanging steel guitar, whose songs I couldn't remember ever really listening to, but which, when I heard them years afterward, I had seemed to have known forever. These voices were all American voices—Hank Williams, the geologist-writer Clarence King, Ernest Hemingway, Gertrude Stein—as the boy and the old man in the picture were Americans. But of all the Americans you could name, what strung them together so that they seemed to make a connection in my mind? As I worked, the photographer E. J. Bellocq and the painter Jackson Pollock joined this group, but by that time I had faintly discerned why I needed to write about these figures and what I had to say.

You could say all these voices, the image of the old man and the bear cub and the boy and Pollock's poured canvases, were in me because of the accidents of who I was, of my own history, my own tastes. And this is true. In almost any kind of writing you are, in effect, finding yourself. But as I worked I began to hear something under the welter of the voices of my subjects and hidden inside their images, something that had an analogue in an unanswered question that I sensed had been under the figures in the George Caleb Bingham painting all the time.

What I heard, if you can express it this way, was a kind of silence. The peculiarly heavy silence of something withheld, of something that was locked behind the omissions of the printed words, and that, in the paintings of Pollock and Bingham, was itself unpaintable. When the answer began to emerge in me, something in my own life seemed to clarify. And I knew I had been hearing that silence for a very long time.

You had to listen very hard. Under the din of Cold War America, the moaning Hammond organs of the soap operas on the radio, the doom-laden news and chattering ads, the silence was difficult to hear. Listening to the Grand Ole Opry with its cowboys who weren't real cowboys, its hillbilly comedians who, you somehow imagined, weren't real hillbillies either, there was a sense of something deeper under the meretricious yodels and the cornball humor. What you heard when you listened for it was a kind of longing, a sense of something lost, lost perhaps even at the moment of gaining it, and possibly irretrievable. It was a silence as compelling as all of the myths of success you grew up with and believed, and perhaps inseparable from them.

I've used the figure of silence for that palpable absence and sense of loss that invade the consciousness of the lives of the people I write of here. Walt Whitman said he heard the smothered sounds of the "long dumb" voices of prisoners and slaves, of the diseased and despairing, thieves, dwarves, the forbidden voices "of sexes and lusts," and claimed to have become a channel for them.[46] But the voices I was hearing and would later try to write about were the voices of those who, in the figuration of the American myth of success, were the inheritors of the land, the winners and the conquerors.

Henry Adams consoled himself by calling the sense of absence so pervasive in his writing and his life failure. It was as if history itself had betrayed the historian and kept him from that place in American life he believed he was born to inherit. But failure, in Adams's particular use of the word, was a code for a protective irony. The full resonance of the silence was really found in the hole his wife Clover left in his autobiographical *Education*. There is no mention of her in that book. No mention of their courtship, of their thirteen years of marriage, of that ghastly suicide. The manikin Adams created and called "Henry Adams" in his little joke on the world is alone.

It is in this solitude that Adams is perhaps most American. Tocqueville viewed solitude as the inevitable consequence of a land where equality had broken down the old connections of caste and class and of family.[47] Every American was new-minted. Every American was alone. Perhaps that solitude is what creates the need for conquest that compels all the denizens of this book, that furious pursuit of what Adams's contemporary William James called the Bitch Goddess Success. The other side of the shining quest, of the mountains that Clarence King climbed and named and of Hank Williams's hits on the country music charts, was something blank and terrible and empty. The theme of failure that inevitably accompanies that dream of conquest runs through these lives like a dark thread.

In one way or another, openly in Adams, with tragic self-unawareness in his friend and idol Clarence King, complexly in Gertrude Stein and Ernest Hemingway and Raymond Chandler, the figures in this book were all at odds with the Bitch Goddess. In Chandler this swimming against the current of the American myth comes close to parody. His Los Angeles is a gangsteropolis filled with a pecking order of crooks and con artists that finally merges seamlessly into the legitimate world of multimillionaire industrialists and studio bosses. It would all be fairly funny except for the detective narrator's straight face and lyrical prose, a kind of inside-out pastoral.

This sense of something lost, of something missing, becomes, in the figures I study, a trope for an incomplete or lost sexual perfection. There are few women in this book, and those who are here—Clover Adams, the missing mother in the Bingham painting, the fictional Indian girl of Hemingway's hero Nick Adams's first sexual experience, the beautiful heiress who gives Chandler's detective protagonist that one perfect night, and who later turns up in a book Chandler was never able to complete—often define themselves as much by their absence as by their concrete presence. Sometimes they are a racial Other: the Old Gold Girls and Archaic Women of Clarence King's half-fictional memories; Prudence Boulton, the Indian girl on whom Hemingway modeled Nick Adams's first love; Debba, the Kamba girl who takes her place in Hemingway's unfinished book on his last safari. Gertrude Stein deals with the psychic loss of her creation Melanctha, the black girl in whose sexual awakening she first began to find her voice, by turning inward and hiding herself in an increasingly coded sexual language that, paradoxically, will make her a literary Caesar, and finally, by becoming that grotesque, sexless monument to herself, a Celebrity. The exceptions to these missing women are the prostitutes Bellocq photographed in New Orleans bordellos around the year 1912. The necessary silence of all photographs is here a kind of screen on which they project their images of themselves, images that speak poignantly of their desires, of who they wish to see in the mirror of the camera. But even here there are those disturbing photographs of women with faces obliterated, the emulsion scratched off the glass plate. All of these strategies are strategies of failure, strategies that embed in themselves the original loss.

Gertrude Stein thought that America was the oldest country in the world. It was, in her quirky way of putting things, the oldest country in the world because, through its massive expansion of business and transportation just after the Civil War, it was the first nation to enter the twentieth century. But there is in Stein's odd language an acknowledgment of the thinness of our history, of how recently we had emerged from what Europeans saw as wilderness to the clearings of history.

It is perhaps this recentness of our history that makes the issue of nature and our inevitable separation from it something that has a particular urgency in the intellectual tradition of this country. The unmapped territory that Lewis and Clark gazed on seems just over the hill of the past, seems there just yesterday. And so its loss is more poignant, and the wound fresher.

Jackson Pollock makes a fitting complement to the questions in the

Bingham painting. Pollock himself, though he studied with Benton and assisted Siqueiros, said he derived his aesthetic pedigree from Europe. But it is the urgency of his need to collapse the distance between himself and nature, the immediacy of that impossible longing, that prompted me to look for an anticipation of his method not in Cézanne or the Surrealists but in the journals of that far traveler in the mind Henry David Thoreau. Pollock, as far as I know, never read Thoreau, or much of anything. Although Pollock named one of the dogs that padded after him like familiar spirits Ahab, he could never finish *Moby-Dick*. But he kept starting it, and, like a twentieth-century Ahab, his project was, in a sense, to read those mute hieroglyphics on the blank face of nature. And like Melville's doomed captain, his project was a heroic failure.

In a now-forgotten novel of 1945, *Gold in the Streets*, by Mary Vardoulakis, there is a haunting moment in which a young Cretan, just off the boat in the years before the First World War, is sitting with a compatriot in a factory in Chicopee, Massachusetts, after their shift. A warm sun is streaming through the windows and a black clean-up boy is sweeping the floor, singing. "Listen," the Cretan whispers. "What melancholy is that?" It is a song in a language the Cretan doesn't understand, but the music alone communicates all homesickness and longing to the young Greek.[48]

What he was hearing was, of course, the Blues. The Greek word for that feeling of melancholy and loss was *kaïmos*, and what I have heard might be called the American *kaïmos*. But it is a particularly rootless *kaïmos*, the *kaïmos* of white, not black, America, played off against a sense of history that is not tragic, but optimistic, a melancholy that is not rooted in the deep past and the inevitability of suffering, but in some sense of a utopian possibility that we just missed, and of an unspoiled nature that was almost within living memory.

Timothy H. O'Sullivan (American, 1840–82), *Steamboat Springs, Washoe, Nevada* (1867). Albumen print, 21.3 cm x 28.1 cm. George Eastman House, gift of Harvard University.

One

The Inner Geology
of Clarence King

DESIRE

This mountain doesn't exist. The Sierra Club doesn't know about this mountain. The Nature Conservancy is unacquainted with it. It is not on any of
the inventories kept by the Wise Use movement. No sheep have gotten lost
in its side canyons in October blizzards, no stray steers have dropped off
its ravines and broken their necks or gotten caught belly up in its scrub for
cowboys to swear about. There are no sheep on this mountain. There are no
steers. There are no cowboys. No tourist could take a photograph of it. (If
there were any tourists. If there were any reason to take a photograph of it.)
Off-road vehicles have not scarred this mountain's side hills, miners have
not pocked its crevasses, oil and gas companies have not drilled exploration
holes into its strata, fossil hunters have not hammered sauropods out of its
ledges, archaeologist have not discovered flints or remains of ancient cooking pits in its flanks.

Rock-hounds haven't carried away its pebbles in their pockets.

No one has bumped into it on a dark night.

This mountain has slipped through the nets of the government planners, the geologists, the writers of Environmental Impact Statements. It has escaped the word-pits of the attorneys, the jargon-bogs of the politicians. It is not on any chart of mineral resources or on any range management grid. It not rated on any scale for potential industrial development nor does it figure in any proposal for removal or inclusion or land swap to or from the public domain. Because, in the sense that politicians and cowboys and tourists and scientists think of things existing, it isn't really there.

Oh, it's there in the way that other lumps of sandstone and conglomerate thrusting up out of their own rubble are present—it's present like them physically. Pilots have flown over it, and it appears in the photographs taken from satellites. It has been translated into the intricate whorls and elevations of an excellent set of relief maps (1:24000) published by the USGS. It is there as a precise set of coordinates expressed in degrees, minutes, seconds of longitude and latitude. (Using GPS technology you could find where you were on it to within a couple of feet.) It is there as what physicists might call a unique event in time and space, a flat-topped peak rising nine thousand feet above sea level between two canyons at the edge of the Uintan Uplift, pine-stippled on its north face, a mountain much like many others in this part of the shelf of the Rocky Mountains. It is not particularly tall, not particularly beautiful. It isn't much of a mountain.

But this isn't the mountain we are talking about. This is a shadow of the real mountain. Nothing that can be put on a page adds up to the real mountain, which looms out of the sagebrush like some palpable mirage, the mountain that you expect to float away at the next bend in the dirt road. The real mountain, the mountain we are speaking about, is not made out of dirt and rock, not created by plate tectonics and local stress and erosion and time. The real mountain, the Diamond Mountain, has been made by desire.

You don't get to Diamond Mountain any conventional way. General David Colton was brought to it blindfolded in the summer of 1872. A month or so later, after wandering around the Utah-Colorado-Wyoming borderlands lost for four days a delegation from the San Francisco investors who had dispatched Colton arrived at a flat sandstone rock below a timbered mesa. The two seedy prospectors who had led them across the desert told them this was a likely spot to dig, and the delegates and their mining specialist

Henry Janin went to work with picks, shovels, and pans. After a few minutes an English adventurer named Rubery gave a yell. He held up something that glittered in the sunlight.

> *It was a diamond, fast enough. Any fool could see that much. Then we began to have all kinds of luck. For more than an hour diamonds were being found in profusion, together with occasional rubies, emeralds and sapphires.*[1]

The wonderfully named Asbury Harpending, who was there and who wrote this account (and who may have known a bit more about how the diamonds happened to be in this unlikely spot than he ever let on), later wondered why a few pearls weren't thrown in for good luck. Probably an oversight, he concluded.

That night the investors were in high spirits. "There wasn't the usual row over who should cook supper, who should wash the dishes, who should care for the stock, which little incidents of camp life had brought us to the verge of bloodshed during the three previous days," Harpending recalled. On the contrary, good will and benevolence were "slopping over."[2] They were rich. That bag of glittering gems that the two rough prospectors had not-so-secretly deposited in Ralston's San Francisco bank that winter had turned out to be no delusion. What they had found was a mountain made of diamonds. Louis Tiffany had squinted at little chunks of it through his loupe in New York and Ralston the banker had run bits of it through his fingers, but here the mountain itself stood before them. The very anthills were loaded with gems. For another few days the San Franciscans dug up diamonds and rubies and staked off claims. Once, on a still day, they thought they heard the distant hoot of a railroad engine whistle. It was impossible. The railroad was a hundred miles away.

A little less than three months later, six other men made their way up a barren gorge in the high desert on the Utah-Colorado border called Vermilion Canyon. They did not know precisely where they would find it, but they knew what they were looking for: a field of diamonds beneath a mountain between Browns Park and the Union Pacific rail line.

At the head of these men was Clarence King. There were few men who knew more about what secrets the mountains of the American West held in their folds, who had the keys to such unimaginable wealth in their pockets. He was thirty years old. At this early age he was just completing one of the most ambitious government scientific surveys to that date. His work as a geologist had helped determine the age and strata of the gold belts of California, and would lead to millions in recovery from the ores of the Comstock and in the exploitation of the almost inexhaustible coal measures of eastern Utah and the Wyoming desert. The government survey he headed would directly and indirectly lead to important collections and studies of the flora and fauna and geology of a broad swath of the United States along the fortieth parallel from the Rockies to the eastern slope of the Sierra Nevadas. King's comprehensive scientific work, Systematic Geology, which would be completed a few years hence, would place him in the highest ranks of his scientific contemporaries, while just published in the East was a little book of local color sketches of California and tales of terrifying mountain climbs that reviewers would look to as the beginning of a significant literary career.

The little party made its way up the barren canyon, fighting the icy wind and the exhaustion of their pack animals. There were a cook, two camp men, King, his associate Samuel Emmons, and Emmons's topographical assistant, Allen Wilson. Already it had snowed. Emmons wore four flannel shirts and two pairs of socks. King had brought them all big woolen mufflers. It was bitter cold. The legs of the worn-out mules were encased in balls of ice from crossing the thinly frozen mountain streams, and Emmons remembered them rattling against each other like castanets.[3] The wind blew a gale over the elevated plains. To keep others off the scent, King had chosen a roundabout route. He pushed into Browns Park, where his party forded the Green, taking four days to make a journey that, started from the other side, would have taken one. King's reputation, the reputation of the survey he had headed, were at stake. Someone else had come to this godforsaken tract of mother earth and exposed the secret wealth hidden in the barren canyons. King should have known it. The survey should have plotted it. Now in San Francisco the directors of the diamond company were only waiting for spring and the opening up of the fields to release that blizzard of shares that, perhaps more than diamonds themselves, would make them richer than their most unspeakable dreams.[4] King and his men had put together their notes—hints gleaned from offhand conversations with the diamond hunters, glimpses of city men in rough field clothes getting off trains in out-

28

of-the-way stops—above all, their profound knowledge of the vast tracts of desolate country and geological probability. The diamonds weren't, as rumor had it, in Arizona at all. If anywhere, they were at the foot of an unnamed peak ten miles north of Brown's Hole.

King's party entered a winding valley called Red Rock Pass. A forlorn white horse, left by some absent hunters, persisted in following them. On the fifth day out, they started before dawn in a driving snowstorm. About noon the party found itself camped on a clear spring in a narrow gulch at the western end of a denuded sandstone plateau. They left the cook and the two packers behind to set up camp and began to reconnoiter the canyon. In fifteen minutes they found a fresh blaze on a lone cottonwood tree and below it a notice claiming water rights to the gulch. It was dated June fifteenth, Golconda City, and signed "Henry Janin." Now they knew they were warm. They began to circle around for tracks. They found no diamonds, but they found a trail that would lead them out of the canyon. Half an hour later they were on top of the mesa, where they came upon fresh stakes and a paper notice laying out ten- or twenty-acre mining claims. Beyond this half mile they came upon a bare, iron-stained table of coarse sandstone about a hundred feet long. Here all the tracks converged, the elegant Janin's narrow footprints conspicuous among them. They threw down their reins and began examining the rock on their hands and knees. Almost immediately Emmons found a small ruby.

Dusk was coming on. The wind blew across the mesa and the three men searched the sand for diamonds in a fever of excitement. Digging with their pocket knives among the grains of quartz of the table rock, they found it hard to make out the steely tinge they were looking for in the fading light. Then, just before dark, they found three diamonds. Their fingers were so numb with cold they had difficulty picking them up.

That night, Emmons wrote, they were full believers in Janin's reports and they went to bed dreaming of immeasurable wealth.

There is this about desire: it blazes up in the mind's darkness like some cold, lambent flame that is always dancing away, that is always just out of reach. In the darkest night you dream of holding the thing you want in your hands, it is there, and the flame of desire slips like water through your fingers, But it never exhausts itself. It shimmers and grows; it feeds on impossibility; it is a kind of rage. A man like King builds his personality around desire. Fold on fold, he builds outward layers of his person; he studies, he climbs mountains, he leads men, and around the campfire he tells his stories. But at the heart is that cold flame. *It is a kind of rage.* The dream that becomes the nightmare, the diamonds that you struggle to pick up with numb fingers amid the grains of sand, that you can't pick up, that lie all around you. The mountain retreats farther and farther away from you in the dying light. Finally it is gone. At midnight you wake up and look out through the flaps of your tent; the wind howls over the flats. The mountain rises up in front of you, a black silhouette cut out of the curtain of stars.

The next morning King sent the camp men off hunting and brought out magnifying glasses and sieves and shovels. They worked for the next few days. The diamonds turned up inevitably in a suspicious ratio to the rubies, one to the dozen. They sieved the earth and found it held gems only where it had been disturbed. The test holes they dug showed the diamonds lay only on the surface. (One diamond sat so delicately perched on top of a rock that the first storm would have blown it away.) And they lay only where footprints showed men had trod before them. In the fabulous anthills there were signs that the gems had been pushed into the earth with a stick. In the trodden places their shovels were turning up diamonds, rubies, garnets, spinels, sapphires, emeralds, amethysts—it was an association of minerals impossible in nature. The mines were a swindle, after all.

Before long, like some odd hallucination, a portly man dressed for the city showed up, having tailed them from Fort Bridger. Berry—the city man—took the news that the fields were salted with mature aplomb as a wonderful chance to sell short. "No, it's bad enough as it is," King said.

The next day King set out before dawn with Wilson, who knew the country best, to ride straight through to the railroad, which, it turned out, was less than fifty rough miles away due north. He and Wilson caught the westbound train a little east of Rock Springs, stowed their mules in a boxcar, and headed straight for San Francisco. On the evening of his arrival, King found Henry Janin and laid out his proofs. The next morning he went before the directors of the San Francisco and New York Mining and Commercial Company and forced them to halt all transfer of stock. There was one more quick trip to the diamond fields by the company's representatives, but King had averted what could have been a disaster before the stock came on the market. The glittering diamonds and rubies turned out to be cheap, second-rate gems bought in bulk in London and Paris. The two "simple old prospectors" (perhaps with a little help from Harpending and the slippery Englishman Rubery) had salted the claim. But more important, they'd salted the minds of a ring of clever money men in New York and San Francisco and even London, for Baron Rothschild had his own man on the board. They had salted the United States Congress with some favorable mining legislation through General Ben Butler, who had been awarded his own little souvenir of the mines in the form of a block of stock. But Clarence King became the King of Diamonds. He had trumped them all.

The Diamond Mountain existed somewhere in the imagination of 1872 because it had to be there. "America is a very large country," the nebulous Asbury Harpending claims Baron Rothschild had told him in London. "It has furnished the world with many surprises already. Perhaps it may have others in store."[5] So desire creates its own mountains. It maps its territories with names, names like those on the maps of the San Francisco and New York Mining and Commercial Company—Diamond Flat, Sapphire Hollow, Ruby Gulch, Discovery Point. So desire would create in the paradoxical mind of the scientist who had exploded the myth of the Diamond Field, his own myths—veins of gold and silver and riches of the imagination he could almost feel in his hands.

NEWPORT

First there was the house. It was an old house, full of rooms and women. You imagine the weird carvings of dragons and demons and chests and cabinets that had little enameled landscapes on them of mountains and forests and little people in strange hats coming out of small, queer houses and crossing little arched bridges over rivers that were a few rippling silver lines. You imagine that sometimes a man would be fishing, or a boat would go by. A crane flies over a pine tree. The mountains are very near. You imagine the child longing to touch them.

Sometimes one of the chests would be opened in front of the child. Then, for a moment, the secrets they held would be revealed. Inside the boxes lay cloth of amazing colors, like the shimmering rainbows in pools of oil, iridescent birds who spread their beautiful tails, and great flowers, gold and blue and dark blue like the purest night. Then the cloths were folded up and the boxes were shut. The strange scents that came out of the boxes faded, until they were only faint hints, in the ordinary smells of the house.[6]

There were names in the house. The name of his father: James King. The name Jesus. Names of the places where the boxes and the beautiful cloths and the carved little old men and children and delicate ivory bridges came from: Canton, Formosa, Peking. There was the name Amoy, the place where his father had died. The smells and the things hidden in the chests were connected to his father.

The women taught him to pray. They taught him about the crime that lay on the land, the crime of slavery. Of places where the poor Negroes were whipped and hunted down if they tried to run away. His nurse had a dark skin and the child loved her.

He would not be allowed to touch the silks in the chests, nor allowed even to open the chests. His father had died in a Pagan land. He had caught a fever and died among the Heathens. His nurse held him in her arms and sang to him.

Beyond the doors of the house, the cobbled streets of the old town led down to the wharves with their carts and sailors and workingmen and the high-masted ships and the smells of the sea, timber, rotting things, tar. Once the boy saw a diorama. The hidden showman cried, "Let there be light!" And suddenly the gas jets flared up and the melodeon started to play and there were planets and the sun and then across the stage marched to the slow music of the melodeon a parade of beasts, and the man with the rod pointed them out and explained how God had made everything.[7]

At the age of six the boy moved with his mother and two infant sisters to Connecticut so he could begin school. Dr. Park had a rod, like the man who showed the diorama. But he fired his pupils' ambition. The boy, Clarence, was a good student. He was everything to his mother, who had been widowed at twenty-eight. Because he was everything, he must succeed. His mother loved him. She could be firm from her love. She was making a mind. Once in the wintertime the boy took her to show her something he had found. They walked across the frozen snow for a mile and he showed her the impress of a fern in a stone wall. He asked her how it got there. She did not know, but they looked it up in Hitchcock's *Geology*. Her rooms in the boardinghouse in which they lived became filled with curious stones, plants, seeds. She studied Greek and Latin and the modern languages to help him.[8]

The boy grew up to be sturdy and bright. He liked sports. He liked to lead.

At the Sheffield School at Yale, he captained a baseball team, rowed stroke oar on the crew, studied the sciences. When the war came he did not enlist. He struggled with his conscience, with his abolitionist inheritance, with his need to show himself a leader. But he could not drive a bayonet into a man. A short time after he graduated, he listened to Professor Brush read a letter from California. Scientists had climbed Mount Shasta. They had taken instruments and measured it and had stood on the top of the world. Through the haze of the valleys below and the clouds that now and then rolled partially away, they caught occasional glimpses of the magnificence below them.

> In the west, a wilderness of mountains stretching to the Pacific, chain beyond chain—all dim now, however—many streaked with snow, others black with chaparral, the valleys filled with smoke, the tops more or less obscured by clouds. In the northwest the valley of the Klamath River and mountains beyond . . .

All in the east, toward the great escarpment of the Sierras, was obscured. The great Sacramento Valley was filled with haze. Rising above it, Lassen's Butte, nearly a hundred miles away, seemed like an isolated island-peak of black rock and white snow rising from a sea of smoke.[9]

By April of the year 1863, Clarence King was on his way west.

MOUNTAINS

Bear Valley, California, in 1863, consisted of three barrooms, a couple of billiard saloons, two inns, half a dozen shanties. There were two laundries, a bathhouse, a French restaurant, and the Cafe Garibaldi. At the edge of the village were the shacks and canvas-roofed booths of a population made up of roving adventurers, Chinese, Mexicans, and the Miwok Indians, called by the contemptuous term "Diggers." The village itself contained the scarcely better dwellings of the miners and clerks and mechanics of the mines. Dust was everywhere. When Frederick Law Olmsted, through whose eyes we are seeing the Mariposa, came to California to manage the mines and first entered this country of rounded hills and narrow ledges of slate, he saw what he thought were masses of children's graves. They turned out to be the tailings of the placer miners left over from the rainy season. Everywhere were signs of the terrible drought that had ravaged the country for two years. The valleys were plowed, sometimes ten feet deep, for gold. Wherever there was a rivulet, no matter how small, wherever there was a puddle, no matter how thin, there were the Chinese in their straw hats and pantaloons, digging and washing, throwing up heaps of gravel and building ditches and little dams to prepare for the rainy season. Olmsted saw the same kind of treadmill he had seen in the paddy fields of China used to raise water for a Long Tom. Often he would greet the Chinese and they would answer him in some insolent word—it was the only English they had learned, and they thought it was the custom of the country. He employed twelve of the Chinese at the mine and paid them half what he paid the other miners. The mines were nearly bankrupt. The previous owner had dug out the richest veins in order to recoup his loans to Frémont, who had held the Mariposa before him. Nothing had been invested in long-term development.

It was a rough little culture, there in Bear Valley. No one felt fixed or settled. Men walked about with their gear tied up in a blanket, ready to take a house, a shanty, a tent, or tree, as it might happen, when night came. Over in the graveyard lay the one man who'd died in bed—an unnatural death, as Bear Valley saw it. The town was filled with Pikes and Secessionists.[10]

Sundays on those clear January days, Clarence King climbs Mount Bullion, which lifts itself above the shabby gold town. At the age of twenty, he had come west with a drove of mules. He had arrived in California penniless, with a Bible, a book of sermons, and a table of logarithms in his duffel and had joined the California Survey under Whitney and Brewer.

While the war rages in the East and the town below erupts in its Sunday explosion of horseracing, gambling, and drinking, King gazes at the horizon. Far to the south there rises above the mass of the sierras a vast pile of white peaks, which he and his friend Hoffmann judge lie near the heads of the Kings and Kaweah rivers. They are always there, at the margin of his imagination. One day he will stand upon them.

"I believe that fellow had rather sit on a peak all day, and stare at those snow-mountains than find a fossil in the metamorphic Sierra," the survey paleontologist had said of King. The remark had stung King, made him ask himself if he had fallen to the level of a mere nature lover. Perhaps he had. He had read Ruskin before he'd seen a real mountain.

He imposed a penance on himself for those lyrical afternoons on what he called his "Sunday Mountain." The penance was work. One afternoon, he knelt in a dreary, monotonous ravine called Hell's Canyon, wearing out geologist's hammers. Jays squawked and flittered about, scolding him and each other, eating the nuts the careful woodpeckers had stored in the oak trees. For a time he was an industrious woodpecker, pecking away at the Jurassic strata of the hollow. Then he split a rock and found inside a fossil form.

"There he reclined comfortably upon his side, half bedded in luxuriously fine-grained argillaceous material,—a plump, pampered cephalopoda (if it is cephalopoda), whom the terrible ordeal of metamorphism had spared."[11] Carefully King proceeded to chip his victim out whole. When it chose to break in two, King was easily consoled, reflecting that it would do as well gummed back together. The age of the gold belt of the Sierras could now be firmly placed. He had given a name to dumb nature.

King sees the snow-covered peaks in the distance once more. The surveying party makes its way out of the drought-parched Central Valley of California and up the pine-covered hills. Above the Kings River gorge he climbs to the top of some granite crags and lies down among the roots of a little family of alpine firs. North and south, as far as he can see, lie the broad green waves of the forest plateau. Due east, on the horizon, a tall pyramid of granite rises, trimmed with buttresses of fantastic spires of rock. For several hours he stays among the firs, sketching the outlines of the summits, studying their systems. He wants to hold them in his mind, so that he can afterward recognize them from other points of observation. He knows that he has not deceived himself about the great height of these peaks. The wide fields of snow, his guess as to the elevation, tell him this. The shadows in the canyon deepen, the expanse of forest behind him darkens to purple, the glow of the mountain heightens. It is the forerunner of twilight. When he gets to the horses and heads back to camp, the darkness of the canyon, in contrast to the light streaming from the peaks, is almost nocturnal.[12]

The mountains that rise out of books are like the mountains that rise out of dreams. Transformed from piles of shard, the granite spires and broken pinnacles become, in the act of writing, ideas. Rising from the dusty valleys and the river gorges, the Sierras are more than the geologic history of the earth. They are the focus of longing. When Clarence King sat down to write of his ascent of Mount Tyndall,[13] his climb became a morality tale, a work of mythology. After the arduous trek that takes him and his partner Richard Cotter to what will be the beginning of their journey, King looks across the chasm they must cross to reach the foot of the gigantic mountain wall that rises beyond it, the highest, he thinks, in America. It is as if, he writes, he were contemplating the purpose of his life, and for just one moment he would have rather liked to dodge that purpose, or to have waited, or to have found some excellent reason why he might not go. But he does go, of course. For his purpose is to reach the highest peak in the range.[14]

Brewer describes King as he was then: "King is enthusiastic, is wonder-fully tough, has the greatest endurance I have ever seen, and is withal very muscular. He is a most perfect specimen of health."[15] He was something on the short side, blond, with a light beard. But his hazel eyes in the early pho-tographs have the soft, far-off look of the daydreamer. He was twenty-one on the eve of the climb.

After they had seen King and Richard Cotter off on their expedition, Brewer and Gardiner and one other member of their party once more climbed the high peak from which they had sighted the towering regions into which the two climbers had gone. They retrieved the instruments they had left there earlier, planted an American flag, and left their names and a record of the height of the peak in a bottle. That night in their camp the remaining three men sang "Old John Brown" alone in the solitude. It was the Fourth of July. They had heard no war news for over a month. In the empty fastness of the Sierras, they heard not a gun. They did not know of the terrible carnage at Cold Harbor, were dying men lay untended on the battlefield for three broil-ing days while the gallant generals Grant and Lee exchanged notes on the niceties of flags of truce. Brewer began composing a letter to King's family. He could not get beyond "It becomes my painful duty to inform you."[16] King had gone into the mountain a dead man.

Up King and Richard Cotter climb; above the dragon-tracks of ancient glaciers, into the region of naked rock and snow. Although it is full day, the sky is grave with nocturnal darkness. The earth blinds them with its light. The climbers look up into an infinite vault from which no brightness seems to ray, only the vast yawning of hollow space. Nowhere is nature so little maternal than in this place of rocks and snow, echoes and emptiness. It is not death. This silence is more terrifying. It is vacuum. It is like the waveless calm of space. It is the emptiness against which King strives to signify himself, to build in this vastness the small figure of a man against that awful sky.

After a freezing bivouac and a terrible and dangerous climb, King rings his hammer upon the topmost rock. Cotter and he clasp hands. He names the peak Mount Tyndall.

But there is always one more mountain.

Sweeping the horizon with his level, he discovers two peaks equal in height to the mountain he stands upon, and two rising even higher. The one that looks the higher of these two is a "cleanly cut helmet of granite" about six miles south of Mount Tyndall, upon the same ridge. It was probably the highest point within the United States. To King its summit looked glorious, but inaccessible.

CONQUEST

Often there is a man in these photographs. Maybe the photographer put him into the picture to serve as an anchor or focus. To measure against the rock or the mountain he is trying to record. The man measures nothing. He does not stand for us. He is simply lost against the vast landscape that floods the lens. Lost and little and irrelevant.

Often the man is posed against the rock, or the white, featureless sky in a landscape with no foreground, no middle distance, only the vast, unimaginable horizon.[17] Sometimes it is only a part of a man that tries to give something a scale. A leg. A torso extending, absurdly, into the image the ground glass has caught, lying next to a steaming pool, or a bodiless head perched uneasily above a grotesque spout of tufa. Sometimes the man is gone. He leaves a coat. A bottle. A ruler absurdly stretched across an inscription some other man left carved on a cliff two hundred years before. He leaves a camera perched on a rock, photographed by another camera against the vastness of space and time.

And always there is the landscape. Whether the man is there, or not, there is this vastness, this awful space that goes on beyond the frame of the photograph, beyond the horizon. Waterless, cracked, almost without a tree, without a shrub. A landscape baked and folded and twisted into horrible shapes. How has this happened? The horrifying eruptions and fractures in the earth's crust, the boulders spewed like cannonballs across an empty desert? It is the evidence of a gigantic battle waged in the past, of the armies of Gog and Magog in their passing through some doomed, apocalyptic world. We do not know who won or lost.[18] There is only this empty field. We do not know where we are seeing this from. We do not know where we are.

1867. The war is over. The young man who had lazed away his Sunday dreaming of mountains had pushed himself up to head a great scientific survey that was to take place along the fortieth parallel of the North American continent. Serving his apprenticeship in California, he had idled away some of his time doodling insignias and mottoes for the expedition he dreamed of leading. At twenty-five he had emerged from Secretary of War Stanton's office with a commission in his pocket that the secretary claimed four major generals coveted.[19]

Like the other surveys in, or about to take, the field—Wheeler's and Hayden's and Powell's—the Fortieth Parallel Survey was to be a scientific appliance to the exploitation of this unclaimed land. The harsh mountains of the West were not sterile "but full of wealth," King had written. "The deserts are not all desert; the vast plains will produce something better than buffalo, namely beef; there is water for irrigation, and land fit to receive it."[20] All that was needed was to explore and declare the nature of the national domain. The Survey, like the transcontinental railroad, had come out of the war. It was, in some sense, an extension of the war. Generals who had fought on battlefields now followed the rails, harrying the Native Americans who lay in the way of the tracks, slaughtering their buffalo, driving them onto government reservations. The Survey was an instrument of conquest.

With the Survey was a young photographer named Timothy O'Sullivan. O'Sullivan had followed the war with his heavy camera, working for Brady and Alexander Gardner. Now his work was to provide with his photographic plates a supplement to the great geological map of the heart of the West that King and his Survey were drawing.

At Fredericksburg and Acquia Creek and Fairfax Courthouse and Petersburg, O'Sullivan had photographed the dead stretched out, bloated, mouths agape, limbs twisted. Like the phantom twitching of an amputated limb, the awful stillness of those battlefield photographs remained to haunt this empty landscape of the West. The scientists of the Survey chipped away at fossils, collected plants, took geological samples, building up a library of data that would be catalogued, analyzed, turned into the volumes of the final report. O'Sullivan photographed the tents of the expedition, and men standing or sitting outside them, the scientists and draftsmen and packers, almost parodying the sober and self-conscious military men he had caught on his plates during the war. Under the hood of his camera the baked terrain of this unimaged land lay upside-down and frozen on the ground glass. The shutter opened, swallowing the immense, empty flood of light, then it blinked closed. Somewhere in the Carson Sink he photographed the ambulance he had converted into a mobile darkroom. Lost beside a dune, the mules look like toys in the sand. Footprints lead from the bottom edge of the photograph to the ambulance, connecting it to the world of men, but we know they will be blown away.

There are a few tranquil lakes in O'Sullivan's photographs, a few timeless rivers; the rest is a desiccated and awful land that lays itself open as if it were flayed. While Bierstadt was painting imaginary mountains and Watkins was recording the Eden of Yosemite with his camera, O'Sullivan shows a scorched and blasted landscape. The Eden of the unspoiled West, with its transcendent promise, was a nowhere, was an imaginary place that lay on the other side of the exploitation that would surely destroy it; a kind of alibi. That stirring letter written, almost, from the peak of Shasta that had sent King West had left out what greeted the climbers at the top: a mixture of tin cans and broken bottles, a newspaper, a Methodist hymnbook, a pack of cards, an empty bottle, and "various other evidences of a bygone civilization,"[21] what Brewer called the "California Conglomerate," that could be found at the edge of any mining town. Beneath the clouds that covered the valley and the foothills, on the Sierra slopes and in the Comstock beyond, lay a land already gouged and washed away by hydraulic hoses and wasted by the mines. It was as if O'Sullivan's photographs were following King's survey like a ghostly double. Alan Trachtenberg asked if the photographs might be a kind of countertext to the ambitions of King's reports, suppressed in its published volumes.[22] There is no evidence that O'Sullivan saw them as anything more than accurate illustrations of landscapes, mines, buildings. But the photographs go beyond subversion. They are images of the hallucinatory world of dreams or of war. Their terrible vastness and the stillness of their depiction show a land strangely like that described by those who have

39

been in the midst of battle, where time slows to a gelid stream. A subaqueous world where every action takes place as if detached, weighed down by terrible lethargy, where the noise of cannon and scream of shot become a strange, cottony silence. In these photographs the works of man, the mills and mines with their shabby, impermanent outbuildings and their grandiose names— Empire, Imperial, Confidence—are oddly still, as if they are abandoned fortresses; the heaped-up anarchy of building is visually the same as the disorder of destruction. O'Sullivan descends into the mines of the Comstock. He takes with magnesium flash the first photographs of men toiling under the earth; almost the first underground photographs. Men work wedged against the rock, their thin candles stuck in spikes in the crevices; work in unbearable heat, sweating, trapped. They stand by ore cars with blank, livid, dirt-streaked faces, about to descend into living tombs. A cave-in snaps heavy beams and pillars like twigs, tons of rock crush through the roof of a room, as if the roof were broken by a bomb. It is an industrial war, the terrible war of matter against spirit.

In 1867, about the time Clarence King was beginning the first year of his survey, twenty-nine-year-old Henry Brooks Adams was brooding over the fossil of a primitive fish on Wenlock Edge. Diminutive, troubled by indecision and morbidity, which he covered by a pose of jocular nonchalance, burning with ambition and burdened by his name and his heritage, Adams had come to Wenlock Edge, as he put it, "in search of a father," an ancestor who could make sense of himself and his moment in history. Four years later, editor, muckraker, teacher, and still trying to find himself in the wilderness of America, Adams stumbled up to a rude cabin at the entrance to Estes Park. What he found in that cabin was neither a father or a self, but Clarence King, and, as he put it, he fell into his arms.

They talked until dawn, a banquet of talk, of geology and literature and their admiration for Agassiz and—to the repressed Henry Adams's profound admiration—of women. For King knew women. He knew even the New York woman, which, as Adams wrote, "is saying much." In his *Education*, Henry Adams would compare King to an Alexander, an Alcibiades. And indeed, like Plato's Socrates in his feelings for the golden, ill-fated Alcibiades, Adams's would always be in some sense not lacking its erotic side, in love with Clarence King.[23]

For Adams, King had stepped on to the theater of the United States after the war unburdened, as Adams said he himself was, with an education fit not for the next century, but for the last. A photograph taken of King outside camp near Sacramento in 1867 shows him debonair in striped pants, vest and cravat, and jaunty little bowler hat—an American King, indeed. Adams had sat on Wenlock Edge looking for a father. Fatherless, King had invented himself. Owen Wister, Frederic Remington, Theodore Roosevelt—other patrician young men from the East—found, or were soon to find, the West. They had come there to find a man, part myth, part reality, who could stand as the exemplar of independence, competence, leadership. A storyteller and a ladies' man, an expert. Wister, the writer, imagined him. Teddy Roosevelt impersonated him. Clarence King became him. "Whatever prize he wanted," Adams wrote of King, "lay ready before him—scientific, social, literary, political,—and he knew how to take them in turn. With ordinary luck he would die at eighty the richest and most many-sided genius of his day."[24]

Adams knew, looking back in 1905, this was not to be. King himself might have suspected it. But just as the images that emerge from O'Sullivan's wet plates show a landscape that gives the lie to the mythology of conquest that the Survey extends, so do they parallel in some haunting way the riven interior landscape of Clarence King himself. In Nevada, in 1867, O'Sullivan takes a photograph. A great crack opens the earth. Steam rises from it, obscuring the figure of the man who stands beside it. The man is a ghost. The man could have been Clarence King.

THE INNER GEOLOGY OF CLARENCE KING

In the fall of 1873, King was thirty-one years old. For ten years he had climbed peaks and descended into canyons. His body was already showing the strains of mountain bivouacs and lightning storms and forced marches and kicks by balky pack mules. He had been captured by hostile Indians, had nearly died in blizzards, and, on Job's Peak in Nevada, had been temporarily blinded by lighting. Now he had come home and set his men to finishing his scientific work.

Already he had written one book, a small masterpiece of local color and Ruskinian sensitivity. *Mountaineering in the Sierra Nevada* had had as its hero a young and spirited American, whose jaunty observations and triumphs in the raw, new land of California it chronicled. It had been a book about peaks climbed with reckless courage; of eons of geologic history dramatized and of landscapes described with lyrical power; of local loungers and teamsters and Indians sketched with the wit of Bret Harte or Mark Twain. Poised on the edge of the Pacific, the young nation might embody itself in just such an Anglo-Saxon as King, ringing his hammer on the highest peaks, a man who measures himself against the degenerate races of the frontier, greaser bandits and "Digger" Indians and retrograde hog-drover Pikes and subhuman Chinese. There is a hope in King's book that the rough generation of gold-hunters in time shall somehow evolve into a noble race, but the reader is not convinced. What the reader remembers is what King finally sees, a drought-parched land with its rude scars of mining, yawning trenches, disordered heaps of overburden and sifted gravel, softened by King's consoling hope that all this is slowly being transformed, that rain, wind, and flood, slowly, surely, were leveling all and covering it with a compassionate blanket of innocent verdure. It is a final dream of sleep, of Nature healing the humble earth, and of God, who is also Nature, molding and changing man.[25] A profound sense of homelessness haunts the hollow triumphs of this youthful book. And there is, in the thrilling tales of climbing, as in King's life, something that came close to hallucination.

In June of 1877, King returned to Yale to deliver the commencement address at the Sheffield School. For King, catastrophic violence, as well as the slow, inevitable processes of geological change, had shaped the earth. He rejected what he called Darwin's "gospel of chance." "Mere Malthusian struggle was not the author and finisher of evolution" in spite of Huxley and that little proto-horse that his own Survey's Othniel Marsh examined in Nebraska. The gaps in the geologic and paleontologic record were not accidents, but the very ruptures through which God showed his creative hand. "He who brought to bear that mysterious energy we call life upon primeval matter bestowed at the same time a power of development and change." The old myths of fire and flood spoke to King. They were survivals of terrible impressions "burned in upon the very substance of human memory."[26] He saw them engraved in the evidence of rocks and plains; perhaps he sensed them engraved deep in his own history. It is as if the harsh landscape of cataclysm and rift rises out of King's inner geology as well.

In October of 1868, King had led a small party from the Survey across the

Goose Creek Mountains of northwestern Utah into the lava-strewn desert of southern Idaho. On the second morning they came to the canyon of the Snake River. Even before they got to the brink, a dull, throbbing sound had greeted them. Its deep pulsations had seemed to come from the ground beneath their feet. It was the sound of the falls of the Snake. Cutting through the piles of jet-black lava two hundred feet below the olive and gray stretches of desert was the sheet of dancing foam that was the falls. For once O'Sullivan's camera failed. It was a scene from Dante, and called up in King a profound sense of emptiness and despair.

> *At the very brink of the fall a few twisted evergreens cling with their roots to the rock, and lean over the abyss of foam with something of that air of fatal fascination which is apt to take possession of men . . . Incessant roar, reinforced by a thousand echoes, fills the cañon. Out of this monotone, from time to time, rise strange, wild sounds, and now and then may be heard a slow, measured beat, not unlike the recurring fall of breakers.[27]*

It as if the ground had suddenly rent and called up this interior hell. And, perhaps, for King, in some sense it had. After sleeping at the edge of the falls, King was glad to climb up to the plain once more, where the obtrusive ugliness and acrid smell of the sagebrush—that smell he had always hated—banished what he called his melotragic state of mind, and the bright, cloudless sky "arched in cheerful vacancy over the meaningless disk of the desert." He was a man who had come away from some interior brink.

Deep under the debonair and insouciant leader of men, the leader ready with the right quip to lighten a cheerless bivouac or an empty plate, there was another man. For there had been spells of depression from his childhood on, when his mind grew weary and again and again needed to be lifted by an effort of tired will, when he found himself taking on "the old wounded beast way" that he had of hiding himself when he was "sore and unsuccessful."

He bought and sold a vast cattle ranch, became for a short time the first director of the United States Geological Survey, then he left science, went off to Mexico to the mines, founded a bank in El Paso, went to Europe for capital, spent and borrowed fortunes. He filled his rooms with art, purchased with the dreams of riches he had not yet uncovered. Chinese urns and antique altar cloths. Paintings by the fashionables of his day, Fortuny and Bierstadt and the two precious Turners. He sat for Zorn as if he were already a magnate. He spent like a Maecenas, left his offices to their own devices, and was cheated by his bookkeeper. His friend Henry James saw him as a "queer, incomplete, unsatisfactory creature . . . slippery and elusive, and as unmanageable as he [was] delightful."[28] And in the end, what had he accomplished? His affairs sank into ruin. He poured other people's money into his failing mines until there was no more to pour. In 1890, five men had died, John Hay wrote to Henry Adams, each ruining King, the last two kicking over buckets of milk King had been a year in drawing. His books stood on the shelves: the volumes of the Survey's work, his own *Systematic Geology*, the slender volume of his stories. They were something from another life. The pages of the novel of women he always wanted to write lay in a drawer. He lived his life as if it were a fiction.

To see into the earth was the privilege of science; but beyond sight, that distances the world, and makes its secrets coherent, there lies the deeper sense, inchoate, primitive: touch.

He spoke of it only in roundabout terms. There was a woman—her name was Dean. A western girl. King had met her in the rough town of Virginia City, where she was teaching school in the winter of the Fortieth Parallel Survey's first year. In the fall of 1869 King went east to obtain his mother's permission to marry. There, in a house, haunted by China and his father's death, his mother denied him.[29] King's father had been no lover to his wife, no hope to his son. Lost in the land of pagans, he was cut off. He had abandoned his son to the harsh discipline of Newport, its Bible, its one woman, who had vanquished her rival with a command.

King had confided in that little notebook marked "personal and confidential" that he kept with him in the first years of the Survey a view that "physical mergence" was the essential part of marriage, that "*Love*" was the "fulfilment of the law."[30] Now it had ended. The erotic hope was dashed.

At Copples's Hotel at the crest of the great Sierra wagon road, the Chinese waiters scurry through the crowded dining room, balancing twenty or thirty plates on their arms and shooting them dexterously over the tables with a crash and spatter, while foul-mouthed, swaggering teamsters clean their nails with their forks, clear their throats, blow their noses, drum upon the bottom of their plates. Of Copples himself—"Cut-Off" Copples, after his much-amputated leg—only the joke of his name, a pious New England widow, and his debts remain. And over everything in the dinning room is "a faint Mongol odor,—the flavor of moral degeneracy and of a disintegrating race." Copples's hotel is the site of an unholy consumption.

Through the windows of the kitchen, the glare of red light pours, a Chinese cook's head is silhouetted against the lurid glow. It is a kind of Hell. A Hell "run," says King, with the careless racism of his age, "on the Mongolian plan." Illuminated by the light of the kerosene lamps we see the inner recesses of a demonic womb, the kitchen, the secret center of the hotel. It is from here that issue the teamsters' awful fare, the "beans swimming in fat, meats slimed with pale ropy gravy."

But King does not risk the fare at Copples's. At Copples's the "red papers with Chinese inscriptions, and little joss-sticks here and there," the "spry devils"—the cooks and waiters—and over all, "that faint, sickening odor of China" that pervaded the room, combine to produce a sense of deep and sober gratitude that he had not eaten the meal about to be set out for him.

Now and then, King has told us, at a friend's house, he has happened to dine upon artistic Chinese cooking, and he knows that all who come home from living in China "smack their lips over the relishing *cuisine*," but there in that old house on Church Street with the "priceless fabrics and porcelains" that he was ever fondling, with the strange scents of a strange land, he had turned away. The comestible Western girls of the world, with their "smooth brilliant skin and ropes of soft brown hair," are not for him. The proffered meal, the relishing cuisine, becomes a meal of disgust.[31]

King played his allotted role of brilliant bachelor, as he played all the roles that fell to him—mountaineer, man of science, writer, politician, capitalist, raconteur—with cleverness and verve, but underneath was a profound ambivalence. "To kiss a woman and feel teeth through her thin lips paralyzes me for a week," he wrote a friend. "This snarl is because I am just in from passing Sunday at Tuxedo, and my grievance is that I didn't want to kiss the beings there. Their little minds squirm and contract under the [stimulus] of light conversation, as a dead frog curls up his wiry toes at the galvanic touch, but I am not deceived by their involuntary simulation of life: I know they are dead."[32]

Yes, they were dead—to Clarence King, at least. But there were other

45

women, women of a darker hue than the maidens of Tuxedo, to whom King turned in his fantasies and in his life.

So the deepest part of him could only emerge in the images of what Adams called "the archaic woman" he conjured up for his friends in his letters and his writing. The "bewitching black and tan sister" thrumming her guitar on the shores of Lake Nicaragua while his chocolate boils, the shining girls of Hawaii, bathing in a waterfall, "Luciana" the Indian woman with whom, he writes Hay, in imagery out of some lurid version of *Ramona*, he comes "as near it as I ever shall"[33] (whatever he meant by that), the Indian madonna he sees nursing her child . . . these are as imaginary as the bandits he outruns on the wonder-horse Kaweah, as the inventions that gild his stories in the clubs. *Locksley Hall*, Tennyson's potboiler about pure young love thwarted by the sordid world of money and society (but King forgets that *he* was the one who jilted the girl), with its renunciation of the world in favor of (momentarily) a dusky native maiden and colonial war, became a model for his imaginative life.

> *I will take some savage woman, she shall rear my dusky race.*

And always in King there was the dream of some earthly paradise, where far from the strictures of the fallen world, the old gold girls, as King named the women of his fantasies, bathed forever in pools of light. He wrote about it:

> *Whoever has strolled at dusk where palm groves lean to the shore, and watched the Indian women sauntering in the cool of evening with a gait in which a ripple of grace undulates—whoever has seen their soft, dark eyes, and read the expression of tenderness and pathos which is habitual on their faces, can but feel that here simple nature has done all she can for woman.*[34]

And beyond that golden light, there was sleep. The stillness of the desert was death. The soundless vacuum at the crest of the peaks was the waveless calm of space. The stillness of the sea was sleep. The sleep of tropic night, the deep, impressive silence, the heavy air that soothed the brain and nerve; sleep that was the deepest, the most dreamless oblivion.[35]

> *Ah, dearest, I have lain in my bed and thought of you and felt my whole heart full of love for you. It seems to me often that no*

*one ever loved a woman as I do you. In my heart there is no place
for any other woman and never will be. My whole heart is yours
forever.*[36]

The letters were yellow and crumbling by then. They come as a sort of
shock to read today, as if some ghost were speaking through a phonograph,
in an empty room. The woman had kept them for over thirty years.

Sometime late in the year 1887 or early in 1888 King had met in the house
of an acquaintance in New York a young black nursemaid. In September
1888, in the home of her aunt, King gave her a wedding ring. There was no
marriage certificate. King called himself in this secret union James Todd.
By giving himself his father's name, he bequeathed to the children he would
have by his wife that same absent father he himself had had, that father who
would die far from home, in the country of a strange race.

The existence of his marriage, the house he had bought for his wife in
Queens, with its orchard of rare trees and its servants, his worries for his
family, the death of his eldest child, Leroy, who bore in his given name the
secret of his father's identity, the death of a daughter—all this was hidden from the white world in which he continued to make his way as the
confirmed bachelor Clarence King.

In marrying Ada Todd, King had crossed a line that would irrevocably
separate him in his own mind from his social world. Henceforth King's life
was cut in two. He became the public man of the clubs and the Pullman
cars, expert witness, capitalist. And there was his secret world, his house
in Queens, his children and his wife. His mother still lived. The fact of
his marriage, were it to come out, would ruin him in her eyes and in the
circles in which he needed to move to keep his family fed. But more, it would
destroy the division that, perhaps, he himself needed, that subterfuge that
kept him from becoming whole. Almost to the end, this friend of the black
race, this father of loved mulatto children, was distorting his longtime black
servant's impeccable English into minstrel-show dialect for the sake of a
story. That long-meditated, unfinished novel begins with the same kind of
racial travesty.[37]

There was something not right about King. Henry Adams thought King
had failed for want of money. The younger Agassiz had put off his scientific
career to go up to the copper mines of the lakes and had made them all rich—

shouldn't King, so much more gifted, so much more charming, make them—
and himself—even richer? Others had married money—men like John Hay
or Whitelaw Reid. But Adams, who, when he looked back on King's life, was
brooding on his own failure in marriage and bearing the silent rage of the
cuckold—cuckolded terminally by that old seducer, Death—would only hint
at the secret marriage his friend had made. King could have played out his
hand on the near side of the color line safely. Many were the brown girls to
be had for casual enjoyment, to be had for a new hat or a bit of cheap jewelry or purchased in discreet establishments catering exclusively to white men
with his tastes. What his society demanded was not the extinction of the life
of the senses, but, as Oscar Wilde was so horribly to discover, its social con-
tainment. So King might have followed the lead of Adams's friend Dickie
Milnes, who of a Sunday morning at his country house might direct a favored
guest to some choice bit of pornography in his vast private library, and then,
in his character as Lord Houghton, drive off to church with his lady.[38] What
such a divided life may have cost is figured in the monstrous Doubles who
haunt the tales of Stevenson and Wilde and Conrad and Poe. But, perhaps,
there was in King too an element that fed on the secrecy, the necessary sepa-
rations. An element that could express itself only in violent, but secret, con-
frontation with the genteel world. There was another man under the debonair
aristocrat, a man who went out at night in New York City with a heavy stick,
wandered past Washington Square and into the rough jungles of "Africa"—
the Thompson–Sullivan Street region, looking for a fight.[39]

> Darling: Yesterday I went over to Brooklyn to get the rent money
> from Mr. Thomas to pay next Monday, and there I got your love
> letter. My darling, I knew all your feeling. I knew just how you
> love me and how you miss me and how you long for the days and
> nights to come again when we can lie together and let our love flow
> out to each other and full hearts have their way.[40]

He was living much in clubs in those days. In smoking rooms and at banquet tables he wove his stories, fabulous stories, that began in some magi-
cal middle and ended nowhere.[41] He was a fascinator, Henry James would
say.[42] He fascinated the men he led up mountains and through awful deserts,
the men he told his wonderful stories to around campfires in the Rockies
and over cigars in the clubs of New York and Washington and London. He

48

fascinated generals and Sierra muleskinners and Cuban revolutionaries and the English Rothschilds and artists and eager young men just starting out on their scientific careers. He fascinated John Hay, something of a prodigy himself, who had gone beyond being Lincoln's secretary to making himself, as one historian has put it, the Henry Kissinger of his age (it was Hay who, quoting Shelley, called King "the best and brightest" of his generation). Fascinated that rare bird Henry Adams, who not much else in his benighted age could fascinate out of his lifelong snit. Fascinated old John Ruskin, poking about in a London picture-dealer's—fascinated *him* out of a couple of choice Turners—"one good Turner deserves another," said King, always prompt with a dreadful pun; fascinated a Spanish *posadera* out of a beat-up barber's basin and fascinated the Prince of Wales and Henry James, whom he took slumming, and whom he imagined buttoning up a few choice invitations in his inner pocket, so there'd be no mistaking the social position of his corpse should violence befall him; fascinated the girls in the Cross and Blackwell's pickle factory and those Soho barmaids James imagined mourning Kings' absence in plaintive helegies and who-knows-how-many women of what ages and what colors and on what continents, but in the end could not fascinate enough investors out of enough gold, or enough gold or silver out of his drifts, or enough water out of the chugging pumps that were trying to bail out those poor drowning mines in Mexico. He was a fascinator still, and the chief victim of his fascination was himself.

The laughter rose like the smoke of the cigars. It was the Hen and the Gondolier, or simply the account of a streetcar ride, elaborated like some tale out of the *Arabian Nights*. He was a liar, and they knew it. Once someone questioned him about the height or the pitch of a mountain in one of his tales: he offered to negotiate a discount in return for a flat acceptance. King watched his life unfolding as formlessly as one of his stories, swirling and breaking up: what was it now but smoke? He wrote to Hay that he had resolved and had "thus far succeeded" to smother and hide his pessimistic hate of civilization and to be "as straightlaced and wooden and fatuously American as anybody."

> *I shall go to the Metropolitan Club and make myself beloved of all the stable boys whom fate has raised to the nth power and chum with all the huxters manquées and carry off the role of a good practical sensible American bourgeois cad, to the queen's taste.*

49

He was now going "with a singleness of purpose, an early and late devotion" to the New York struggle for money. "No matter how much I hate the people and the life," he wrote, "no one shall see it or know it. . . . I have sinned, I own, in allowing my nature to influence my life. I shall do it no more till I am able to say to my nature, 'at last it is your turn, be free!'"[43] But he never was able to say it.

The secret life, the life of the passions, lay hidden, known only to Hay, a few other men; perhaps not even yet to Henry Adams. It lay hidden like the paintings and treasures he had stored in the little dark room on Tenth Street. He might daydream of a suitable setting for them, a dream-palace with its frieze of stained glass, which he constructed in his mind for his friend La Farge,[44] as he might dream of a safe haven for his wife and children in Canada. The dreams never came to pass. The expeditions to consult on mines in rough towns in the West and as far as the Klondike took their toll. His novel on women remained a few poor pages in his execrable handwriting. Howells thought he would have never finished it anyway. For a man so profoundly afflicted by the pathos of nomadism, the house he had made for his wife and his children became something he had to avoid, and he wrote Ada he had not come for fear of talk, for fear boarders were around.[45] He clung to the hope of some small legacy from his aunt. He was sick of an old spinal injury in those days, sometimes shabby, and had lost weight. The Bitch Goddess Success had raced far from him. In 1896 Homer Plessy, with his Caucasian looks and his one-eighth black heritage, was told by the U.S. Supreme Court that the Louisiana railroad that denied him a seat in the coach reserved for whites had not erred. The decision effectively ended any hope Clarence King might have had that his children could become fully a part of the new America he had helped to make. The railroad trains of Louisiana could safely curtain off that one table in the dining car for the black citizens the country did not want to see. It was a curtain like that King had drawn over his own family, after all. Only in 1901 did he write to Ada his real name. He instructed her to keep it in the Bible, in case she forgot it. He was in Arizona learning how to die.

Once, King had written a slight little essay for a friend in San Francisco. He shared with his friend a passion for Cervantes. It was an odd taste, perhaps, for a man so vigorous, so much in the world as Clarence King. In Spain he had gone down to the barren country where the old Knight of the Sorrowful Visage had lived his imaginary life, and had purchased there just that sort of barber's basin, green with verdigris, with its chin notch, that Don Quixote had dubbed the fabulous Helmet of Mambrino. He had sent his friend, a ruined speculator, the bowl, with the essay as an envoy. But the story touched something deep in King, something that had lasted him longer than his science, which had been eclipsed, or the peaks he climbed and named in his youth. Let the Sancho Panzas of the world laugh: Quixote knew the true worth of the helmet that had by some strange accident fallen into someone's hands who had not recognized its value, and had melted down the half of it that was pure gold and made of the remainder something very like a barber's basin. Like the true secret of the helmet, this thing inside King was there all along, if only he could see it, his vocation for failure, which he had fought desperately against; more enduring than the fortune that he had failed to seize, that had slipped through his fingers.

"I have been at times all but morbidly aware of the power of local attachment, finding it absurdly hard to turn the key on doors I have entered often and with pleasure," he had written in his youthful first book,[46] and now, at the end of his life, he might have looked back on the dead and dying gold towns of California and their pathos as he had described them then, those hundred towns and camps with their empty buildings standing in rows, no nailing up of blinds to hide the vacancy, the houses standing with wide-open doors, their cloth walls and ceilings torn down to make squaw petticoats, the cheap squalor of the Chinese streets, the pigs prowling the empty roads.

The fund he'd told Ada he had set apart for her and her children, like so much in his life, turns out to be a fiction. (It is Hay, in the end, who secretly supports Ada and, in a final irony, that mother from whom King had so long hidden his marriage.)[47] King's bank fails. His mines fill up with water and the ore plays out. He buys up the plates to Mountaineering, tries to suppress it. His stories sail up into the cigar smoke of the clubs. He will die insolvent.

G. Hunter Bartlett, *Administration Building at Night, Worlds Columbian Exposition; Chicago (Ill.); 1893.* Chicago Historical Society, ICHI—13854.

I went to the animal fair
The birds and the beasts were there.
The big baboon by the light of the moon
Was combing his auburn hair.

The monkey he got drunk
And sat on the elephant's trunk.
The elephant sneezed and fell on his knees
And what became of the monk?

American minstrel song

Two

Henry Adams at the Fair

MAXWELL'S DEMONS

Everybody Henry Adams knew was either dead or dying as the summer of 1893 approached. His neighbors most generally sat down on their stairs, or wherever came handy, and died. Somewhere he must go, and the quicker, the further, and the more quietly he went, the better. He thought of Europe or the Yellowstone.[1]

He was wrestling with kinetic theory and Maxwell's sorting demons. The trouble was his brain, which would not sort. At the observed rate of dissipation, say twenty million years, any molecules must be dead. But Maxwell gave no definition of a dead molecule. The dead molecule, Adams wrote, was really himself. He could not bounce violently enough to understand the kinetic theory.[2]

In May he went to Chicago with Senator Cameron, his beloved (by Adams) wife Elizabeth, and their party in the senator's private car. On the edge of the lake whose great city had been named for the wild onions the Potawatomis harvested there, another race had erected an ideal city of plaster and steel to celebrate the four hundredth anniversary of its arrival on the continent. In spite of the economic rumbling that had accompanied the opening of the Fair, the crowds flocked to the ideal city. They toured the exhibits housed in the neoclassical buildings that had risen from Lake Michigan mud, it seemed, overnight. They visited the Midway and rode on the Ferris Wheel and gaped at the muscular allegorical statues that were the sum of artistic production at the approaching end of a century of power. At the presentation of the first sketches of the Fair by its architects, Augustus Saint-Gaudens had looked around the room and said, "This is the greatest meeting of artists since the fifteenth century!"[3] "Sell the cookstove if necessary and come," Hamlin Garland wrote his father. "You *must* see this fair."[4]

The mental excitement and disturbance upset Adams's usual balance so much that he found it hard to write on the subject. The two days he spent there were hardly enough to take it in. Who would have imagined that Chicago would suddenly and without apparent cause or consequence lavish millions and infinite effort to produce something that the Greeks might have delighted to see, and Venice would have envied?[5]

But then he was off to England. His depression returned. He wrote to John Hay from Wakefield, "As for me, I crawl in corners and lie in dark holes like a mangy and worn-out rabbit, and play pretend to be alive when noticed; but it is rather ghastly." He wished Hay were there to protect him.[6] For one who made no calls and never dined out, London at the height of the season was a grisly desert, full of weary sandwiches at a club. He sat in corners and wondered why he came and he thought of the long, long years when he thought it amusing and wondered who was alive and which was the ghost, the rest of the world or himself.[7]

By July he was on his way home, summoned by telegram from Switzerland by his brother Brooks. The financial crisis that had rumbled in May had not abated, and a full-scale panic had ensued. European investors were abandoning the United States, and their business houses were sucking up American gold like siphons; banks and railroads fell every day. The Adams family trusts were in serious danger: he had been called home to help.

In Quincy, Adams found everything in disorder. His personal fortune had been untouched, and his family's would survive, due in part to some timely work on his part with railroad bonds, but the strain of the panic had broken men down by the score. It was as if the whole generation had had notice to quit.[8] He hadn't heard from Clarence King, but could only assume he'd

54

gone up in flames as usual, though this time in a "numerous and respectable New York society."[9] Adams's nerves were broken up. He saw everything black and he wanted to change the scenery. Boston always had that effect on him. He was in a panic of terror about finance, politics, society, and the solar system, with ultimate fears for the Milky Way and the Nebula of Orion. The sunspots scared him. Ruin hung over the polestar. Of course, he wrote Elizabeth Cameron, this meant the approach of old age and senility, but he saw nothing optimistic in that.[10]

In October he was back in Chicago, staying at the Hotel Windermere at the very door of the Fair. He was with his brother Charles and his wife, their daughter Elsie, Looly Hooper, and his housekeeper, Maggy Wade. Brooks came for a day, but, difficult as always, fled with the excuse of rheumatism.

Chicago, on this second visit, was even more amusing for Adams than it had been in May. Twenty skyscrapers, their skeletons all of steel, rose into the air, and the city, as he'd observed on his first trip, had seemed twice the height it had been on his earlier encounters. Visitors gawked at the Auditorium, the Rookery, the uncompleted Stock Exchange building. Hyperbole, a scholar has said, was Chicago's native idiom.[11] It was true. Twenty-two years before, the city had been reduced to ashes in the great fire; seven years before, it had shuddered under the fear that an anarchist was under every bed. But here it stood, puffed up with boosterism, concrete, and steel. Still, it was the White City of the Fair that engrossed Adams. He was like someone who had seen a vision, blinked, and blinked again to make sure it hadn't gone away. He gazed out on a pure white temple on the pure blue sea with an Italian sky, all vast and beautiful as the world never saw it before and in it the most astonishing, confused, bewildering mass of art and industry, without a sign that there was any connection, relation, or harmony or understanding of the relation of anything else anywhere.[12]

The chain linking him to his father, and a world based on moral law, had seemed to have snapped as well. In the midst of the Civil War, acting as his father's secretary at the Court of St. James, Adams had visited Wenlock Edge, for it was there, Lyell had told him, reposing under the Ludlow shale of Adams's favorite abbey, that Adams's earliest ancestor, a fossilized armor-plated fish called *Pteraspis*, lay. Brooding there, with that fratricidal war at his back, young Adams could not attach to *Pteraspis*'s appearance or disappearance any moral meaning. "Out of his millions of millions of ancestors, back to the Cambrian mollusks, every one had probably lived and died in the illusion of Truths which did not amuse him, and which had never changed. Henry Adams was the first in an infinite series to discover and admit to himself that he really did not care whether truth was, or was not, true. He did not even care that it should be proved true, unless the process were new and amusing."[13]

Adams had come out of the conflagration of the Civil War morally singed, bearing off his aging father and what few of the household gods he could conveniently get hold of on his narrow back. For almost thirty years he had been sailing around the world trying to find his America—that new Rome. So he stood there, in those bright fall days toward the end of 1893, on this shore that had sprung up before him with all the strangeness and delight of discovery, having emerged like some new Aeneas from his private hell, holding the brim of his hat piously in his hand, as he gazed out across what had once been barren swamps and sandhills and into the dream city that would be the American future.

And for the first time in years (if we can make inference from his response), there was a lightness on his shoulders, that burden he had been bearing had lifted; perhaps had lifted from all of his peers, post-Darwin, post–Civil War, post-Grant.

He was fifty-five. Small, with high bald forehead and dark eyes, insomniac, with delicate hands. Here, on the shores of Lake Michigan, with the Fair shimmering in the water before him, his life was suspended between two silences, the one at his back, and the one that stretched before him.

CLOVER

Before Clover Hooper married, she had a horrible dream. She dreamt that between her and her sister Ellen there had been for ever so many years a wall of ice, and that when she tried to look through it she saw something in her sister that was so like herself that it made her cold all over. Marriage had warmed her sister's side of the wall; now its prospect had begun to warm Clover's as well. At first she had snapped her fingers at that warmth and tried to ignore it, but by and by it got so warm that she tried to move and couldn't. Then came a day where, about sunset, the sun blinded her so that she had put her hands up to her face in terror, and when she took them away, there sat Henry Adams, holding them, and the ice had all melted away. She was a Hooper, and if a feeling was very pleasant she felt as if it were wrong. But now she was going to sit in the sun as long as it shined.[14]

Her mother had died when she was five years old, and she had been brought up with a sister and brother by her valetudinarian father, a physician who no longer practiced, among Sturgises and Hoopers in patrician Boston. She was small, intelligent, serious—not quite pretty, with what could be a biting wit. She had made an alliance with the perfect man.

As he strolled along the Midway that fall, the sights and smells of that ersatz street in Cairo the promoters had set up might have caused Henry Adams to think of his own Egyptian travels, and that long, slow journey by dahabeah up the Nile twenty years before. It had been his wedding journey. He had watched the shores as he drifted by, awed by the silent monuments of an ancient civilization. Nothing he had seen in the world was equal to the temple of Ramses at Abu Simbel, he enthused. But after a while Clover—his wife—did not enthuse. For the first time on her honeymoon she felt the madness that had run through her family begin to beat its wings over her.

All of America was going up the Nile that winter. The Wards of Boston, the Roosevelts of New York, with their bespectacled fourteen-year-old son (who seemed interested only in shooting and stuffing exotic birds), George Bancroft, Emerson. Otto Friedrich, Clover's biographer, had the happy idea of following Emerson as a way of imagining the Adamses' trip. We might follow as well. Emerson was recovering from a stroke, and even in his own language he was having trouble finding the right word to fit his thought. The obelisks, the temple walls, defied him with their histories, which he could not spell. The journey was a perpetual humiliation, satirizing and whipping him for his ignorance. He watched the endless shore, that thin ribbon of green on either side of the river. Day after day and week after week of unbroken sunshine, and though you might see clouds in the sky, they were merely for ornament, never for rain. At every landing, blind beggars appeared, led by their children. Flies roosted in the eyes of the babies and the boys. They did not notice their presence. The people walked with the grace of ancient philosophers going to the School of Athens. The monuments oppressed him. Their ancientness was a weight on an American, his transcendental wings held down by the oppression of time, time so ancient that the foundation stones of the temples had writing on their undersides, for they were built on the ruins of even older civilizations. Every new object only made new questions for each traveler to ask the other, and none could answer, and each sank lower in the opinion of his companions. The sphinxes scorned dunces. The old man grew satirical. Could anyone argue wilder insanity than leaving a country like the United States to see this bareness of mud? Look! There is some water, and see! there is a crowd of people. They have collected with a purpose of drowning themselves. At Karnak he left the river and returned to Cairo by train.[15]

On the river the joy of sunny, perfect days gave way to tedium for Clover. The wind blew cold, forcing them to cower on shore. Clover never seemed to get impressions that were worth anything. She felt as if she were blind, and deaf and dumb. Everyone around her was so intelligent and cultivated. Everything appealed to them, but she was disgusted at her want of curiosity and hated the process of seeing things of which she was hopelessly ignorant. She found it impossible to get her thoughts straightened out at all.[16] She wrote her father and watched her small, balding husband fiddling with the lens of his camera, or reading in the shade of the boat's awning, and Egypt and its endless flies and sand and dirt and beggars drifted by.

At Karnak, perhaps, towered over by those ancient, speechless stones, something happened to Clover. What it was is obscure. There was a spell of something, some deep depression, some nameless thing. Only a little Bible with a mysterious coded inscription remains.[17]

And then they were home with their trunks of bric-a-brac and paintings and the gowns from Worth and their love. They had chosen Washington as a place to set down their roots. There on H Street, with Clover's Turner over the mantelpiece and a visitor—perhaps it was Henry James, hands under the tails of his coat, warming his backside at the fire—the couple whom James called "the little Adamses" held court. And they were, in some sense, little—like very precocious children, in that house whose diminutive furniture was chosen to fit their statures—children who touched a world, but only, it sometimes seems, in a kind of pantomime.

Adams installed himself in the Library of Congress to work on his history of the Jefferson and Madison administrations, that book which he hoped would make him the American Gibbon. Beyond the walls of H Street, the Capitol, presided over by the unfinished phallus of the Washington Monument, sank into the mud, a bog of corruption and intrigue. Perched on its edge, Adams and Clover railed and mocked. Their friend James satirized them in a story: "Hang it . . . let us have some fun—let us invite the President."[18] They filled their salon with the wits and *élégants* of the capital: John Hay, Lamar of Mississippi, Aristarchi Bey planting his cynical Greek feet on Clover's yellow carpet, Carl Shurz playing deliciously on Clover's piano. Afternoons they rode out to Rock Creek. They came back in the fecund spring bedecked with flowers, like a pagan bridal couple.

Clarence King had taken leave from the United States Geological Survey in order to seize the fortune in gold and silver that he, best of all men, could see beneath the folds of the earth. All through the winter of 1880–81 they had reports: King was ill in Arizona, desperately out of pocket. He had gone off to Mexico to look into the mines at Prietas . . . And then he turned up one Sunday in February, very well and jolly, after a fearful fourteen-hundred-mile trip on mule-back through Mexico. He'd been swamped in a flood, lost all his papers and money, but he had come through, and here he was, like spring itself, full of stories and inside tips on mining stocks, sitting late by the fire with them, and babbling while Clover tried to finish a letter.[19]

Clover was the sort of woman King could be satirical about. A New England bluestocking with an "unabridged dictionary of a mind," as he'd said of the type—not the kind of woman one could imagine kissing, or much else. But he cared for her, and, it may be, more than Henry Adams, knew her. Beyond the banter and the wit and the social shine Clover held out to the world, King might have recognized a deeper kinship. In the library, set apart from the Bonnington, the little Reynolds portraits, the Turner with its shepherds and castle, was the horrible image of Blake's Nebuchadnezzar—something Clover and Henry had brought back from their honeymoon, hideous, but too good to pass up. Distracted a moment from the gossip of the tea table, one King scrutinized another. Fallen from his glory, naked, crawling, his hands turned to claws, eating grass like a beast of the fields, Nebuchadnezzar was mad, stricken with the insanity of the world, the blindness of materialism.

In Washington the Adamses continued their round of dinners and receptions, commenting wryly on the comings and goings of presidents and senators. With King and the Hays they made a select little circle they called the Five of Hearts. Their lives were in perfect regulation. But all the while Clover was slipping away from Adams.

They were childless. Whatever their sexual life had been, it now became the study of tomes on reproduction and sterility—sterility in the female—of consultation with physicians, with experts. There was something almost childish about them in itself.[20] No matter how large their own ambitions or productions or how brilliant the company gathered around their table, they were playing at life. Detached from posterity, they floated free. They were just what they had created themselves as: a unique couple, isolated in their very exclusiveness, in their aversions and discriminations. It was as if they were burdened by the need to mirror themselves and their life at every moment, to hold its glass up to their narcissism, to force it to tell them that they were themselves. They were to be only that terrifying moment, cut off from history, cut off from the future.

Clover took up photography. She filled her notebooks with chemical formulae and records of exposure times. Washed in waves of the developing fluid, the same faces and figures that had filled her house appeared as ghostly negatives of themselves. The artist La Farge, George Bancroft, Francis Parkman, John Hay, Oliver Wendell Holmes Jr., who a little more than ten years before had thought he had died at Ball's Bluff, but now sat confident and mustachioed, a hand casually in his pocket. Little Jerome Bonaparte straddling a chair and tooting a toy trumpet. It was as if she wanted to fix them all, to catch them as they rushed across the curve of her camera's lens. Adams himself she could not fix. He'd taught her the rudiments of the camera, but loathed to be photographed himself. She caught him sometimes informally. At his desk or with one of the dogs. She photographed herself in her study. "15 sec—hideous but good photo," her note read.[21]

And all the while death was rushing toward her. She must have heard it under the chatter of the tea table, under the music of an embassy reception, like the roar of some mighty cataract. And she was hurrying about, desperately trying to snatch those faces, those people she knew, from death's oblivion, Henry and Boojum and Betsy Wilder, her father and Secretary Evarts and the good General Miles, so concerned about his poor Indians, to snatch them from that rushing precipice. The albums filled up with the faces she knew, caught in little rectangles of frozen light. She was making a necropolis of her world: stone faces staring into the future from the land of the dead.

Outside, on Lafayette Square, opposite the White House and a kind of deliberate affront to its vulgarity and ambition, rose their own house, and that of their friends the Hays. Austere, fortresslike (Clover said it was done in Richardson's neo-agnostic mode), it took shape. She may have known she would never live in it. Sundays she still sat down to write her smart, chatty little letter to her father. She wrote about the dogs, the dismal winter. About Henry. The letter opened up the Sunday stillness like a wound. The ice barrier she had dreamed and had imagined melted had come again to stand between her and the world. She and Adams were in hell.

CHAOS

Forty Ladies from Forty Countries: The World Congress of Beauty

In dirndls and djellabas, in togas and tiaras, the forty ladies smiled and smirked, sparkled and beautified. (They were, it turned out, remarkably backward in their forty native tongues, but remarkably fluent in German as it is spoken in Vienna.) Adams had seen much of the world's women by 1893. He had been paddled about Tahiti by delicious teenagers (it was said, for a smile they'd do more than paddle, although he never tested that) and had sipped tea with many a countess. He had seen the women of Japan, who struck him as doll-like and mechanical, and there were the Americans, smart and pert—but the American woman, he thought, was a failure. It was a question that loomed large for Adams, this question of women. A nineteenth-century man, he saw them as a different species.

Yes, American women were failures, but it was the men who had failed them. Years before, Adams looked back on Boston. "In this Arcadian society sexual passions seem to be abolished. Whether it is so or not, I can't say, but I suspect both men and women are cold, and love only with great refinement. How they ever reconcile themselves to the brutalities of marriage, I don't know."[22] He was questioning himself.

At the Exposition Adams wandered among neo-Greco-Roman statues, Victorian anecdotes, the last bubbling effusions of an era hardened into stone. He might have been amused to see himself, duly embossed and catalogued, on the covers of his books in the display of the American Library Society. It was a different man, he knew, who had hunched over the manuscripts of those pages, one he scarcely recognized anymore. He had become a spectator of himself. Solemnly, methodically, he labored through the great buildings and looked like an owl at the dynamos and turbines. All the time he kept up a devil of a thinking. He remembered Sargent's portrait of Mrs. Hugh Hammersley that had been exhibited in London that summer. The fashionable hostess with the thimble-narrow waist sat draped in red in her drawing room, her little pointed chin and sparkling, mocking eyes presenting themselves for pleasure and admiration, at once witty and predatory—was it a defiance or an insult to our society, this portrait, or a rendering in good faith of our civilization, or a conscious snub to French and English art, or the artist's despair of reconciliation with the female of the goldbug? Well! The architecture of the Fair, Adams decided, was precisely an architectural Mrs. Hammersley. The ornate white buildings, the statues, were an appeal to the human animal, the superstitious and ignorant savage within us that has instincts and no reason, against the world as money had made it.[23] So Adams gazed and gaped. Endless allegories in plaster and hair gazed down at him from the pediments of the buildings. Fountains spumed and spouted in Olmsted's lagoon. Naked as God—or Nature—made her, *Columbia* plopped her plump nether cheeks on the throne of her barge of state (*Fame* at the bow, *Time* at the stern) as Triton spewed and dolphins frolicked—Bernini after a bad night—while at the far side of the lagoon, stern, togaed mother *Republic* (fair-goers called her Big Mary) looked on disapprovingly and raised her liberty cap and orb as if to clobber the revelers at the other end. All about the White City, froth turned miraculously to stone—but it wasn't stone—it was only a gypsum-and-hair concoction called "staff" troweled over a framework of steel. The entire City was made of it—Roman columns, Venetian domes, Greek peristyles, and Florentine galleries, with their statues and entablatures and bas-reliefs—and all sprayed one single shade of glittering white by huge hoses wielded by men in overalls and goggles. It was some ersatz Europe, permanent as marzipan. A Europe without a history. A dream issuing forth from the Ivory Gates.[24] "All trader's taste smelt of bric-a-brac," Adams concluded. "Chicago tried at least to give her taste a look of unity."[25]

Within the art galleries Dickens looked down fondly at Little Nell, statesmen disposed, Orpheus raptured, Indians gazed nobly through their marble, unseeing eyes, and buffalo browsed. And always there were the nymphs, clothed only in their innocence, who turned plump marble shoulders to Adams, or presented their nude flesh on canvas, their lubricity redeemed by coy charm. Here a Bouguereau simpered pinkly, a Sargent exotic turned her backside toward him, wearing nothing but her long, swaying hair—a sort of Nilotic Mrs. Hugh Hammersley, without the gown. This was art. (But the frankness of Eakins's heroic portraits of Drs. Agnew and Gross, who cut beneath the living flesh of half-undraped patients, was too much for Chicago. The *Tribune* was stern: the accessories of the paintings—meaning the surgeons' bloody fingers—made them unfit for public exhibition.[26] Nor was there, at the Fair, among all those pudgy French nudes, and despite a few Degas dancers, anything like Manet's *Olympia* of 1863, coolly appraising a customer—or the gallery viewer—while dangling a sandal from one naked foot. A telling lapse in a city where one crusader counted thirty-seven houses of ill fame in one precinct alone.[27] This was America, and Americans liked their realism cut with moralizing and their sex carved out of lump sugar or veiled by the invisible veils of the Ideal.)

Columbus had discovered America, said the head of the Board of Lady Managers, the self-confident Chicago society woman Mrs. Potter Palmer, but even more important, the United States had discovered woman.[28] Well, that may have been so, as far the government was concerned, with the Fair's Woman's Building rising above the lake, designed by women, decorated by them, inhabited by their arts. But as for Adams, he was still searching. And there was in him that deep emptiness left by the absence of his wife, that perfect little artifact of his age, and his own unacknowledged, speechless anger and pain.

In the spring of 1884, with his and Hay's house being drawn up, Adams had published another book. As in his earlier satire on Washington, he took a female pseudonym—the gender change amused him—which called up the formidable Puritan bluestocking inside him that he loathed and could not reconcile himself to. The book was called *Esther*. It was not art, this book. He was not twanging with a vengeance, as James would say, the aesthetic lyre. It was, like Clover's photographs, an attempt to seize something that, for all its seeming solidity, was a shadow moving across the glass. The cruelty of the book was an expression of his own pain. He put them all in it, Clover, Clarence King, La Farge, himself . . . It was strange. He himself became King, the scientist, the man of action—with King's resolution but without King's heartfelt Christianity. And he was the clergyman who loves the girl Esther, Esther who in turn loves him but cannot have him because she cannot, ultimately, believe, and whose own passion cannot be fulfilled, for her art is condemned to the eternal limbo of the amateur. It was as if in this book Adams were reversing the narrative of his and Clover's union, unwinding its skein, trying to set himself and Clover free.

He had given Clover a novel by Howells as a wedding present. A honeymoon book that ended at Niagara. Adams's book too ends at Niagara, but its issue was not marriage, but rejection, incompletion. In *Esther* Henry Adams prophesied it all—the end of Clover's happiness, the death of her father, her despair. The last thing only he did not write, perhaps because he did not see it, or would not see it. Only Clarence King rooted it out of those anonymous pages. He told Henry Adams that in those last pages at Niagara when his heroine rejects the clergyman who loves her, that Esther should have thrown herself into the falls. For King might have known her better than Adams after all. In Idaho once he too had stared into a falls, and felt the demons rising in him.

When it came, it came swiftly. On April 13, 1885, Clover's father died. She did not recover from the shock. She had never given herself, really, to anyone else, and then he was gone. She was crushed by her unworthiness, her insignificance, the sinful things she had done, her awful omissions. All of it rose up against her, accusing her. "Ellen I'm not real," she cried out to her sister. "Oh, make me real—You are all of you real!"[29]

On Sunday, December 6, 1885, Henry Adams found his wife dead. She had swallowed the potassium cyanide she used to retouch her photographs.

Henry Adams burned all of Clover's letters, all the photographs he had of her, got rid of her belongings. She lay buried in Rock Creek Cemetery under an enigmatic statue of a hooded woman he had commissioned from Saint-Gaudens with no inscription on it, not even her name. As for himself, his own public existence, his own search for a place in an active world, had ended. With Clover's suicide he commenced what he called his posthumous life. He would keep on leading it until 1918.

On Chicago Day, Adams crowded through the gates of Jackson Park with his fellow fair-goers. "The Exposition itself," he later wrote, "defied philosophy. One might find fault till the last gate closed, one could still explain nothing that needed explanation. . . . Since Noah's Ark, no such Babel of loose and ill-joined, such vague and ill-defined and unrelated thoughts and half-thoughts and experimental outcries as the Exposition, had ever ruffled the surface of the lakes."[30]

All day long the statues of the fairgrounds were black with crowds hanging on them to watch the parades. There would be floats, a balloon ascension, a tightrope walker, and in the night, fireworks. From the roof of the Administration Building the Court of Honor was a sea of umbrellas.[31] And everywhere roiled all of Chicago, shoving and spitting, sweating under picnic hampers and boxes, pulling its children by the arms. Crammed into the lanes of the Midway Plaisance, between the great buildings in which the dying century announced, although it did not know it, the terminal hurrah of its ideals, the Chicagoans had thronged the alleys of the Streets of Cairo, with their sword swallowers and camels, had ogled Eskimos and the Fon of Dahomey in their wattle huts, had lost themselves in the mirrors of the Moorish Palace and watched Muybridge's horses gallop across a screen and a flickering fragment of life stutter through Edison's Kinetoscope.[32]

Adams wondered if the twenty million visitors carried off the same sense he did. Probably not, for he had long recognized the same chaos in his own mind and knew it when he saw it, while they probably felt it for the first time. They would think of it as education. Precisely what education was, he didn't know. Perhaps it was to learn chaos when one saw it. He preferred to treat the Fair as amusement.[33] The Midway Plaisance was a sweet repose, he thought somewhat grimly. He reveled in all the Midway's fakes and frauds (in the Java village one could look at the Missing Link; then, there was the Ostrich Farm, of course), and he did not think anyone understood the real wicked-ness or, even less, the genuineness of the Fair.[34]

Looking at the map of the United States made entirely of pickles, say, or at the fifteen-hundred-pound chocolate Venus de Milo, or that monstrous cheese from Ontario, a visitor might understand how Adams could think one might decline to take the Exposition seriously. Adams wasn't quite sure that it wasn't all a joke (he'd heard of people base enough, and immoral enough, to affect to regard even Boston as a joke). Surely the Fair was a seductive vanity. There was something about it strangely unreal to Henry Adams. It reminded him somehow—and he wondered if this were so for the architects and artists who had made it—as akin to the only real art left nowadays: scene painting for the theater. Anyway, its beauty was the same, whether it was solemn earnest or play. Of course he didn't understand it, the meaning of this dream of beauty. But then, he didn't understand anything—not even Beacon Street. His business was to look on and wonder at everything on the earth and off it.[35] Still he thought he found, amid the cacophony and chaotic jumble of displays, and the riot of education they proclaimed, a sort of clue, both for the future and, though he would not be a part of that future, for himself. He sat under the dome of his friend Richard Hunt's Administration Building to ponder the leap this crass commercial city of Chicago had made "directly over the heads of London and New York" to become one with Corinth and Syracuse and Venice. "Was it real, or only apparent? One's personal universe hung on the answer, for, if the rupture was real and the new American world could take this sharp and conscious twist toward ideals, one's personal friends would come in, at last, as winners in the great American chariot-race for fame."[36]

Night and day the great dynamos purred, spinning out Tesla's alternating current. Here was the heart of the Fair, if any could see it, beyond the confectionery domes and towers, the lagoons, the gondolas, the humorless allegorical statues. It was power. Henry Adams lingered long before the dynamos.[37] The raw energy stored up in a society and sent out by wires to light the buildings and the fountains, the numberless globes turned the Fair, at night, into a vision. But who was to control that energy? Where was it tending?

The armies of laborers who had drained the swamp at Jackson Park, the wheelbarrow pushers and carpenters and groundskeepers and masons, were gone. Inside the halls and beside the great machines, or safely locked up in the scale model of George Pullman's ideal community in the central court of the Transportation Building, the toil imbedded in the goods that spilled out from every corner of the Fair was invisible. It was as if that latter-day Roman Triumph by the lake, with its parade of booty and conquered peoples, had somehow left out its marching legions. But that August past, whether it wanted to or not, Chicago had seen its workers. For days the unemployed had been meeting by the statue of Columbus across from the Auditorium. On the thirtieth of August, the building trades unions in Chicago organized a mass meeting at the sandlots north of the Art Institute. The crowd, as many as twenty-five thousand men, with some women, marched behind the Carpenters' Band and the six wagons that would be platforms for the speakers. Everywhere were police, breaking up little knots of men if anyone

66

started to speak, moving the crowd on. Earlier in the day, they had driven off a crowd of six thousand men who had gathered around the Columbus statue, some of them armed with barrel staves and newspapers hiding iron bars and coupling pins. A thousand Italians had been driven away from Louis Spizzirri's store on State Street, demanding Italian flags. "I have men enough to crush out any riot which could start today on the Lake-Front," Chief of Police Brennan said. "But those fellows on the Lake-Front this morning were not laborers. They were foreigners, men who knew no law in their own countries and knew none here. They should be made to know there is law here, and law that will reach them. I have no fear but that we can suppress them." The marchers followed the band and the wagons to the sandlot. Well-dressed people stared out from the balconies and windows and the roofs of the great Michigan Avenue hotels. At the Second Regiment Armory the sidewalks were patrolled by uniformed guardsmen bearing rifles and fixed bayonets. The roof was covered with armed men. In the middle of the hall artillerymen were working about two Gatling guns and a pair of Napoleon cannons. At the sandlot speakers rallied the marchers from the wagons, Samuel Gompers declaiming and Henry George calling as ever for the single tax. Clarence Darrow mocked the idea that men were made poor by patronizing saloons, the idea that public employment agencies would solve anything. A man named Tommy Morgan, who showed up in his overalls and jacket and leather apron, climbed up on a wagon. His clothes were no bluff, he said. He had just come from work. He told the unemployed men and women to bear all the burdens heaped upon them as long as they could. When the limit was reached, then do what they must. He had no advice for them after that time came. They knew what to do. Robert Steinert spoke in German. He saw Mayor Harrison at the edge of the crowd, just coming from the fairgrounds. Steinert reminded the laborers that they had built the Fair, and asked how many of the thousands gathered at the Lakefront had had the chance to see the Fair even once. Steinert urged the workers to remain quiet, endure their suffering, and walk the streets like hungry cats. Bishop Fallows claimed the public officials were one with the workers. After all, where did the police come from? "Ireland," three or four hundred people shouted to cheers and laughter. The crowds dispersed.[38] Not a few might have gone home remembering the four Haymarket martyrs hanging from nooses in the Cook County Jail five years before, and August Spies's last words:

"There will come a time when our silence will be more powerful than the voices you strangle today."

In those hot evenings that past August, Brooks and Henry Adams had sat in the study at Quincy that had been used by two presidents and talked endlessly about the panic, about history, and about their own family. During that season that wore away amid an excitement, Brooks later wrote, verging on revolution, Brooks had presented Adams with a manuscript. A strange, blunt document that presumed to show the great centers of the Western world going through inexorable cycles of consolidation and dissolution, expanding and being split into atoms as the cycles of accumulation and debt followed one after another according to laws as rigid and unarguable as those of physics and biology. Brooks's long series of investigations, which had taken him all around the Mediterranean basin, had forced upon him the conclusion that all history was governed by unmitigated oscillations between fear and greed. Fear expressed itself in war, and in the great edifices of religion and religious art. Thus, fear was productive of beauty and empire. Greed expressed itself in the sin of usury and, in the end, in the destruction of empires, nations, cities. All life was a ruthless competition, it was a war in which slavery was apt to follow defeat.[39] Which, then, in Chicago, in the autumn of 1893, was it to be? Blindly some very powerful energy was at work, doing something that nobody wanted done.[40]

The great Ferris Wheel on the Midway might have given much to consider to any historian, but especially to Henry Adams. The cycles of consolidation and disintegration Brooks had found were working themselves out in his own family. A whole race was exhausting itself, disintegrating under the demands of history's laws. The question between Brooks and Henry Adams was, assuming the general law of the past held, whether their family could keep solvent until relief came, or whether they should go under like the Roman peasants or the British yeomen. Henry was inclined to think they should be crushed. Brooks thought with good luck, courage, economy, and patience they should be able to hold on until relief in some form came, and they would crawl in with the bankers on the rise.[41]

And then where would they be? In Henry Adams the old Calvinist anxiety about whether one was or was not enrolled in the books of Heaven had been transformed into an anxiety about whether one was or was not one of history's chosen. John Quincy Adams, that grandfather who had once, when

Henry was a child, led him firmly to the school he had rebelled against, had ended his life with such horrible doubts. Betrayed by his countrymen, who had chosen Jackson, slavery, and the West over himself, the old ex-president had in his anguish come near to renouncing the Providence that, he clearly saw, had renounced him, and had come to the edge of death with the agony of those doubts of himself, even of the Savior, in his heart.[42] Childless, occupationless, wifeless, ever the eternal uncle, his grandson Henry feared that, as far as history went, he was only along for the ride. An Adams-Come-Lately to the America of the nineteenth century—he had been, really, educated for the eighteenth—he'd cast off the Republicans to throw in his lot with the Democrats and Reform, but now Cleveland and the gold standard were kicking him out of the Democratic Party. Well, then, hurrah for Silver and for Populism! Hurrah for the West! No more goldbuggery for him!

Always prone to seasickness, Adams might have felt a little queasy as the great wheel rose and fell, lifting above the masses of people who seemed, on this beautiful fall day, like so many molecules, thronging and swirling according to laws one might someday learn. Below the feet of the middle-aged historian the white, ideal city was laid out like some vision. Then the wheel dropped to earth amid the swarming of the multitude, the smells and sounds of the Midway, the primal chaos that was, after all, where everything was leading.

The previous July the American Historical Association had met at the Fair. They had named Henry Adams (as usual, in absentia) president, and sat down to hear papers. Among those papers, though little noted at the time, was one by a young professor named Frederick Jackson Turner. Where Brooks Adams had sought for a science of history in the laws of economic exchange, and Henry Adams was groping toward a model based on the laws of physics, Turner found his in the laws of biology. The great adventure of the West was over for the United States. Three years before, General Miles, grand marshal of the parade that had opened the Columbian Exposition, had sat in his office in the Pullman Building directing his troops by telegraph wire in the offensive that wiped out the Ghost Dancers of the Dakota Plains. The Ghosts had not risen out of the ground to help the tranced dancers drive the whites from the hunting grounds. The Sioux and the Cheyenne and the Arapaho and the Pawnee were driven back to the reservations. Sitting Bull was killed, and Big Foot. In 1890 the director of the census had declared the frontier phase of white settlement closed.

The stern virtues Turner saw as the frontier's legacy to America—coarseness and strength, acuteness, inquisitiveness, that practical turn of mind, that restless, nervous energy, and, above all, Democracy—had been shaped by the struggles of the white frontier. And now the movement was over. Hamlin Garland had told his father to sell the cookstove if he must to see the Fair: he might well have told him to sell the farm, for the industrial might that was the real subject of the Exposition was making the family farm an anachronism in a country increasingly urban, increasingly based on the power of the machine. In the Hunters' Cabin, the Boone and Crockett Club's contribution to the Fair, the Philadelphia patrician novelist Owen Wister was polishing up that consummate westerner, the Virginian. But even the Virginian had put away his six-gun and his hanging rope and ended his days contemplating his coal lands and his investment portfolio in a high collar and made-to-measure suit. What would be the new America? Was it the frozen dream palaces with their hidden hearts, the dynamos throbbing in the Machinery Building? The world that the robbers of State Street and Wall Street and Beacon Street had spawned? It is difficult to tell what Henry Adams might have thought of Turner's paper had he heard it. His own *History of the United States of America during the Administrations of Jefferson and Madison* had ended on a note that called the new American states to an unlimited future. United both politically and socially, free from the contentions of Europe and its nobles and great men, homogenous in population, America could be a laboratory for the establishment of a true science of history, whose laws would be derived "not from the complicated story of rival European nationalities, but from the economical evolution of a great democracy."[43] That optimistic future might not have been so assured in Chicago in 1893, with its roiling masses of fair-goers neither ethnically or racially homogenous nor socially uniform and the country in profound economic crisis. Since the Calvinists, in various forms and permutations, the country had seen itself as bearer of a special providence. It was a view of history Adams had abandoned in his reading of the history of his family, his country, and above all, himself. The triumph of the West and all it stood for had spelled the end of his family's hopes for its version of the American republic. Under Turner's thesis, for all the crudity and violence of the successive white frontiers, was buried a myth of Progress—the sense that all history was carrying America to its destiny. Henry Adams had smelled out how easily—after a bad night or two—Darwinism was assimilated into the established virtues of the English middle classes thirty years before.[44] In Chicago he might have smelled out the suspicious virtue under the myth of progress in Turner as well.

Another man at the Fair that year was pointed toward the future. Neither Adams nor Turner would have known him, but as clearly as anyone, he had seen where that frontier myth could lead. Drought and bankruptcy and ruptured dreams had driven him out of Dakota Territory, and he was living in Chicago trying to support his family as a drummer for a crockery manufacturer. He'd slipped into the Fair with a delegation of Spanish diplomats, because, according to one family story, he was wearing a silk hat and cutaway to meet a client.[45] Henry Adams's urgent question about whether the Fair was real or only apparent would have seemed to that phony diplomat like barking up the wrong tree. He was a new kind of American, a step ahead of the closing century. The question for L. Frank Baum, as it would be for his Wonderful Wizard in that other city made out of flimflam and tinted light, was if the illusion would sell.

The chaos that history was tending toward in Henry Adams's mind in those days of panic and splendor was exactly what Chicago thought it had put behind it on that bright autumn day when the Fair celebrated its city. The fire was only a memory, the anarchists were all hanged, and August Spies's silence was drowned out by the brass bands and the speeches from the podium and the tinkle of coins in the counting trays. Mayor Harrison, distinguished by his ever-present cigar and his little gold-headed cane, clanged the Liberty Bell, looked over the treaty with the Indians that had ceded Chicago to the whites for three cents an acre, and diplomatically claimed descent from Pocahontas. Old Chief Pokagon spoke. His voice was so weak that after a few words his speech had to be read for him. The Great West had been swallowed by white men, Pokagon told his people. By adoption the red men were children of this great republic. They must give up the chase and live like the whites. They must teach loyalty to this nation, to their children, and solemnly impress upon them that the war path led only to the grave . . . But Chief Pokagon was too feeble to tug the clapper of the Liberty Bell. It had to be done for him by a younger man. Out on the grounds, the Bureau of Indian Affairs had erected a model of an Indian boarding school, with boys and girls from the reservations studying or reciting, working at trades. Neatly organized and labeled were calumets and beadwork, bows and hunting spears, all immobilized and pinned like specimens under glass. Over on the Midway some entrepreneurs had lugged Sitting Bull's cabin from the Rosebud. There was a sign on it: WAR DANCES GIVEN DAILY.

In a sense the Fair was an elaborate instrument to hold at bay the very forces that were threatening its dream of power. In the Anthropology Building a Harvard professor had created his own exhibit: he had painstakingly measured twenty thousand college students and collated their anatomical details into two ideal statues, the new American Adam and Eve. Were they the future? But the Fair defined its world not only by what it included but by what it left out. The industrious Harvard professor had not measured any of the fairgoers who had come on Colored People's Day to hear the Jubilee Singers sing spirituals, and to listen to old Frederick Douglass call the Exposition a whited sepulcher, or any of the ex-slaves neatly tying up little souvenir bales of cotton in silk and satin ribbons, or any of the fifty thousand Poles who had pushed through the gates on Polish Day, or any of the Miniconjous who had lain heaped up in windrows at Wounded Knee three years before. On the Midway Plaisance, Laplanders and Algerians, Turks and Armenians, crowded each other in some awful freak show, a kind of living gallery of history's losers, while the crowds stumbled and pushed their way to the Ice Railway or the Ferris Wheel. Inside the draped rugs of the Algerian theater the hootchie-kootchie dancers gyrated to the droning music of another world and the King of Dahomey sat dozing in his compound while a slave held an umbrella over him, coal black and fat, as Hubert Howe Bancroft described him with the requisite racism, dreaming of his conquered kingdom while warrior women postured and quivered to the war-drums.[46] And all the while Adam and Eve stood roped off in their pavilion, removed from each other and every one else, chaste, naked, and cold. But lest the Algerians or the sleepy King of Dahomey or the Winnebagos in their village, or even the fifty thousand Poles, forget who was calling the tune at this Fair, rooted into the muddy bottom of Lake Michigan was a deceptively real-looking model of the battleship *Illinois*—and who was to know its thirteen-inch guns were made of wood and concrete?—that towered above the replicas of Columbus's three poor caravels and Leif Ericson's longship, while over at the Krupps Pavilion, hard by the Indian School, was the largest cannon ever cast, with the mute but sufficient evidence of its power in the exhibit of eighteen-inch steel plates ruptured by its 2,300-pound shells, while under Karl Bitter's plaster allegory

The Glorification of War, Captain Blunt compared the modern infantry rifle, with a velocity of two thousand feet a second, with the older weapons and Surgeon La Garde illustrated his remarks with anatomical specimens showing the superiority of the modern steel bullet, which was both more effective than the old lead varieties and more humane.[47] In a world defining its lessons by arcs of power, explosives taught most, Henry Adams mused. But they needed a tribe of chemists, physicists, and mathematicians to explain.[48]

And above it all the great Ferris Wheel moved through its cycles, propelled by engines of a history that the small, balding man in one of the cars was trying to understand. "I went to the animal fair," he'd hummed of his trip to the Exposition that May past, and maybe he was still humming as the wheel moved through October, for the Fair was still there and so was Henry Adams. Yes, he'd gone to the Fair and then he'd gone back, but what had become of the monk? He'd been asking himself that ever since the elephant sneezed and fell on its knees. Precious little was left of him; he was a used-up animal. But he'd been to the animal fair anyhow, and gotten very drunk on it.[49] And perhaps he was still drunk, drunk with it all, as the Ferris Wheel rose and fell.

The fair-goers spilled over the White City's limits, laughed at the Keep Off the Grass signs, filled Chicago's streets, clung to the roofs of its streetcars, slept in hallways and in lobbies and three to a bed in its hotels, and crammed the seats of Buffalo Bill's Wild West Show. The soot-stained city of packing houses and steel-girdered skyscrapers and endless slums was like the troubled sleep of the White City by the Lake. While the bands were playing Souza marches on the Midway, in the Black Hole and Little Cheyenne and Satan's Mile and Hell's Half Acre they kept pouring the drinks and rolling the suckers and the trained parrot at South Clark Street kept squawking "Carrie Watson. Come in, gentlemen." And in a bar somewhere in the Tenderloin an itinerant black piano player named Jess Pickett was rolling out a rag tango called "The Dream."[50]

Night opens like a magician's bag. A White City reflected shimmering in the black waters of the lagoon, its domes and cupolas and columned porticos crisscrossed by searchlights and outlined in halos of electric bulbs, a lucent city floating on the dark water, a city delicate as a fairy web, that shimmers and dips and might disappear in the blink of an eye. *Ooooooo!* A dull boom and a phosphorescent shower of sparks explodes high above the domes and pinnacles, doubled in the dark water on which the magic city floats. *Boooom!* Another burst of fire, opening like a Chinese peony against the black silk sky. For a moment the White City is shattered in the dark waters of the lagoon by a sudden wave, broken into a thousand fragments of light, then it rocks together, gently remaking itself on the dark tide. Somewhere the whistle of the holiday boat toots. From the Midway come the mingled sounds of a distant marching band, the cries of the throng. The Ferris Wheel turns above the crowd.

On October 31, the Fair ended. The closing ceremonies were a subdued affair, not the triumph they had set out to be: a few days before, Mayor Harrison, who had swaggered his little gold-headed cane and dinged the Liberty Bell, had been assassinated at his own front door. Mourners filed past Mayor Harrison's bier and the Fair closed its gates with one last, drunken binge on the Midway.

But even through its heyday, the Fair had been full of a kind of melancholy in the knowledge that it would not last. Twenty-one-and-a-half million people had poured through its gates. Almost twenty-nine million dollars had been booked in its accounts. And it was over now. The words of the five thousand nine hundred seventy-eight addresses of the Congresses had been read. Women and Peace and Religion had expressed themselves. Royce and Dewey and Swami Vivekananda and Booker T. Washington had spoken and old Frederick Douglass had thundered and Susan B. Anthony and Jane Addams had raised their voices and Samuel Gompers had temporized and a young radical named Debs had said some hard things. Earnest and good, the City of Words that had risen beside the White City had been dispersed to the winds. The two thousand cops and firemen at the Exposition had been sent home, the three thousand water closets and two thousand urinals had had their last flush. The Security Department entered its final report: Arrests: nine hundred fifty-four. Convictions: four hundred thirty-eight. Acquittals: ninety-four. Escapes: one. Number of reports on children lost: thirty. Number of reports on children restored to parents: twenty. Number of reports of attempts to gain admission with fraudulent passes: thirty-three. Number of reports of suspicious persons: five hundred thirty-nine. Number of reports of finding fetus on grounds: three. Number of reports of Zulu acting improperly: one.[51] Even before it closed, the paint had begun to peel from the plaster columns of some of the buildings.

The exhibits were crated up and sent back where they came from. The statues had been carted away to museums, parts of some of the buildings had been sold, the plaster frogs and fish and lizards that had ornamented the Fisheries Building were being cut up for souvenirs. (The Krupps, their eyes as usual on the ledger, donated their fifty-seven-foot gun to the City of Chicago, presumably to help should Chicago decide to settle things once and for all with Cleveland or Milwaukee.)

All winter long the abandoned buildings of the exhibition had been inhabited by the homeless. The great halls where the giant dynamos had hummed, powering the electric lights that had lit the Court of Honor, the statuary, the lagoon, the endless expositions, were empty except for the gray figures who had lit fires to keep warm. Already the Casino, the Peristyle, and the Music Hall had burned. With the coming of summer the unemployed who had poured into Chicago to build the Fair, and who had been abandoned when it closed, filled the parks, sleeping in the open. The Midway was gone, the Ferris Wheel dismantled, the sounds of the bazaar and the belly dancers' finger cymbals, the snorts of camels, and the blaring of the brass bands were forgotten by the black waters of the lake. The human wreckage left by the closing of the Fair and the depression could be seen gathering in crowds, polyglot, shabby men and shawled or hooded women, their market baskets high above their heads, hundreds of them, dull, persistent, weary, chilled, hungry.

On May 11, 1894, workers at the Pullman Car Works—that self-advertised workingman's utopia—had gone on strike and Eugene Debs had called the newly formed American Railway Union out in sympathy. Now, in the first weeks of July, Debs was under indictment. In Chicago strikers had overturned boxcars in the stockyards and defied the federal troops that had come to keep the mails running. Perched on the cowcatchers of the engines with the bolts of their rifles drawn and their mouths filled with spare cartridges, federal soldiers moved the trains through the crowds of strikers and jeering women. Chicago was a city under siege.

On the morning of July 5, soldiers attempted to move a train from the stockyards. When word got out strikers swarmed from all directions, only to be driven back by the fixed bayonets of the infantry company opening the tracks. At Wentworth Avenue strikers overturned a car across the track; they turned over twenty-three more up and down the line, blocking the engines before and behind. When the troops retreated to the tents, the strikers set the cars and the switch towers afire. A gang of them made an attempt to burn down the Rock Island roundhouse. It was not considered safe for the commuter trains to go beyond Grand Crossing.

From his office, General Miles talked of martial law. "This thing has got beyond a strike. It has become a dangerous riot. The crowd at the Stock Yards is naturally gathering within itself the vicious and criminal classes. If it is not dispersed a grave crisis is before Chicago." Miles did not think those people knew what they were doing. Fifty of his soldiers could mow down two thousand of those people in a few minutes. In the yards the artist Frederic Remington passed hundreds of burning cars. When he walked among the campfires of the military bivouac at the Lakefront, he saw men of the Seventh Cavalry he recognized from Pine Ridge in '90. He paused to chat with Captain Allyn Capron, whose battery had cut down the Miniconjous at Wounded Knee.[52]

Then, in the midst of the strike, on the evening of July 5, the White City, emptied of its ideas, and holding only the tramps and homeless men and women who had found shelter in its vacant buildings, burned. The plaster-and-hair surfaces caught like tinder. The fire spread from building to building.

By 6:30 the Sixty-fourth Street entrance to the fairgrounds was crowded with bicycles. But soon the electric lines and cable roads began dumping people in hordes at the Stoney Island Avenue stop and the cross streets. Thousands came to watch the White City burn, crowding the cars that were overloaded because the strikers had closed down the Illinois Central. They came like people headed to the exhibition on a fete night. There was no regret. Only a feeling of pleasure that fire, and not the wreckers, would end the Great Fair. There was no excitement in the waiting crowd. They stayed and watched the destruction of the great buildings like the fireworks that had lit up the sky during the nights of the Exposition. When some beautiful cornice or row of columns or piece of statuary wavered, then fell into the flaming mass, they oohed and aahed. "Wasn't it grand?" they said. "What a glorious sight!" There would be no salvage. The iron that was not melted was torn and twisted into impossibly tangled skeins. The massive girders of the Administration Building, which were supposed to withstand almost anything, were bent like coat-hanger wire. The allegorical statues were crumbled to ash. For a while, at the Terminal Building, the blackened figure of an Indian gazing to the north loomed up atop a pillar through the fire and smoke until all the building was burned. Then, at the same instant that the Administration Dome collapsed, the statue pitched forward as the crowd cheered.

In the darkness five thousand people watched the flames reflected in the black waters of the lagoon as the dome of the Liberal Arts Building crackled, then broke and sank into the ground. There was a great, long-drawn sigh from the spectators, and then the clear voice of a girl said, "Oh, it's all over."[53]

Traveling as usual, Henry Adams would miss the December meeting in Washington of the American Historical Association—he was fit, as he said, only to be an absent president—but he took the occasion to send an address from Guadalajara. He wrote on the urgent question of the coming of a science of history. As a matter of taste, he greatly preferred, he would say in 1905, his eighteenth-century education, when God was a father and nature a mother, and all was for the best in a scientific universe,[54] but taste was not an option. The future cast its shadow before him, like the shadow of the great wheel in Chicago; that future in which science would find the meaning of history, without a God, without a Providence, but one with the same iron laws that governed the swarming molecules. What would that science bring? Looked at dispassionately, it could bring anything, and what then would be the duty of historians? If it required them to announce that the present evils of the world—its huge armaments, its vast accumulations of capital, its advancing materialism and declining arts—were to be continued, exaggerated, over another thousand years, no one would listen to them with satisfaction. In whatever direction Adams looked he could see no possibility of converting history into a science without bringing it into conflict with one or more of the most powerful organizations of the era. If the world were to continue moving toward the point it had so energetically pursued during the last fifty years, it would destroy the hopes of the vast organizations of labor. If it were to change its course and become communistic, it placed such professors as he in direct hostility to the entire fabric of their social and political system. If it went on, he must preach despair. If it went back, it must deny and repudiate science. If it went forward, round a circle that led through communism, he must declare himself hostile to the property that paid him and the institutions he was bound in duty to support. Should the crisis come, historians must face its dangers and responsibilities. But until then, beyond a doubt, silence was best.[55]

What Clarence King might have thought of the great Colombian Exposition, or if he went at all, is unknown to me. The White City's architecture—the fin de siècle domes and facades, might have charmed the sybarite in him, or offended the aesthetician. He had once written an article about the proposal for a tomb for General Grant.[56] America's experiences were those of civil war and conquest, he had said. The proper model for American architecture was not Greece but Rome. So it is difficult to know what he might have thought, whether he might not have wanted the Exposition's architecture to be made of sterner stuff; or what he might have thought of the exhibits of the United States Geological Survey, which he had founded, and from which he had taken his leave. He would not have missed, in the galleries, the relative absence of the Impressionists (his taste in painting was thoroughly unadventurous). And one can't imagine him having much good to say of all those taffy-colored nudes. But at Sargent's Egyptian Girl, with her great dark eyes and inviting nakedness, he might have given a start. Of course he would have cast an appraising eye at the mining equipment in the Machinery Hall—God knows he could have used the latest pumps in Mexico—and at the fabulous ores in the Mining Building. You imagine him lingering long over the Japanese art, and, like the young Frank Lloyd Wright, being charmed by the Japanese buildings on the Wooded Isle. But what he might or might not have thought of the Fair is irrelevant. By 1893 his affairs were in hopeless disorder, his health was ruined, and he was bearing the killing psychological burden of a life that was cut in half.

On October 30 the papers reported that a well-known New York clubman named King had been taken into police custody for causing a disturbance in front of a large crowd in the Lion House at Central Park the day before. There was some kind of altercation with a black butler from a house on Madison Avenue. The two men carried their argument into the baseball diamond nearby, and King was arrested. On October 31, the day the Fair held its final ceremonies, King signed the papers committing himself to the Bloomingdale Asylum.[57]

He went off with Henry Adams to Cuba in February of 1894 to recuperate, and spent a good deal of time fraternizing with revolutionaries, to Adams's chagrin. Then he was back in the United States, and the killing grind of trying to make a living. In the spring of 1897 Henry Adams received his last letter from King, a plea that he reconsider his decision not to accompany his friend on a trip to Mexico. "I grieve that you cannot go to Mexico with me," King wrote. "All I lack is a pessimist addicted to water-colors and capable of a humorous view of the infinite." If only Adams would go along, King offered to admit in the secrecy of the primeval woods the truth of all Adams's geological criticisms of him; he would even execute in advance an assignment of half the brown girls they met. He would read Adams's complete works, go to England with him in June to sustain Hay under the sodden weight of British aristocracy (Hay was then serving as McKinley's ambassador to the Court of St. James) . . . King would do anything, in short, if Adams would only sing "that little Cuban song: 'Yo me soy contigo!'" It was one of the regrets of Adams's life that he could not go.

"We were touching sixty years old when he wrote this," Adams recalled.

> He was struggling desperately under a load which was sure to break him down; and as for girls, brown, black or yellow, they had about as much interest for us as a phonograph. If he wanted me with him it was because he knew that I was anything but a gay companion, and that with me he need make no effort. Yet it was instinctive with him to call for companionship on his own youth, and he was really thinking not of me, but of the pine woods of 1870; the Sierras; the Rockies; and the brown girls. We both knew that it was all over; that thenceforward his energies were to be thrown away; that the particular stake in life for which he had played was lost.[58]

In 1901 Clarence King died in Phoenix of the tuberculosis that had haunted his last years. It had taken science, with its new discovery the x-ray, to look inside a man who, for all his skill in mapping the hidden strata of the earth, had depths that remained a mystery to his friends and perhaps himself.

John Hay, his friend, died four years later, at the height of his prestige as secretary of state. Henry Adams lived on. What had become of the Monk? he had asked, tipsy from the ride history was giving him at the Chicago World's Fair in 1893. The Monk had become a witness to his age. In a very few years after the Fair closed its doors, he had seen the United States rise out of the panic as an Empire. The planters in Hawaii had revolted against the queen,

and in 1898 the United States had gone to war against Spain: the same diplomats who had been feted in Chicago had become the butchers of Cuba.
Soon the gawky boy Adams had met on the Nile so many years before was
charging up Kettle Hill at the head of a group of cowboys and would-be cowboys called the Rough Riders, General Miles had claimed Puerto Rico for
the Stars and Stripes, and in Manila Bay, Dewey's very real battleships had
blown Spain out of the Pacific. John Hay had opened the door to Asia: our
empire faced East, and in the jungles of the Philippines, the Krag-Jorgensen
rifles that had been displayed as the ne plus ultra in Chicago were being used
to shoot down Aguinaldo's freedom fighters.

Where King had lived the terrible paradoxes of his culture, Adams stood
apart and took note. And he was silent. When he was not traveling—and
always travel was the great anodyne—he divided his life between Paris and
that massive, fortress-like house on the Washington DC block he shared with
John Hay. He became a student of the Middle Ages. He found the unity he
could not see in his own era in twelfth-century France and, agnostic that
he was, in Thomistic theology, and he solved the terrible paradoxes of his
frustrated eroticism by displacing it to the perpetual worship of three unat-
tainable women: his dead wife, Lizzie Cameron, and the Virgin of Chartres.
So he became in old age a kind of chaste and doting *cavalier servente* to
the charming and now-separated Mrs. Cameron, subsuming the rage that
had always been in him just under his ironic and amused pose into uncon-
summated love, and aestheticized what was left of his passion in a kind of
latter-day Maryolatry. And always there was the memory of Clover Adams.
About history, about the terrible and bloody deeds that lay under the consolidation of the American empire under his friend Hay, he pretended to say
nothing.[59] Silence became a kind of consolation for his ambivalence about
power, which he so furiously desired and from which he so fastidiously dis-
tanced himself. The family that was at the center of the history of its nation
ended up producing in Henry Adams a marginalized student of history, who
was, finally, a student only of himself.

In 1908 Adams met Frederick Jackson Turner, whose paper he had missed
in Chicago in 1893, at a luncheon for historians in Washington DC. Turner
called the Adams of these years a "lovable personality," despite his "prickly,
hedgehoggy outside." But underneath this benevolent posture was another
Adams. His rage and self-loathing spilled out in a virulent anti-Semitism.

Like other American patricians, he might have discovered an emotional affinity with the Jews, those bearers of a tradition even longer than Boston's (if that were possible) and who, like Adams, belonged nowhere in the world. He did not. The Jew became for him the epitome of the goldbug, and he forgot about his friend Berenson and the kindness of the London Goldsmids and Cohens and poured the filth inside him on the people who professed to be clean and ancient and apart. It was as if the Jews mirrored the Boston inside him he was always trying to run from. "Had he been born in Jerusalem under the shadow of the Temple, and circumcised in the Synagogue by his uncle the high priest, under the name of Israel Cohen," he wrote in his *Education*, "he would scarcely have been more distinctly branded, and not much more heavily handicapped in the races of the coming century."[60] He saw himself as "a sort of ugly, bloated, purplish blue and highly venomous hairy tarantula which catches and devours Presidents, senators, diplomats, congressmen and cabinet-officers, and knows the flavor of every generation and every country of the civilized world."[61] He thought of his younger brother, whose manuscript he had worried over in the year of the panic, and whose solutions to the chaos Henry Adams saw around him were increasingly authoritarian and cruel, and cried out, "Brooks was right."

In those years he was writing a secret book. It was the story of his life. He made himself the ironic observer of that manikin who was called Henry Adams. The manikin, he claimed, was only a convenience, a kind of geometrical figure for studying relation. It must have an air of reality, he wrote, must be taken for real, must be treated as though it had a life. Who knows? Possibly it had.

He compressed all his silence and anguish into this fiction named Henry Adams, a voice without a body, the ghost of his own history. Wrote about him as if posthumously, in the third person, since he, Henry Adams, the manikin's creator, was already dead. He had died that day he had come home to find Mrs. Henry Adams slumped over with the poison still on her lips.

He devised for his book, which, as he intended, would not be published in his lifetime, a strategy of failure. His education had failed to prepare him for the nineteenth, let alone the twentieth, century. It—and he—were failures. No doubt the picture of Henry Adams in the pages you are reading is a caricature—but for more than sixty years he had caricatured himself, perfecting in his letters and now in his secret book a discomfort with the world that masqueraded as an edgy sort of devil-take-the-hindmost bonhomie, a jolly, rollicking procession toward the grave: the death's head under the fool's cap was the truest image of the manikin. The world had gone to hell. Filled with goldbugs and Jews and vulgarians and the chaotic collision of molecules, it was a world in which an Adams rattled around on the edges with no permanent role, no place to rest. But the secret of the book was that the failure was not failure at all. In such a world, to fail was in some curious way to succeed: it wasn't Henry Adams who had failed the world, but the world that had failed him. To be a random molecule, buffeted by chance, offered, in its own way, a justification, and even a kind of pleasure. If the world had no place for an Adams, it wasn't worth having.

And at the center of the book was a silence. Not one word—not one line about Clover. He could not face her absence, which was the one failure he would not write about. For if the world had failed Adams, Adams had failed most profoundly his wife. What was left? What was left for this ghost, this manikin, Henry Adams, but to be amused? *Amused.* It is the word that surfaces again and again in his book, the only permanent value, the word that comes at moments of keenest bafflement. "Ça vous amuse, la vie?" Hay had written him of King's lonely death, and Adams's answer was that it must. It is in boredom, after all, that one hears most clearly the ticking of the clock, suffers most acutely one's own anguish, rage, and embarrassment.[62]

Henry Adams lived long enough to see the balance of power, contrived in so great a part by John Hay, break apart. World War I commenced with the assassination of Archduke Franz Ferdinand, who had not made himself popular among the immigrants in the Chicago of the World's Fair. Adams's last days saw the Bolsheviks triumph in Russia. He died in his house in Washington in late March 1918. He had destroyed the journals he had kept since youth. He was buried in the Rock Creek Cemetery under the same Saint-Gaudens statue, with neither name nor date, that held the remains of his wife.

E. J. Bellocq, untitled photograph, ca. 1912, of a prostitute in New Orleans, from *Storyville Portraits: Photographs from the New Orleans Red-light District, Ca. 1912*. (New York: Museum of Modern Art, 1970). Gelatin silver printing-out paper print (printed ca. 1966–69), 9 $^{13}/_{16}$ in. x 7 $^{13}/_{16}$ in. Gift of Lee Friedlander (978.1969). © Lee Friedlander, courtesy Fraenkel Gallery, San Francisco. Digital Image © The Museum of Modern Art / Licensed by SCALA / Art Resource, New York.

They did a lot of uncultured things there that probably couldn't be mentioned, and the irony part of it, they always picked the youngest and most beautiful girls to do them right before the eyes of everybody. . . . People are cruel, aren't they?

Jelly Roll Morton on Emma Johnson's
Circus House, New Orleans, c. 1900

Three
The Cruelty of Seeing

VENUS UNSEEN

For sight is the keenest of our bodily senses, though not by that is wisdom seen. . . . But beauty only has this portion, that she is at once the loveliest and also the most apparent.

Plato, *Phaedrus*

Floating above the waves, pushed by the gentle winds, Venus in her nakedness makes her way to Paphos to be born. As soon as she touches shore she will be covered by the cloak held out to her by the solicitous Hour. In order to set foot in the realm of time and space, she must be clothed, for her ideal beauty is not meant for human eyes, just as Botticelli's painting is, in its way, imaginary, a dream of a lost original.

For Beauty turns her back to the world. Venus, as Velásquez paints her, lies facing away from us, unconscious of our eyes, which follow the lovely curve of her back as she gazes at her face in a mirror held by Eros, her son. But her face is obscure to us, for we who see her are irrelevant. It is as if there is an endless circularity in her gaze, as if absolute Beauty can only see herself in a reciprocal current of knowing that is without time and without longing. What is Venus thinking? What can she think?

In these cold, clear Platonic realms, only ideas can see themselves. But finally we turn away from that elegant back and the eyes that refuse to see us. Perhaps we are secretly nauseated by ideas. Perhaps what we long for is the world.

THE PIANOS THAT ONE HEARS IN THE BETTER NEIGHBORHOODS

Allez, stériles ritournelles,
La vie est vraie et criminelle.

Jules Laforgue

The polished surfaces and gilt mirrors of the houses on New Orleans's Esplanade Street reflect the probity and lovely possessions of the good husband. The wife, that sensitive instrument of production (the production of children, first communions, piano lessons), whose emotional vagaries must be managed by a combination of patience and address, like the fluctuations of the cotton market, wanders from room to room, adjusting something here or there, giving instructions to the servants. She has her children, of course. She has her duties. She declines to think about that darker family elsewhere in the city who bears her husband's or her own family's name, cousins, half-sisters and half-brothers—it may be her children's siblings. Perhaps she paints a little, or reads. She has her charities. On its pedestal like a confection on a doily is a reproduction of Hiram Powers's *The Greek Slave*, naked and wistful in her chains as she looks out at her unseen Turk. Henry James used to see the Slave in various parlors of the higher sort in Albany and Manhattan, "so undressed, yet so refined, even so pensive, in sugar-white alabaster, exposed under little glass covers in such American homes as could bring themselves to think such things right."[1]

In just such a home on Esplanade Street Kate Chopin's Edna Pontellier marinated in ennui thirty years after the Civil War, her life an endless repetition of cards left and received, of visiting days, of waiting for the return of the pleasant and accommodating stockbroker she had married, and of the exigencies of her children and their mulatto nurse. Trapped in the vitrine of her possibilities, Edna Pontellier sees the world as a series of lovers. She will weary of them, as she has wearied of herself. The disagreeable Mlle. Reisz has her art, and nobody can play Chopin like Mlle. Reisz, just as no one can play Edna Pontellier like Kate Chopin. But whom can Edna Pontellier play? Edna Pontellier might outrage the social world, but she cannot turn outrage into another self. Finding no solution in her life, Madame Pontellier had walked naked into the ocean to her death in some sort of *Liebestode* with the sea, like Venus returning to the element that gave her birth. But the ending is no real ending at all, it solves nothing. Light floods Mlle. Reisz's dingy apartment with its magnificent piano and its miserable gasoline stove and its dust-hooded bust of Beethoven scowling on the mantelpiece. The faded fake violets that are her only ornament are like the possibilities of a world measured against the beauty of her playing.

Stretching out from the windows of Mlle. Reisz's dingy top-floor apartment was the curve of the river with the masts of ships and the tall chimneys of the Mississippi steamers. The river carried land broken off from the Ohio, the Missouri, the great rivers that entered its channel with all their commerce and violence, bearing with them hogsheads of sugar, pork, salt beef, lumber, the cotton that arrived at a cluster of offices where brokers tested its quality with practiced fingers, as, in 1873, Degas had painted them. Beyond the river, beyond the Cotton Exchange and the Vieux Carré, were zones where the differences of race and sex were negotiated in a constant play of social adjustment, the half-white world of the old free Creoles of color—shopkeepers, cobblers, editors; the *petites maisons* of the kept women of mixed race; the District where white and black mixed in a constant adjustment of pleasure, gambling, sex. In the midst of her anguish Kate Chopin's heroine had paid a call on the lovely matron Adèle Ratignolle, whom she found with her maid sorting a bundle just back from the laundry.[2] It is just what the Basin Street madam Nell Kimball and her housekeeper would be doing only a few years after the publication of *The Awakening*. Basin Street is not so far away, after all, from the Vieux Carré. The body of Edna Pontellier is no different from the bodies of the prostitutes of the District. It is the site of neither redemption nor shame.

Hidden behind a curtain at Emma Johnson's Circus House, a seventeen-year-old mulatto piano player named Ferdinand Lamothe, who has not yet become Jelly Roll Morton, is rolling out effortless arpeggios and singing about sis out there on the levee doing the double twist. She's trying to be bad but she doesn't know how.

On Esplanade Street wives and daughters are practicing their scales.

Running a whorehouse, Nell Kimball thought, was as hard as running U.S. Steel. She had come off the farm in southern Illinois. Her view of rural life was not the tender eighteenth-century engraving envisioned by Jefferson or Hector Saint John de Crèvecoeur. "We lived poor and simple," she wrote, "but were not happy or clean or hopeful."[3] She'd pulled herself up by her own garters, had established a paying business, and she wasn't about to let it go to hell. She was, above all, a manager. The whores had the damnedest taste for froufrou and feathers, and Nell had to monitor their dress. She wasn't partial to the way they wanted to pile up their hair with rats and pads, unless she had a customer that had a taste for hair. It took some of the whores a while to get used to the baths she made them take every day. Nell made them take cascara and rhubarb for the constipation that was endemic among prostitutes. She had to watch out for the johns who'd try to stiff her. She had to watch out for the girls who were lushes or coke fiends. Suicide was always hanging over her (she'd found one girl hanging from the rafters naked as a plucked chicken). She might allow a little sexual recreation between the girls, but if she found a dildo they were out—they had to save it for the paying customers.

Clarence King might have seen the upper tiers of New Orleans bordellos as mirror reversals of the society boudoirs he satirized, whose "neo-Pullmanic" décor looked like the *disjecta membra* of once-important bank accounts, and whose very chairs, King imagined, were stuffed with curled coupons.[4] For the brothel wants to be a salacious parody of The Home, the madame a kind of louche major-domo, and the prostitute-houris serving only as instruments of the production of pleasure. On the red-silk walls of the brothel parlors, flickering in the light and caught in the many mirrors, are paintings of nymphs and satyrs, classical orgies. Vesuvius erupts in an ejaculation of fire and ash, scattering poor Pompeians, who, after all, just wanted to live their mundane lives, pursue their pleasures, tally up their accounts. For Nell Kimball the bordello was a club where gentlemen, freed of the constraints of their daylight world, could talk as men, relieve themselves of their social and sexual burdens. Going from front parlor to back parlor, keeping an eye on the girls, her body pinched in her corsets, her feet killing her, Nell thought it was amazing how much peace of mind a man needed, after a certain age, to, as she put it, fuck properly.

Nell liked, she said, a little color, the girls who called themselves Cubans or Spaniards, but if they didn't pass she turned them over to what she called "a nigger house." She had to keep up the social standards as much as any matron in the Vieux Carré. (In the cribs in San Francisco, she found the girls priced along national and color lines: "Cost for a Mexican two bits. A nigrah whore, Chinese or Japanese asked fifty cents. All those who claimed they were French, seventy-five. A Yankee girl cost a dollar."[5]) The young whores were often wild girls, a bit batty upstairs. If a house got the reputation of having girls who didn't act right with the customers, you might as well close up and turn out the lights in front of the place and throw the key away: like all of the arts, the arts of the erotic require discipline. "I'd punish the girls with fines, and if they got feisty or out of line, I'd have Harry work them over, but not to bruise them."[6] The house was virtually a prison. Sometimes she'd let the Catholic girls go to mass.

Costumed like schoolgirls or jockeys, or in filmy gowns, the prostitutes move through the parlors, with the sound of a piano in the background. It wasn't just the sex, Nell Kimball realized; what a girl was really selling was an illusion, the idea that the john was *some* guy and that the girl was just crackers for his kind of work.[7] For the men seated on the couches and divans, the moment of choosing is exquisite. A gentleman nods to one of the women. The rest disappear into nothingness, for, after all, they are dreams.

By three in the morning the crowds at Nell Kimball's house have started to trail off. The all-night johns are tucked away in bed and on the third floor there might be a show going on—the girls naked or in frilly underwear. By five, Nell Kimball has the lights turned out downstairs and gets out of her corset and into bed with a cup of hot milk and nutmeg. As she grew older she became a poor sleeper. Sometimes she would take one of the light-skinned maids to bed with her and they would lie there and lazily talk with a nightlight burning, talk about the johns, where the maid came from, and when the maid saw Nell was woozy she would get out of bed and Nell would sleep until ten or eleven. But sometimes she wouldn't sleep at all, and she'd just lie in bed, half-out until the first light came in through the shutters. She'd think about how she was getting old, without family, with no true friends and only herself to turn to. She hated to get up. "What the hell—what for, why? To support a house of snotty whores?" But in the end, when she heard the girls coming downstairs or Harry testing the shutters outside, she would groan out of bed, coughing and hawking, yell for black coffee and a drop of rum, and go downstairs to count the night's take and read the papers to see who was at the good hotels.[8]

SILENCE

Mornings a house is like a tomb. Smells of body powder, Lysol, dead cigars, the woman smell of it always heavy; sweat, scent, piss, armpits, medical douche, and spilled liquor.[9] At Dago Tony's and The Frenchman's and the dance halls on Perdido Street and at Jackson Park and in Funky Butt Hall the music has ended. The orgies of the night, the liquor and whorehouse laughter and the hop, are finished.

For now it is quiet and the house is restored to its prosaic business of feeding and washing, unmysterious and ordinary, like an empty theater seen in daylight. In a few hours the whores will be up, yelling down for their coffee. They will have a few hours to themselves, while they sit and smoke, do their hair, lie to each other, brag, look over magazines or astrology books or the funnies. Nell Kimball found them mean, but sentimental; they would cry over dogs, kittens, kids, novels, sad songs.[10]

The rooms in these photographs are plain, and have a faded, shabby quality to them. Daylight has exposed the illusion of the opulence the houses projected with the red-shaded lamps and closed curtains. The rooms are somehow part of the pathos in which the women who are the subjects of these photographs are seen. The camera frames the corner of a bed. A table. A spittoon. The doors are wired shut, as if to keep the inner world inviolate while these tender photographs are taken. There are ordinary pictures on the walls, only a few of which seem to be erotic. Pennants: Vermont (*Freedom and Unity*). East Saint Louis. Sometimes a word or phrase we can decipher: "Oh bébé please come." There are often mirrors. Everything is ordinary in the house, caught in the prosaic morning or afternoon light. Women play with their pet dogs, or sit in their rooms.

Lee Friedlander, who bought these glass plates and patiently found a way of printing from them, paralleled the mundane details of these rooms in his own series of nudes, so different with their flashlit immediacy from these softly lit whores of the New Orleans of ninety years ago. The lamps and cheap bedsteads of hotel bedrooms in which Friedlander caught his models seem to invoke a viewer who is sixty years in the future, who would see in these details of the daily life of the mid-twentieth century the same pathos, the same clutch of reality we find in the whorehouses of 1911 or 1912. The dark edges and fissures where the emulsion has peeled away from the glass plates that record those earlier rooms and their occupants pull us away from them and into the present, as if life itself is so fragile that it peels away from what holds it to the world.

You would like to know if the photographer paid these women. Usually in the published images,[11] they are alone. When they do appear together they are playing cards like college girls in a dorm—an image far from the acrobatic duos of erotic stereopticon slides. Often they are quite ordinary. They put on a fancy blouse or hold a bouquet. One dressed for the street in a picture hat and high button shoes visits a friend whose sleeping head just enters the photograph (perhaps, as the writer Rex Rose has suggested, it is a hospital ward for venereal diseases). It is almost as if these women pose as much for themselves as for the camera. Grinning with pleasure, one very young woman drops her covering to expose her breasts. Another raises a glass of rye—the label is plain on the bottle—in a toast to what or to whom? The photographer? The prospective client? Rye whiskey itself? The names of these women do not appear on the plates.

Gazing into a heavy, framed mirror above a bureau, plump, naked, except for her shoes, a young whore stands with her back to us. For a moment she catches sight of something reflected in the glass. We do not know if she is looking at the photographer, standing beside his camera with the plunger in his hand, or at the hooded instrument that holds her in its darkness.

Looking over the shoulder of this woman before the mirror in the photograph, we can only imagine the woman she longs to see: in front of us there is only a pudgy whore, in bangs. In the long moment of the exposure of the photographic plate, her face is mobile with the thoughts and emotions that move across it. Thoughts we can only guess at, for they remain her own, a private world, a world the camera does not enter.

For years Ernest Bellocq, the man who stood under the hood of the camera, was imagined as a kind of monster, a "water head," as one prostitute termed him. Others saw him, embarrassingly, as trapped in a stunted body, a dwarf, Storyville's Lautrec.[12]

But in fact, when the camera hood is lifted, what we see is a man of regular height and features, a commercial photographer from a respectable French-Creole family of the upper-middle class. He had grown up in the world of school, communion, the French Opera. His younger brother Leo became a Jesuit priest. On Bellocq's desk is the ordinary bric-a-brac of the turn of the century, sentimental photographs of women, a few that we would now call soft porn. It looks like the bachelor's desk that trompe l'oeil American realists were fond of painting. Reflecting on the image of this desk, Rex Rose speculated that perhaps Bellocq was trying to reproduce the saccharine lubricities of his era with the models available to him: his art was a failure of banality.[13]

The tale of Bellocq as monster was false in a literal sense, but it called up a kind of truth about his art. A monster is something to be exhibited, a portent, a warning. In his shame at the horror he instills, he wants to hide himself from the world. But just the same the monster is voracious in his need to see. Hidden himself, only through seeing can he know who he is. Like the Beast in the fairytale, his house is full of mirrors, but none of them show his face. Yet for all his privacy, Bellocq is no pornographer. The pornographer sees the world through a keyhole. He stages circuses of perversion, possesses the sexual secrets of everyone, but his world is profoundly unoriginal, for his images only reproduce in a postcard or stereopticon slide what is already in his mind. Sade's libertines are, after all, literary figures, quack philosophes, full of unctuous blather. For all their whips and dungeons, there is something pathetic and even comic in them, and they are closer to Walter Mitty or to Don Quixote and his imaginary helmet than to Gilles de Retz. And like the johns in Nell Kimball's whorehouse, their pleasure is founded on a carefully orchestrated illusion of potency. In Sade, pain becomes a symbolic substitute for the ability to give pleasure.

Now, there is no more lively sensation than that of pain; its impressions are certain and dependable, they never deceive as may those

of the pleasure women perpetually feign and almost never expe-
rience; and, furthermore, how much self-confidence, youth, vig-
or, health are not needed in order to be sure of producing this dubi-
ous and hardly very satisfying impression of pleasure in a woman.
To produce the painful impression, on the contrary, requires no
virtues at all.[14]

What does the pornographer possess, finally? He seizes an image, spirits it off to a private dungeon of the mind, but it is only an image, a few words, a shadow, a thin smear of film on a piece of cardboard.

It is Bellocq's refusal to impose his own dreams of power and need on the women of his photographs that gives them their unique tenderness. Under the hood of his camera, the women float upside-down in the safekeeping of his privacy. This is his darkness, the place he has made for himself, the place from which he summons to the realms of his solitude the beauty and pathos and plenitude of the world.

TOUCH

Yet when we came back, late, from the Hyacinth garden,
your arms full, and your hair wet, I could not
Speak, and my eyes failed, I was neither
Living nor dead, and I knew nothing,
Looking into the heart of light, the silence.

T. S. Eliot, *The Waste Land*

A naked woman stands drawing a butterfly on a wall. Her face has been obliterated by a black smear. Another woman stands wrist on hip, against a dark background, a white door in front of her. Her face has been blacked out too. It is as if these women had been decapitated. It was once believed that Bellocq's brother the priest scratched out the faces of these women when he acquired the negatives. But no one knows if Father Leo Bellocq ever had them in his possession. Experimenting on a small corner of one of the glass plates, Friedlander found that the emulsion would not scratch off with the broad strokes of the defaced images. The plates must have been defaced when still wet.[15]

As far as we know, Bellocq never made these images for sale. They lay in his private collection and in his store of memories or were given to the women he photographed. So we do not know if he scratched out the heads of his subjects out of anger or cruelty or to protect the privacy of these women, who might have been his friends, and who might one day slip back across that tenuous line between the District and the respectable world of proper houses. Lifted dripping from the chemical tank, only the image of a woman's body is left behind, beyond the reach of touch, in the realm of memory and desire. On the plate, that smear of black in the print is a clear space, a window wiped clean.[16] It is like scraping the silver from the back of a mirror. Or like the breaking of a spell.

THE CRAVE

War might have been good for business, but Nell Kimball hated it. She didn't buy any interest in dying for a flag, or history or politicians. She hated people being shot, boys being killed for slogans, or for more land for United Fruit or Whatsits Name Sugar or the *New York World*.[17] War made sex a kind of disease. The idea of dying made a man want to have it as much as he could. It was a kind of nervous breakdown that could be treated only with a girl between him and the mattress. Nell had heard the drunken soldiers singing "Damn Damn the Filipinos" in her house in San Francisco during the Philippine Insurrection. Now the guns were booming in France. She dreamed one night that the whole city of New Orleans was sinking into a lake of sperm.[18]

In 1917, while Jelly Roll Morton was on the Coast knocking them dead with a jazz tango he called "The Crave," the U.S. Navy shut down Storyville and tricks weren't walking anymore in the District. Soon the war would end a whole era and Nell Kimball would see everything blow up in speakeasy booze, flappers, bootleggers, and sticky sex in the backseats of Marmons and Pierce Arrows. Things got too loose and easy for her. The country club girls were giving it away free and it got to be almost respectable to be screwing in roadhouses, necking in Stutz Bearcats, and weekending with someone else's wife. In the District the old discipline and order had gone out the window. The color lines were bending, even breaking, in the houses. At midnight, November 12, 1917, it was all over and Nell Kimball watched Storyville go out in one crazy orgy of violence and frenzy. She was tired, feeling stiff in the joints, and the sporting world wasn't classy anymore. The war had changed things and she could see they would change a lot more. On the way to the railroad station to catch the Florida train, she saw the streets filled with torn paper and broken bottles. Someone had set an old laundry wagon on fire.[19]

Sin, which had given a spice to the whole thing, had ceased to exist. "Society," she wrote, "came off its high steps, mixed with the gangsters, the artists and the singers and the fairies. The whole morality, so carefully stuck together by my old world for me went out the window."[20] At the pictures you could watch Joan Crawford shimmying into her underwear in *Our Dancing Daughters*, and the artists, the black singers and dancers and the fairies, the whole lot of Americans who had been pushed out or scared out or were just looking for some larger world, would discover Paris and London and Berlin. For that generation of white expatriates who found themselves in Europe after the Great War, haunted by the land they had left in order to realize themselves, expatriacy had given clarity to the rhythms of landscape and even speech of their home. But even more, of all that separated themselves from it. The war had ended any of the moral certitudes they might have brought out of their native land. Who were they, after all? Situated in the psychological paradox of being of a land but not in it, they looked into the mirrors of art to try to find themselves. Feeling in their own souls this strange dislocation at the margins of a society they no longer believed in and that did not believe in them, the white American expatriates who came to gawk at the Revue Nègre might have seen in these black performers, marginalized and denied by the country of their birth, exotics in a land that wasn't their own, a version of themselves.

By the time the United States came back from the war, Bellocq's photographs of prostitutes, like Storyville itself, were finished. Bellocq grew old and fat and descended into senility. He had wanted to see what was forbidden, but for him the forbidden was behind the social screen that made the bodies of women figments of a masculine dream. The only thing remaining of his personality is a picture of him in his jewelry and his loud ties in the days when he sported in the District and photographed its women. And those photographs themselves, with their tenderness and their singular beauty and their scratched-out faces.

It is unlikely we will ever know the names of more than one or two of these women. Or their histories. But they've left, pressed into the photographic plates of a New Orleans photographer, their dreams of themselves. Dreams which, in those haunted rooms where two solitudes met, have become our dreams of them too.

View from East Oakland, 1868. Anonymous untitled photograph. Courtesy of the Oakland Public Library.

Four

Some Versions of the Pastoral

Roots

From the air, the land flattens out. The wrinkles of mountains and hills become a two-dimensional pattern, like a postcubist Braque or a Picasso or a Masson. Looking down, her eyes were full of it, and over the snow hills and then the snow prairie it was unbelievably beautiful, and the symmetry of the roads and the farms and turns and the shadows of the trees on the wooded hills made something that filled her with a lot.[1]

> *I know so well the relation of a simple center and a continuous design to the land as one looks down on it, a wandering line as one looks down on it, a quarter section as one looks down on it, the shadow of each tree on the snow and the woods on each side and the land higher up between it and I know so well how in spite of the fact that the human mind has not looked at it the human mind has it to know that it is there like that, notwithstanding that the human mind has liked what it has which has not been like that.[2]*

The land stretched out into a geography of planes and lines and patterns in the snow, but it was a history too, and history was flattening out for her, becoming something depthless, outside of time, in the pure play of what she called the human mind. In France, in the shuttered salon, the great Picasso portrait was getting to look more and more like her every day, and she was going home, flying west above the wintry landscape. "It has always seemed to me a rare privilege, this, of being an American, a real American," she had written with all the Babbittry of a speech at a chamber of commerce banquet. But for all the embarrassing banality, the self-consciousness, there was something she was trying to get hold of in the country she had not seen since 1904. With its railroads and its coarse power and its corporations, America had, she thought, invented the Twentieth Century. And she, above all, was the apostle of modernity. But the Pioneer Spirit she invoked was the conquest of an internal space.[3] And like most conquests it needed its own massacres and silences.

"Roots are so small and dry when you have them and they are exposed to you," she said. "You have seen them on a plant and sometimes they seem to deny the plant if it is vigorous. Well, we're not like that really."

> *Our roots can be anywhere and we can survive, because, if you think about it, we take our roots with us. I always knew that a little and now I know it wholly. I know because you can go back to where they are and they can be less real to you than they were three thousand, six thousand miles away.[4]*

She said that the essential thing about roots was to have the feeling that they exist. That they are somewhere. But where was that somewhere? And who was the person who bore that place in memory? Since the book that had made her, all of a sudden, a celebrity, she had written nothing. *The Autobiography of Alice B. Toklas*, that gossipy, inaccurate, famously entertaining quasi-fiction, gave her a way of settling old scores—with Pound (he was a village explainer. Excellent if you were a village, but if you were not, not), with Hemingway (he was, after all, 90 percent Rotarian. Can't you make it 80 percent? he'd asked)—and putting in the mouth of her invented Alice one long, extended advertisement for herself. But then there was nothing.[5] If you stop writing if you are a genius are you still one?[6] She began toying with an old nursery rhyme, teasing out its possibilities in her maddening way. I am I because my little dog knows me, said the old woman. Well, at sixty she was on her way to really being an old woman and in France Basket the poodle and Pépé the chihuahua were waiting for her, but who, just *who*, might she be? Circling around a building on Times Square a flashing, insistent electric sign had greeted her return to what she called the oldest country in the world: *Gertrude Stein has come.*[7]

High up, above the towns and the cities and the Burma Shave signs that rushed up to meet you with their little jingling narratives that so delighted her, she pried the human mind from what she named human nature, the mess of existence, with its pain and confusion and its memories, in order to turn the past into the flat, quilted patterns of her prose. The human mind had nothing to do with sorrow and with disappointment; the human mind knew neither memory nor tears. It could forget nothing, but not be remembering.[8]

> *There*
>
> *Oakland's just a place to start from.*
>
> Jack London

Her father always told her that she had been born a perfect baby. It was a reproach he offered up whenever there had been anything the matter with her. She was the youngest of the family and nobody could do anything but take care of her and she liked it and she still liked it. She did not remember Allegheny, where she was born, but Vienna was a place in her memory, the formal garden and the salt caves and the birds and butterflies and insects and the first contact with books, picture books. She remembered shopping in Paris, and seeing her first theater in London with the family on the way back to the United States, and she remembered Baltimore, and it was there that she first began to feel her emotions in English. She remembered a counting poem her mother told her, about one little Indian two little Indians three little Indian boys, four little five little six little seven little eight little Indian boys. And then there was California, the rambling wooden Victorian hotel in Oakland with its teas and its walks and then the big house with its long line of eucalyptus trees and its ten acres of gardens and orchards and its animals and the rose hedge and the dingy working-class houses of their neighbors, and school with the polyglot children of East Oakland, and the beginning of her questioning.

> *And so I was a little girl in East Oakland California and of course one did have to find out that life although it was life there was death although there was death, and you had to find out that stars were worlds and moved around and that there were comets and that there was wind and rain, grass and flowers and birds and butterflies were less exciting in California, but most of all there were books and food, food and books, both excellent things.*[9]

There was a book in the house about the excavations of Nineveh and the enormous heads they had found and there was the Bible. When she was eight she was surprised to learn that there was nothing in the Old Testament about a future life or eternity.

> *It was frightening when the first comet I saw made it real that the stars were worlds and the earth only one of them, it is like the Old Testament, there is God but there is no eternity. And now that is what everything is there is a God but there is no eternity.*[10]

She learned that there had been two other children in the family who had died, and that they were to have been the last. She and Leo would not have existed except for the deaths of those other children. It made them feel funny.[11] Even her name was the name of a dead grandmother. Identity always worried her, and memory, and eternity. Death started history and fears.[12]

While she was growing up in Oakland, the nineteenth century was giving way, the long skeins of its narratives were being broken up, first into pieces so that they could be examined, then the pieces themselves fell off their strings of contingency. About the time she was born, an Englishman named Muybridge set up a line of cameras at Leland Stanford's farm in Palo Alto whose shutters were tripped by a horse galloping over their strings, and the galloping was seen in its pieces; soon Frederick Winslow Taylor would begin holding a stopwatch to the rhythms of work, and shoveling coal would become a series of separate postures; Henry Ford would piece out the assembly of an automobile along a moving track; and the world would lurch into life in Edison's Kinetoscope. For a while, before Einstein showed that time was a relationship, the world would be cut up into little fragments of activity stuttering through a spool.

From babyhood until fourteen, to play in a garden in the evening when it was darkening was a legend; roses and pansies, buttercups and daisies, this was what made a legend. What she meant by a legend was that you did everything just the way you should look as if you did, in that unconscious, self-conscious ease of childhood, without the struggles of later life, and when Leo and she walked and walked into the mountains on the dusty roads, and nothing came in between them, they were legends then, and when they dragged a little wagon and slept closely huddled together, like a page from a book, like *Paul and Virginia*, they were legendary then. Anyone is between babyhood and fourteen.[13]

> *What makes the legend real between babyhood and fourteen is that there is then the first struggle not to die and the first struggle to help kill the century in which you are born. . . .*
>
> *It is a struggle not to die between babyhood and fourteen, not not to actually die, that is a matter for parents and nurses and guardians, but the not to know that death is there, and not to share, that is to be secret and not die, and not to not know why. . . . There is no use in remembering between babyhood and four-teen. . . . When I was between babyhood and fourteen and I was a legend then, of course I was, to myself and to them and of course I was struggling not to be dying that is not to know that dying was dying and frightening was not only frightening but connected with any thing.[14]*

She would learn that she was alone. Alone in the family and in this great young country, with its habits and dress-suit cases, clothes and hats and ways of thinking, walking, making money, talking, reforming, all with a metallic clicking like the typewriting, which was its only way of thinking and edu-cating, its way of learning. "We are all the same all through us," she wrote, "we never have it to be free inside us. No brother singulars, it is sad here for us, there is no place in an adolescent world for anything eccentric like us, machine making does not turn out queer things like us, they can never make a world to let us be free each one inside us."[15] When her mother became ill, the family moved from the old Stratton place with its fields and orchards to a small house farther west. Then her mother died. Gertrude Stein was fourteen and no longer a legend. In 1891 her father, that petty tyrant, that coarse enthusiast, who frightened everyone "because," as she said, "he was too impatient to finish what was not yet begun,"[16] died as well. The family moved to San Francisco. Mike, the oldest brother, returned from Johns Hopkins to run the cable car line and salvage his father's tangled fortunes. The younger children tried to keep up the family, but there was no center. Fathers were depressing. Mothers might not be cheering, but they were not as depressing as fathers.[17]

There was no center anymore, but there were books. There was the Mechanics' Institute Library. There were Richardson and Jules Verne and Lecky's *Constitutional History of England* and *The Mill on the Floss*. And there was the anguish of growing up and learning who you were. What is the use, she wrote, of being a boy, if you grow up to be a man? She never had an unhappy childhood. She never had an unhappy anything. What is the use of having an unhappy anything?[18]

Between fifteen and twenty-four there is so much time in which you do nothing but stand around and wait for it to happen.[19] Fifteen is really medieval and pioneer and nothing is clear and nothing is sure, and nothing is safe and nothing is come and nothing is gone. But it all might be.[20] And the food that was so much a part of one's pleasures might turn horrible. The end of babyhood to fourteen makes the world not a dream but an awakening. When a baby eats and vomits it is not war. But when fourteen eats and vomits it is war.[21]

Autobiography Number V

When I was at college I studied philosophy that was it they did not know what they saw because they said they saw what they knew, and if they saw it they no longer knew it because then they were two. . . .

The minute you are two it is not philosophy that is through it is you.[22]

In William James's psychology laboratory at the Harvard Annex, she experimented on students about memory and automatic writing. A phrase would catch in the minds of the students, repeating itself like a stuck record. There was a place in the mind that kept wanting to tell another story, a story that welled up and overcame one's attention. She herself had no such unconscious reactions. She could not write automatically.[23] There were other such experiments in the laboratory. James said if Miss Stein gave no response then it was as normal not to give a response as to give one.

> *I believe what I know although nobody tells me so, because I know that I believe what I know. But in doing so, there is no time in me and no identity.*[24]

Human nature was not only uninteresting, it was painful. It was the repository of emotions, of memories, of the pain of living, of the pain of being who you were. But the human mind was the place beyond pain and memory, beyond identity. It was the place where masterpieces were made, which purged the world of pain and history and fear and everything else that they took as their subject.

She quit medical school after her second year. The anatomy of the brain and delivering babies in Baltimore's black districts had no more interest for her. A friend admonished her to think of the cause of women. "You don't know what it is to be bored," Gertrude Stein said.

What she longed for was no longer to be bored. No longer to feel the awful ache of who you were eating into you, minute by minute. She longed, although she didn't yet know it, to be a genius.

Both saints and geniuses were never bored. Their business was not the moment, but eternity. To be a saint meant to do nothing, and not being bored. It meant to be half in and half out of doors, not seated and not standing, like Saint Therese in her opera. And it meant not to have to choose, and not to have to have regret. "A genius need not think, because if he does think he has to be wrong or right he has to argue or decide, and after all he might just as well not do that, nor need he be himself inside him."[25] It took a lot of time to be a genius. You had to sit around so much doing nothing, really doing nothing.[26]

Her first book was about her earliest love affair. It was a badly written, stilted book, diagramming a love triangle as ruthlessly as she had diagramed those sentences she loved to take apart in school back in Oakland.[27] In Paris, after she had already started work on what she thought was her masterpiece, the long book that would be called *The Making of Americans*, she put together a little volume called *Three Lives* inspired by Flaubert. She discovered that she could write about herself and that first love affair—what she called the wandering after wisdom—in the disguises of a sixteen-year-old black girl named Melanctha Herbert and her lover Jefferson Campbell. She was bright, curious Melanctha but more, she was slow, deliberate Doctor Jeff Campbell. She had begun to find her voice, and when she found it, it was in the slow layering of repeated phrases. She was writing from the inside now, trying to reproduce the inner rhythms of consciousness.

There was no present. There was no past and no future. There was only that flux of consciousness, that "specious present" that William James had discovered contained both reconstructed past and constructed future.[28] If there was no past, then, really, there was no pain. There were tears, but they were tears shed over literature. The fictive little shards of now layered one on top of the other to make a life, just as the individual cells of image ran through the projector to make the pictures jump and tumble on the nickelodeon screens, but there really was no past, nor future either.[29] There was no past, and there was no future, but you could count: one little two little three little Indians . . . it was always one little Indian, even when there were two little Indians. This is how the mind worked. It worked by tiny accretions of information. Every instant was a distinct instant. Every instant was new, replete with meaning, complete in itself. There was no repetition.[30]

With *Three Lives* finished, Stein turned back to *The Making of Americans*. *The Making of Americans* was to be the story of all the kinds of people there ever were, a crazy typology, the story, in part, of her own family, in Oakland, which she called Gossols. There was something cracked and obsessional about the project, and she filled page upon page diagramming various types of character. In its ritual incantations of the banalities of life, the marriages and deaths and moves, there was something, as well, self-consciously American. She was determined to be quite ordinary, to find her genius in the ordinary. There was to be a kind of brisk American optimism about it all. It was the optimism of the West, and William H. Gass would compare her idea of the Pioneer to Turner's frontier thesis.[31] A kind of Manifest Destiny of the Soul. William James and that many-sided genius Peirce were proclaiming a new kind of truth, whose pragmatic test was absolutely in tune with the manly fortitude that seemed at the turn of the nineteenth century so right for the country. The value of a truth was not some abstract ultimate, but its utility in the market place of ideas, what James called—the phrase was unfortunate—its dollar value. There is in Gertrude Stein this same determination to be sensible, and right, and cheerful and American. But there is often a pathos informing her work that is at odds with this cheery Americanism, muddled and anguished for the most part in *The Making of Americans*, in later works swimming up to the surface in haunting moments of clarity. Americans had to have so much optimism, she said, because the land goes away from them, the water goes away from them, they go away from everything and it is all so endless and yet they have all been from one end to the other end of it. Europeans did not know anything about disillusion.[32] Finally, *The Making of Americans* became a Book of the Dead. It concluded with a long tolling of the funeral bell that is the ultimate end of the History of a Family's Progress. If everyone was a real one for her, so too could anyone, and any family, come to be a dead one. Can and will, you could add.

While she worked on *The Making of Americans* she began composing experimental portraits of the people she knew, Picasso, Mabel Dodge, Alice Toklas, the Cone sisters. It was as if the pain of Melanctha and *The Making of Americans* frightened her. Her work turned inward, became difficult, abstruse. Henceforth it would be a kind of emotional hieroglyphic, where the deepest parts of herself would be encoded in a private language—a language made public in plays, in novels, in poems.

It was a hard thing, she said, to kill a century, the nineteenth century into which she had been born, which was so sure of evolution and prayers and Esperanto and its ideas. Her battle was not with social conventions or ideologies, but with the forms of language that held them in place in the cluttered Victorian parlor of literature, bursting as it was with inherited bibelots that made of the expression of the human mind at play a morgue-museum full of stuffed birds, claw-footed pianos, antimacassars, and ponderous vases filled with the ashes of dead emotions. The novel was dying, choking on its own irrelevance and sentimentality. Those books she pored over in the Mechanics' Institute Library might soothe her, but they were not interesting.[33] By the time she had begun to read them, Uncle Tom was dead and Little Nell and Clarissa and Paul and Virginia and even Maggie Tulliver. Stein sensed that in a world without gods their suffering couldn't elevate itself to the tragic, nor could it be a revolutionary tool in the hands of its comfortably middle-class readers. Their suffering was, finally, superfluous. Sick of those dying heroes and heroines, Flaubert had turned his back on the agony. What he was left with was irony. But irony itself was no answer, it was a *position*. It was sentimentality held at bay. And beyond irony, what was left? What was left for literature was a delaying tactic, a procrastination: the examination of its own form.

Then there were the words the books were made of. The words themselves were wearing out. Adjectives were dead and nouns just about dead too. The names of things had ceased to be anything but sterile reflexes, the punctual cues to habitual responses. "Long before the cuckoo sang to me I wrote a song and said the cuckoo bird is singing in a cuckoo tree," Stein teased, "singing to me, oh singing to me. But long before that very long before that I had heard a cuckoo clock."[34] The words themselves had to be reclaimed.

In the Bateau-Lavoir, Picasso and Braque were reinventing painting, freeing it from its conventional referents in a kind of teasing, brutal play with reality and with its own conventions, rearranging its terms so it could play in the mind and on the canvas without being snared by its own bad habits. In just this way Stein began to play with language. Already the play was incipient, was there in her recasting of the conventional and banal prose of *Q.E.D.* into the haunting repetitions of *Melanctha*; and it began to emerge in *The Making of Americans*, that bloated whale of a book floating around listlessly on her writing table, looking for someone to harpoon it.

> Bear it in your mind my reader, but truly I never feel it that there ever can be for me any such creature, no it is this scribbled and dirty and lined paper that is really to be to me always my receiver,—but anyhow reader, bear it in your mind—will there be for me ever any such a creature,—what I have said always before to you, that this that I write down a little each day here on my scraps of paper for you is not just an ordinary kind of novel with a plot and conversations to amuse you.[35]

So she turned back to the language. She threw off the old language habits as she threw off her corsets, freeing her great, formless mass to find its own destiny. She made herself willfully a child (she had in many ways always remained a child, the baby of the family). It was as if she were always learning the language, like a child in a new country. Her English, with its odd, faintly Germanic syntax and her pleonastic constructions, had a deliberate strangeness, an awkwardness. In the early work at times she would snidely imitate some bad eighteenth-century novel, dear reader—or perhaps, still finding her way, she simply couldn't write any better. (The prose of her college themes is abominable.) The effect was to make the language really present. So she forged on, never correcting, never looking back, bending the language to her will. Leo thought that Gertrude was basically stupid.[36] If she was, it was a stupidity with a method. As if she were some stubborn, perverse, destructive child, she had to take her words apart just to see if she could put them back together in new ways. Repeating them again and again and again, like holding your breath until you went blue in the face, the words become something else, become *anything* else. It was a way of denying the authority of the inventor of these valuable toys, these words, of that patriarchal poetry she made fun of. She would make up her own language. It was a lifelong, low-intensity tantrum against the word.

She insisted that her art was an art of surfaces, an art of the visible, that she had no inner world. And, in a way, she was right. It was as if, like some glove turned inside out, she exposed the inside of her mind: that inner world was now the outside, the raw material of words, puns, codes. It is the reader who bears the burden of its meaning, the reader who bears her unconscious. There was an essential primitiveness—like the primitiveness of Picasso—in her.

Take her love of puns.

Duchamp once made a disk of one long string of puns, to be played on a phonograph turntable; Joyce wrote a whole novel as one endless punning exfoliation. But for Stein puns were not ways of deepening meaning, of creating the model of an unconscious with multivalent layers of myth and language and history; puns were ways of evading history and time itself, of hopping from thought to thought like a pigeon pecking at microscopic bits of nourishment on the pavement. So she worked, unpeeling nouns from their meanings, like some willful child locked in her room peeling away the roses on the wallpaper. It would be *her* room, she would make it that way. And it worked—for the most part—badly. But there were moments of astonishing lucidity that emerged from the maddening eccentricity of her language. Poetry was calling upon the name of a thing until it had an existence of its own, like Adam naming the animals in some new Eden. A word was what a thing *was*. And when she wrote a rose is a rose is a rose is a rose, she thought that not since the Renaissance had a rose really been so red on the printed page.

Her audience was herself. "I write for myself and strangers," she once had said. And then the strangers, too, were gone. Nobody entered into the mind of someone else, not even a husband or a wife. You may touch, but you did not enter into each other's mind. The created thing could only mean something to one person and that person was the one who wrote it.[37] But the audience is a creation of the self, a self she could not quite believe in, that she needed to invent, as she needed to invent the persona of her written voice. And we, the readers who would come to her in spite of herself, are compelled, if we enter her world, to bear witness to her self-inflicted talking cure—no, not talking cure, her *writing* cure—for her language was always meant for the eye. She had noticed that the portraits of the great statesmen and writers of the past all had their mouths firmly shut. Like some marble bust of Caesar or Shakespeare on a library shelf or a photograph of her much-admired Ulysses S. Grant, nothing would escape her mouth. She wrote to see, and to be seen, not to be revealed. The sexual power of words as love-charms, as incantations, was hidden in a coded language of seizures and cows and the tender buttons of sensual pleasure. And, in a way, she wrote to still the emotions that welled up in her. She was walking in the Luxembourg gardens once and it was the end of summer and the grass was yellow. She was sorry that it was the end of summer. She saw the big fat pigeons in the yellow grass and she said to herself, pigeons on the yellow grass, alas, and she kept writing pigeons on the grass, alas, short longer grass short longer longer shorter yellow grass and she kept on writing until she had emptied herself of the emotion. It was like a mother talking to her child in a bath, she kept talking and talking until the emotion was over. That was the way, she said, a writer was about emotion.[38]

History as Geography

She was bothered that in an airplane being up so high nothing happened. If you went up into the mountains not very high everything happens, you felt funny even if you were not afraid because being so high makes you feel high, but being really high, as high as you could be, did not make you feel high. And all at once she knew and it was true that the air below was solid when you were above it, as solid as water.

She spoke at colleges and schools, talked to students and people she met on the way and always remembered what they served her for dinner. In Chicago she saw a triumphant performance of *Four Saints in Three Acts*, her opera with music by Virgil Thomson. She was enjoying being a genius. She was enjoying being recognized on the street.

In Hollywood she and Alice sat all alone in a projection room and saw the newsreel clip that Pathé had made of her reading the "pigeons on the grass" passage from *Four Saints*. Her image was almost as large as the movie screen, taking glasses off and putting them on again, reading about the pigeons, moving around and talking. She did not particularly like it, particularly the talking. It gave her a very funny feeling and she did not like that funny feeling.[39]

Of course celebrity had its compensations. One of them was getting to meet anyone you wanted to meet. She met Dashiell Hammett—she was addicted to detective stories—and asked him why it was the nineteenth-century women authors who wrote about themselves in their characters, and now it was the men. Hammett said that the men had lost confidence in themselves, they had to make themselves "more beautiful, more intriguing more everything and they cannot make any other man because they have to hold on to themselves." It explained for Stein why it was a woman who was doing the real literary work in the twentieth century. There were no heroes to dwell on in detective stories. They were a kind of book in which the hero was always dead at the beginning. In America the dead were dead and there was no connection with those left living. That had a great deal to do with deserts and religion.[40] The hero was dead, but the detective himself was like Gertrude Stein. He had no inner life, no psychological depth. The detective reassembled a world through attaching one clue to the next, just as Stein reassembled her world through sticking one word next to another. Like the newspapers or radio or the funny papers it was the moment-to-moment emphasis on what was happening that was interesting. She didn't care about solutions.[41] At a dinner party in Beverly Hills she met Chaplin and they talked of their art. Silent film had let you do something that had never been done in the theater—it let you change the rhythm of movement. Chaplin had invented the sentiment of movement and she had invented the sentiment of doing nothing.[42] She found out at last what had been bothering all of them at this dinner when one of the guests blurted out, "What we want to know is how do you get so much publicity?" And so she told them.[43]

Alice Toklas and Gertrude Stein left Los Angeles, driving up the San Joaquin Valley in a rented car. They were going to their California, the California they had come from. Alice's pioneer grandfather had once owned all the land in the San Joaquin Valley, Stein thought, and it was exciting, the names of the places were exciting. They smelled the orchards of oranges and nuts and the fig trees that smelled best of all, and then the land rose a little and they saw the California poppies they had not seen growing wild since they had left home. It gave Gertrude Stein a shock to see them there, it began to be funny and to make her uneasy.[44] The roads in America were lovely. They moved along with no connection with the country, the way the railroad tracks used to be laid, not following the towns, but creating the towns along the line.[45] They visited Yosemite and saw the great redwoods, which, in her telling, had no roots. Then they set out for the coast. The coast looked like all the ordinary nineteenth-century school of California painting, and there was no use looking at it, just as there was no use looking at the Loire, because it looked like mediocre nineteenth-century French landscape painting.[46] They stopped in Monterey, then returned to the road, and the last stage of Gertrude Stein's journey home.

> We left for San Francisco and Oakland there I was to be where I had come from, we went over the green rounded hills which are brown in summer with a very occasional live oak tree and otherwise empty and a fence that does not separate them but goes where the hill has come to come down, it was just like them geographically altogether the hills they had been and a great deal of them up and down we went among them and they made me feel funny, yes they were like that that is what they were and they did trouble me they made me very uncomfortable I do not know why but they did, it all made me uncomfortable it just did.[47]

Then there was San Francisco, and it was quite frightening driving there. *Gertrude Stein Is Here. Is Interviewed, Is Bored, Is Here*, the heading of the piece in the *Chronicle* read. (Stein's prose style, the poor woman sent out to interview her wrote, was apparently infectious.) William Powell and Ginger Rogers were playing in *Star of Midnight* at the Golden Gate that week, and Bing

Crosby and W. C. Fields were at the Warfield. On the comic page Joe Palooka had been kidnapped by Gypsies. Hitler had issued five demands to the rest of Europe. Goering was marrying an actress. In Berlin two Communists were being beheaded for the killing of Horst Wessel. A nineteen-year-old black boy had been hanged at San Quentin through a mistake in his appeal.[48] In San Francisco, Alice met friends she had been to school with and remembered every one. Gertrude had been to a public school and did not remember her schoolmates. "Gertrude never left home in the same way I did," Alice remembered years later. "She was always at home through the language, but I was at home only through her."[49] Yet the language might not be enough, the language might only cover a certain emptiness and anxiety at the heart of things. Well, like it or not, everybody had to do something to fill the time.

> *After all human beings have to live dogs too so as not to know that time is passing, that is the whole business of living to go on so they will not know that time is passing, that is why they get drunk that is why they like to go to war, during a war there is the most complete absence of the sense that time is passing a year of war lasts so much longer than any other year. After all that is what life is and that is the reason there is no Utopia, little or big young or old dog or man everybody wants every minute so filled that they are not conscious of that minute passing. It's just as well they do not think about it you have to be a genius to live in it and know it to exist in it and express it to accept it and deny it by creating it, anyway here we were in California.[50]*

They crossed the bay on the ferry and Goat Island might just as well not have been there and they visited Mills College where she and Leo used to ride on a tandem bicycle in the dust. There was no dust now but Mills did seem dusty enough to be a memory of dust, not that there was that spring, but in the summer there might be dust. And she asked with a reluctant feeling to see the Swett School where she had gone as a child and Thirteenth Avenue and Twenty-fifth Street where she had lived in the big house with the gardens and the drive flanked by eucalyptus trees. Thirteenth Avenue was the same. It was shabby and overgrown and the houses were certainly some of those that had been there in her childhood and there were no bigger buildings and the houses were neglected and there was lots of grass and there were bushes growing, yes, it might have been Thirteenth Avenue when she had been there. The house wasn't there. Not of course the house. The big house and the big garden and the eucalyptus trees and the rose hedge, naturally they were not there.

> *What was the use, if I had been I then my little dog would know*
> *me but I had not been I then that place would not be the place*
> *that I could see, I did not like the feeling, who has to be them-*
> *selves inside them, not any one and what is the use of having been*
> *if you are to be going on being and if not why is it different and if*
> *it is different why not.*[51]

She did not like anything that was happening. She saw it and felt it and it had a tenderness and a horror too.[52] What was the use of her having come from Oakland? It was not natural to have come from there, yes, write about it if you liked or anything if you liked but not there, there was no there there.[53]

Gertrude Stein and Alice Toklas left for France on May 4, 1935. Just before she sailed, Stein sat in her hotel in New York giving an interview, talking about roots, and that to go back to them was only to confess that the plant was dying. "Yes," her interviewer said, "but there is something more. There is the hunger for the land, for the speech."

"I know," Gertrude Stein said almost sadly. "America is wonderful!"

Then, without any warning, she said, "I feel now that it is my business here. After all, it *is* my business, this America!"

Then she laughed with what her interviewer called "a marvelous heartiness, a real lust."

When the interviewer asked her if she would come back, she looked up slyly, still smiling, and opened and shut her eyes with the same expression of zest with which a man smacks his lips.[54]

But she never returned to the United States. Her pose might have deceived her interviewers, but not herself.

Identity a Poem

After her American tour, Stein had gone back to her house at Bilignin and her dogs and her garden and her work. "Come back to anything is always a bother you have to get used to seeing it as it looks all over again until it looks as it did which it does at last," she wrote. Settled down, she worried about identity and remembered the nursery rhyme about the old lady and her dog.

> *I meditated a good deal about how to yourself you were yourself at any moment that you were there to you inside you but that any moment back you could only remember yourself you could not feel yourself and I therefore began to think that insofar as you were yourself to yourself there was no feeling of time inside you you only had the sense of time when you remembered yourself and so I said what is the use of being a little boy if you are to be a man what is the use.*[55]

"I am I because my little dog knows me and I was not sure but that that only proved the dog was he and not that I was I." You lived on this earth and you could not get away from it. And yet there was a space where the stars were that was unlimited and that contradiction was there in every man and every woman and so nothing ever did get settled.[56]

The Occupation found her still in Bilignin. As were so many things, her Jewish heritage was remote to her. She and Alice lived as if they were invisible, as if they were not Jews. She began to translate Pétain's speeches in order to explain him to America. She was protected perhaps by powerful friends, or by her own obliviousness, or by her assumption that she was still the baby of the family and that people would take care of her. They always had. She had gone deep inside herself, where time stands still, and found there an essential detachment from history and from the world: there was only death and the unlimited space between the stars, and what did the Nazis or the Collaborators or the Maquis or anything have to do with that, after all?[57] Someone had asked Stein's Saint Therese if it were possible to kill five thousand Chinese by pressing a button would it be done. Saint Therese wasn't interested.[58] And when, after the destruction of Hiroshima and Nagasaki, someone asked Stein about the atomic bomb, she wasn't interested either. There would still be plenty of people left. And if nothing were left, there would be nobody to be interested and nothing to be interested about.[59] She continued to write, but her new public voice became increasingly split from the literary voice she had cultivated so assiduously. She clung to celebrity, to that overripe public persona of the down-to-earth, straight-from-the-shoulder

Republican Aunt Gert that had been developing since her American tour. But there was the other voice too. The difficult voice that held all her contradictions and uncertainties and anguish.

In Stein's last collaboration with Virgil Thomson, she sees Susan B. Anthony as a living statue. "We cannot retrace our steps, going forward may be the same as going backwards," this woman, now become a monument to herself, sings. "We cannot retrace our steps, retrace our steps." The suffragist had been what Stein had not been, an actor in history. But finally, what does it mean? And what does that laborious life of words mean now that it is finally almost over for her creator? "But do I want what we have got, has it not gone, what made it live, has it not gone because now it is had, in my long life in my long life" There is a silence. A few more words, then another silence. "Do you know because I tell you so, or do you know, do you know." Another silence. "My long life, my long life." The opera ends with a phrase that has no verb, that goes nowhere.

PART 2

HEMINGWAY'S INDIANS

Paris

Working in the morning when he always wrote, in the house above the sawmill, with the rooftops of the rue du Cardinal-Lemoine beneath him, Ernest Hemingway went back to his boyhood. Over his workspace there was a map of northern Michigan. Beyond the pieties and the smug self-congratulation of the Chicago suburb where he grew up, it was his real home. Once he and a friend had walked there from Oak Park, and after the war, here in Paris, with his wife and his baby in the room below him, it was the place he returned to in his mind. It was a landscape of lake and lakeshore and a few resort hotels, and the farms that spread back from the water, and beyond the farms, starting just at their margins, of the woods. The woods themselves were not the original forest, but its remains; for this was the bitter end of an industrial world, with its stacks of hemlock bark for the tanneries, its forests of stumps and slashings and stripped trees and the ruins of abandoned mills, and the ruins of the people of the forest, the Indians, living in shanties in the barkpeelers camps, drinking, and dying. Beyond this, beyond the war and the

116

scars of memory and the burnt hacked land, was another place, an aboriginal woods, a place you could never get to.

He was learning in those days in Paris that a story was something you made. It was more than reproducing some story you had already read, like a Jack London or Ring Lardner. It was more than the neat ironies of O'Henry or the fiction in the *Saturday Evening Post*. Like the paintings he had started to look at at Gertrude Stein's and in Luxembourg, the story had a complex relation to the surface of the world. The story was something that happened in memory and in the imagination.

At 27 rue de Fleurus he sat listening to Gertrude Stein talk. Stein had a talent for collecting. She collected paintings and bric-a-brac and she collected brilliant young men. She was less successful with brilliant women, although there were those too, but it was the men she specialized in, and Gertrude Stein held forth while Alice Toklas talked with the wives about cooking and shirt-waists (Alice would imagine herself writing something titled "The wives of geniuses I have sat with"). Less than a mile away, in the fashionable Faubourg St.-Germain, Edith Wharton, that other formidable expatriate, kept her own court. Farther out, on the rue de Longchamp, lived Wharton's friend Henry Adams during his Paris stays. Wharton and Adams might have been inhabitants of another galaxy. Stein's acquaintance with William James and with the Berensons might have closed the gap, but it was more than a difference of class or of style: it was a rupture in the whole way of reading the text of the world. From her fortress in the city she would come to call her hometown, Stein was giving marching orders to the twentieth century, but the orders were encrypted in a language few could read.

"Gertrude Stein was prodigious," her friend and rival Mabel Dodge wrote. "Pounds and pounds and pounds piled up on her skeleton—not the billowing kind, but massive, heavy fat. She wore some covering of corduroy or velvet and her crinkly hair was brushed back and twisted up high behind her jolly, intelligent face. She intellectualized her fat, and her body seemed to be the large machine that her large nature require to carry it." But she wasn't large at all, only her presence was. She had a laugh, Mabel Dodge said, "like a beafsteak."[60] The crinkly hair was hacked off short now, but the presence remained, and the fat and the laugh. Hemingway thought she dressed like an immigrant. You could buy either paintings or clothes, she told him.

She was reinventing the bourgeois household, with herself as the Giver of the Law and the painters and brilliant young men as her family. Her brother Leo, with his neuroses and his opinions and his condescensions, was gone, along with the Renoirs and most of the Matisses and Cézannes. The eyes he had taught his sister to use remained. She insisted on the rigorous banality of her domestic scene, what she called the "rich, right American living," and her salon was nearly abstemious. Like a good, middle-class American home, her rooms were a clutter of domestic comforts—but on the walls hung the new century, the Matisse portrait of his wife with the shocking green stripe down her nose, which Leo had for some reason left behind, the last rose-period Picassos with their melancholy and big feet, the cubist still-lifes and collages, all presided over by Picasso's marmoreal portrait of Stein herself, with its eyes carved out of a face that was becoming a classical mask. She hadn't thought the portrait looked like her. Picasso assured her it would.

Stein too had been doing portraits. But the portraits weren't observations of a surface *out there*, but of some intensity of movement inside her subjects that the writer in some occult way divined and that set up an agitation in the very language itself.[61] So the portrait was in some sense a portrait of the artist, a portrait of something the artist held inside. Hemingway had stumbled on the power of repetition writing for the newspapers, but now from Stein, he was learning about how it suggested the way a portrait or even a story might be built, in little increments of observation, a bit at a time, like the color-facets of a Cézanne. And musing on his work in the house above the sawmill, he was learning about the uses of silence.

For if intensity of movement was inside the writer, it was inside the reader too, if one wrote well. Everything had to be slowed down on the page, the way fear slows down the rush of time in war, so that that inner place where the real story was happening could be found. You couldn't get there directly. You could only suggest that place, make it out of the little bits and flecks of memory that floated above it, like sunlight glinting on the surface of a pool in some river one might remember, with the fish shadowed below, holding themselves still against the current.

Indians

"But tell me what they were like."
"They were Ojibways," Nick said. "And they were very nice."

"But what were they like to be with?"
"It's hard to say . . . "

Ernest Hemingway, "Fathers and Sons"

The Indians are always there. They are there in the first stories, and in "Big Two-Hearted River," they are there like the war is there, as an absence, something pushed back beyond the edges of memory. They are there in one of the first stories he wrote in the room above the sawmill.

> *"Do ladies always have such a hard time having babies?" Nick asked.*
> *"No, that was very, very exceptional."*
> *"Why did he kill himself, Daddy?"*
> *"I don't know, Nick. He couldn't stand things, I guess."*
> *"Do many men kill themselves, Daddy?"*
> *"No very many, Nick."*
> *"Do many women?"*
> *"Hardly ever."*
> *"Don't they ever?"*
> *"Oh, yes. They do sometimes . . . "*
> *"Is dying hard, Daddy?"*
> *"No, I think it's pretty easy, Nick. It all depends."*[62]

Crossing the lake back to the family cottage, the boy, Nick Adams, comes back to the domestic world with something in him that will not stay unsaid. In his mind are the child and mother his doctor father had saved back there in the Indian camp, and the husband his father could not save, his throat cut by his own razor in the bunk above his wife. Like that pastoral Bingham painting of half a century before, the power of the stillness is in an absence: absence of that place to which the innocent boy Nick Adams is surely going, and an absence of someone missing from those boats.

Perhaps she isn't really missing at all, this fictional mother who remains on the shore we cannot see. Between her and the Indian woman and her newborn child and the dead husband are the boy and the man in the boat. A bass jumps, making a circle on the water. And on that still morning, with the sun just coming up, the boy feels sure he will never die.

Hemingway had caught this woman's voice before. In "The Doctor and the

Doctor's Wife" the doctor's wife lies in a darkened room in bed, her Christian Science tracts and her Bible on the table beside her. In his own room the doctor is sitting on his bed cleaning and loading his shotgun and seething over a fight with a mixed-blood named Dick Boulton.

> *"Was anything the matter?"*
> *"I had a row with Dick Boulton."*
> *"Oh," said his wife. "I hope you didn't lose your temper, Henry."*
> *"No," said the doctor.*
> *"Remember, that he who ruleth his spirit is greater than he that taketh a city," said his wife.*[63]

It was the voice of the returned soldier Krebs's mother in "Soldier's Home" as well. A sweet, cloying Christian voice that had under it all of the smothering malice that the young writer could impute to the Middle West he had fled for Paris. Its cadences were imbedded in him, familiar from his own mother, from, surprisingly, his father as well. A pleading voice, a voice filled with terrible need and disappointment. Present in the writer's own silence, beneath the silent rage and the contempt, there was a certain longing. For the rage was after all, the rage of a hurt innocence. The doctor's loaded shotgun would stand, in the corner behind the dresser, hidden in Hemingway's mind, for thirty-seven years.

Fathers and Sons

His father came back to him in the fall of the year, or in the early spring when there had been jacksnipe on the prairie, or when he saw shocks of corn, or when he saw a lake; or if he ever saw a horse and buggy, or when he saw, or heard, wild geese, or in a duck blind. . . . His father was with him, suddenly, in deserted orchards and in new-plowed fields, in thickets, on small hills, or when going through dead grass, whenever splitting wood or hauling water, by grist mills, cider mills and dams and always with open fires.

"Fathers and Sons"

Nick Adams has been to the war. He has been wounded. He has been to the Big Two-Hearted River, fishing in the solitude, trying to keep from thinking about the things he has seen in the war, the images that keep him from sleeping at night, as his wounded creator could not sleep. Nick Adams is a father himself now, in a car, with his son dozing beside him.

And Adams, at thirty-eight, thinks of his father, thinks of his remarkable eyes, the way he saw literally, the way a bighorn ram or an eagle sees, and the hunting his father had taught him, as he hunts in his mind the landscape outside the windows of the car. Like all men with such a faculty, his father, Adams thinks, was very nervous. Then, too, he was sentimental, and like most sentimental people he was both cruel and abused. He had had much bad luck, not all of it his own. He had died in a trap he had helped only a little to set.

Thinking these things, thinking how sound his father was on fishing and hunting and how grateful he was for having been taught that, Nick Adams thinks how unsound his father was on sex. He remembers how, having been forced to wear a suit of his father's underwear, which he felt tainted with his father's smell, though it was perfectly clean, he had waited behind the woodshed with his shotgun—the gun his father had given him—cocked. And Adams thinks of an Indian girl named Trudy Gilby in a hemlock wood behind the Indian Camp. His son has awakened now, and he asks about the Indians. "But tell me what they were like," he says.

The silence between Adams and his son becomes a bond that connects Adams to his own father, the silence of his life and death, finally, the silence of sex. Nick Adams can't tell it, but Ernest Hemingway can try to write it.

> *Could you say she did first what no one has ever done better and mention plump brown legs, flat belly, hard little breasts, well-holding arms, quick searching tongue, the flat eyes, the good taste of mouth, then uncomfortably, tightly, sweetly, moistly, lovely, tightly, achingly, fully, finally, unendingly, never-endingly, never-to-endingly, suddenly ended, the great bird flown like an owl in the twilight.*[64]

The language buckles, gives way to an urgency that is close to inarticulation, baby talk, releases a metaphor, and then it's over. It is unsayable, finally, unwritable. Daylight in the woods and the hemlock needles stuck against your belly.

Transferred to that drive in a car, located somewhere between fiction and memory, the story is suspended between two silences. On December 6, 1928, worried about his deteriorating health, worried about money, worried, finally, about life, Doctor Clarence Hemingway went into his bedroom in Oak Park and shot himself with his father's Civil War pistol. There was another death. The dead woman's name was Prudence Boulton, the very real daughter of the Dick Boulton who had argued with Doctor Adams in "The Doctor and the Doctor's Wife." She was the daydream of sexual perfection, the Indian girl in the forest, whether real or invented, how can it matter?[65] It is impossible to believe that Hemingway, home from the war, couldn't have known that on February 15, 1918, pregnant, she and her paroled convict lover had committed suicide by taking cyanide in Charlevoix.

Writing in that tiny room with the map of northern Michigan pinned to the wall, Hemingway had found that painful center of absence that his stories needed to build themselves around for them to be true as he conceived their truth. The Indians were there, and then they were gone, but still they remained in the imagination and as a hollow place in the memory.

> So that when you go in a place where Indians have lived you smell them gone and all the empty painkiller bottles and the flies that buzz do not kill the sweet-grass smell, the smoke smell and that other like a fresh-cased marten skin. Nor any jokes about them nor old squaws take that away. Nor the sick sweet smell they get to have. Nor what they did finally. It wasn't how they ended. They all ended the same. Long time ago good. Now no good.[66]

Toward the end of his life Hemingway tried to find Nick Adams once more. It was the last story he worked on, and he never finished it. Running from game wardens and their laws, young Nick Adams heads out beyond the margins of the farms and cottages and resorts around the lake, with a younger sister he calls Littless. It is before the war. Before the lacerations of history and the body. Before everything. The place he heads to is beyond the slashings left by the bark peelers, in virgin forest, a secret place. It is the last really wild stream, except one in another awful country to get to, across the lake. Indians knew it, but they are gone now. Only their firestones remain. It is the last good country.

Hair hacked boylike, stealing for Nick, Littless brings Nick herself, and Nick brings the two of them to a kind of radical innocence that crime has bought.

Nick watches his sister sleep. "She looks like a small wild animal, he thought, and she sleeps like one. . . . He loved his sister very much and she loved him too much. But, he thought, I guess those things straighten out. At least I hope so."[67] Embarrassing, tender, childish as the stories he'd grown up on and had had to leave behind in order to find himself as a writer, it was a daydream. A place beyond the family and its laws, beyond the laws of men. "You should have been an Indian," Nick thinks. "It would have saved you a lot of trouble."

Hemingway could never finish this story. How can a daydream end and still be a daydream? If he didn't finish it, then Nick and Littless would never have to return. They would always be there, in him.

> *First Light*
>
> *There are always mystical countries that are a part of one's childhood. Those we remember and visit sometimes when we are asleep and dreaming. They are as lovely at night as they were when we were children. If you ever go back to see them they are not there. But they are as fine in the night as they ever were if you have the luck to dream of them.*
>
> Ernest Hemingway, *True at First Light*[68]

The place in the mind that Ernest Hemingway could never return to, the Michigan woods of his childhood, became the Africa of his adult years. In the fall of 1934, while Gertrude Stein was crossing the United States by air, Ernest Hemingway was in Key West finishing *The Green Hills of Africa*. It was a book about hunting, of course, as more and more he was writing himself into the page, becoming what he was, half-celebrity, half-artist, that kind of impossible monster that would, in the end, devour both halves of itself in a terrible orgy of fear and drink. The book was an advertisement, a primer on domesticity à la Papa Hemingway (his second wife was along on the hunt), and more than all of that, a kind of retreat into the landscape of childhood, now transported to a new continent.

> *I loved the country so that I was happy as you are after you have been with a woman that you really love . . . and you want more and more, to have, and be, and live in, to possess now again for always, for that long, sudden-ended always; making time stand still, sometimes so very still that afterwards you wait to hear it move.*[69]

123

It was also about art and artists, a way of settling up with his literary ancestors and with Stein for her comments on him in *The Autobiography of Alice B. Toklas* (or perhaps for simply being a version of that compelling, powerful woman he was always running away from). Of all the things that we forget about artists, their quarrels go first; thankfully, art remains: "A country, finally, erodes and the dust blows away, the people all die and none of them were of any importance, permanently, except those who practiced the arts."[70] The slashings in the woods of Michigan, the ruined lumber mills, would be a foretaste of what Africa would be. The celebrity's book, the hunter's book, would contain inside it the seeds of other stories. The Nick Adams stories he had published had ended where they had begun, with a man and a boy between homes, between the women who existed in ways that were never quite real to their author, and those same questions of life and death, of why men, or sometimes women, cannot stand the pain of life and choose to end it. It is that injured, questioning boy that we feel behind the silences of Ernest Hemingway's finest work, but he couldn't go beyond him, and when we can't hear that boy's silence any more, when the reticences of the stories become empty and mechanical and the stiff-upper-lip is all that is left; when the books give way to cynicism and bravado and posturing and that nagging voice of the expert in hunting and drinking and women begins to take over, lecturing as his father might have lectured—then the stories he tells are lost. For if he could not forgive his father, he could not forgive himself. He tried to kill this expert know-it-all, this bloated womanizing drunken white hunter version of himself in the manuscript published as *The Garden of Eden*, as he had tried to kill the more subtly realized version of him in that most beautiful of his stories, "The Snows of Kilimanjaro," but *The Garden of Eden* can't be finished. So we lose the man behind the finest stories and get only the shoddy, invented man who is, finally, less true than the boy he didn't need to invent, only find. "A white hunter is nearly crazy," Gertrude Stein had written in 1913, when the fifteen-year-old Hemingway was still poaching in Michigan. She might have been Nostradamus.

There is one final safari in the winter of 1953–54. It is the years of the Mau Mau insurrection, but Hemingway had not gone to Africa to find politics, or history either. At night, when he woke up in the tent below the flank of Kilimanjaro, and could not sleep, he unscrewed the cap on the quart bottle of Bulmer's Dry Cider, which he drank instead of water. Lying there, in the wake of one of the nightmares that had returned to him after so many years, drinking cider with his holstered pistol between his legs and the smell of a balsam-needle pillow under his neck, he thought he wanted to have a sweet grass basket to keep the pillow in, the kind the Indian women would sell around the resorts of the lake, and the cider reminded him of the cider mill in Michigan and the trout he had caught in a deep pool below the dam of the mill. But his powers of detachment and discipline would fail in the last works and around those patches of wonderful evocation and humor only the despair and the need remained, and the bottle. Moving through a haze of gin and Tusker Beer, that fiction he called Papa could only reclaim in Africa a parody of Michigan, there under the peak of Kilimanjaro, with the closeness of the animals, the hunting, the Africans whom he tried to weld into a kind of boy-gang of drinking partners and pagans, his wife, the teenage Wakamba girl Debba who stood for another brown girl, a long time ago, in another country. "You're hopeless," Miss Mary said to him. "No," he'd said—or at least that fictional man in the manuscript had said—"I'm not hopeless because I still have hope. The day I haven't you'll know it bloody quick."[71] The leopard that had been found frozen climbing toward the snow-peak of Kilimanjaro, the home of the gods, had become in this manuscript a farmyard predator wounded and then shot at point-blank range with a load of no. 8 birdshot on an assignment for *Look*. When it was all over he hadn't even bothered with the photo.

For a while in America the daily ritual of writing continued, even when he could finish nothing. "In Africa," he wrote in that unfinished book on his final hunting trip, "a thing is true at first light and a lie by noon and you have no more respect for it than for the lovely, perfect weed-fringed lake you see across the sun-baked salt plain. You have walked across that plain in the morning and you know that no such lake is there. But now it is there absolutely true, beautiful and believable."[72] His life itself might have been like that, as he looked out on it. Still he doggedly added up the number of words he had completed every morning on a piece of cardboard before he mixed the day's first drink. And then there finally came the days when the alcohol and the fame and the Seconal and the sex and even the writing failed him— those mornings when things were no longer true at first light, or true at all.

PART 3

CHANDLER AND THE CITY: VARIATIONS ON A
THEME BY PROUST

Reading Between Places

We are not good readers of these detective novels. We read them in train stations and in airports, in the anonymous rooms where we wait for something. If we imagine ourselves reading on a plane we like to think it is a prop plane, and it is always night, the plane fighting the wind, with the noise of the engines in our ears, the spinning disc of the propellers catching a slash of light only just visible in the dim illumination of the cabin; or, if we imagine it is a train, it is night too, the train is swaying and clicking on the rails, going into the darkness of some country dimly seen behind our own reflections in the glass of the windows. And if we read them in hotels, it is late at night, and we read them because waiting is worse than reading. We read much as Raymond Chandler read pulp novels of the 1930s, driving aimlessly up and down the California coast with his wife Cissy—at forty-five a failed second-rate poet, failed businessman, a failure, even, at being a drunk, turning the pages of some thriller in hotel rooms at night, and thinking he might write such stuff.

We read as Chandler read, because, in those moments between places, we are most vulnerable to boredom. If we don't, finally, have any stakes in the solution to the mystery, it is a pleasure to watch the detective at work. There is just enough anticipation in the story to keep us going, to keep us from seeing that hopeless terrain that is the landscape of boredom, that landscape in which we are most appallingly aware of the oppression of the self. So we keep turning the pages between the tick and the tick of the clock, in that zero place of who we are. Now and then there are moments that suddenly prickle with danger, or violence or sex.

> *"I'm no bitch in heat," she said between tight teeth. "Take your paws off me."*
>
> *I got the other wrist and started to pull her closer. She tried to knee me in the groin, but she was already too close. Then she went limp and pulled her head back and closed her eyes. Her lips opened with a sardonic twist to them. It was a cool evening, maybe even cold down by the water. But it wasn't cold where I was.*[73]

The moment is over. The book subsides into the ordinary grinding of its familiar mechanisms. Outside the windows of the plane we can still make out nothing on the ground. The minute hand on our watch has moved an eighth of an inch.

The narrative of the detective novel moves backward and forward in time at once, and as we are putting the pieces of some event hidden in the past together, we are moving forward in time, until past and present coincide in an answer; and we forget that we are not going anywhere, really, that the past doesn't matter to us, that it, like the future, is just a version of the present, this moment that layers over other nows and other nows and others, while we are waiting to go to sleep.

So after a while we don't remember the crackle of dialogue and the smart-aleck comebacks, or the false leads, or who the killer really was, if we ever cared at all. And finally all we remember are the descriptions of places; the insides of rooms, isolated from everything else, haunting us like the places in dreams we recall long after the dream itself has been forgotten, that pierce us still with the little stabs of recognition, as if these are places we have known before.

Proust thought such places were embedded in the senses. Turning from side to side in the sleepless night of his imagination, his body, he thought, held impressions of other rooms he had slept in, summoned up by the very kinks and adjustments of his muscles. We have not been in the rooms in Chandler's books. They are places in someone else's memory—if they are memories at all. If Raymond Chandler himself had ever been in them.

Why do they haunt us?

Some Versions of the Pastoral

There is a building in Los Angeles called the Fulwider Building. On the wall next to the elevator buttons are numbers with names next to them and numbers without names. There are plenty of vacancies or plenty of tenants who want to remain anonymous. Painless dentists, shyster detective agencies, small sick businesses that have crawled there to die, mail-order schools that would teach you how to become a railroad clerk or a radio technician or a screenwriter—if the postal inspectors didn't catch up with them first. Beyond the old man dozing by the elevator on a ramshackle stool is the fire door. The fire stairs haven't been swept in a month. Bums have slept on them and left crusts and fragments of greasy newspaper, matches, a gutted imitation-leather pocket book. In a shadowy angle against the scribbled wall a pouched ring of pale rubber has fallen and has not been disturbed.[74]

There is another place. Away from the mansions and hotels of La Jolla there is a beat-up cottage hidden behind an auto dealership. A bulb is burning in a lamp behind the unlocked door. The paper shade of the lamp is split. There is a couch with a dirty blanket on it. An old cane chair, a Boston rocker, a table covered with a smeared oilcloth. Spread out beside a coffee cup and a saucer full of cigarette butts is a copy of *El Diario*. A radio is playing. When the music stops an announcer rattles off commercials in Spanish. On the zinc drain board lie a short length of black rubber tubing and a glass hypodermic syringe with the plunger pushed home. In the sink are three long, thin empty tubes of glass with the corks near them. A parrot keeps squawking *¿Quién es? ¿Quién es? Hijo de la chingada*. Outside in a converted privy a man is hanging from a piece of electrical wire.[75]

There is still another place, a rented house in Palm Springs. It is a very handsome house except it stinks decorator. The entrance hall floor is covered with blue vinyl with a geometric design in gold. The living room carpet is pale gray and there is a Hammond organ built into the bar. The main bathroom has a sunken tub and sliding-door closets big enough to hold all the clothes twelve debutantes could want. The hi-fi system has speakers in every room. The house's front wall is plate glass, with butterflies imprisoned in it.[76]

None of these places is real. There is no Fulwider Building. There is no cottage in La Jolla with a broken front step. There is no rented house in Palm Springs. They are like places in dreams.

But the novel itself is a dream. The waking world lies outside its covers. And inside that dream is another dream, the memory of a past that the dream-present of the book can only long for.

> *I used to like this town . . . A long time ago. There were trees along Wilshire Boulevard. Beverly Hills was a country town. Westwood was bare hills and lots offering at eleven hundred dollars with no takers. Hollywood was a bunch of frame houses on the inter-urban line. Los Angeles was just a big dry sunny place with ugly*

homes and no style, but goodhearted and peaceful. It had the climate they just yap about now. People used to sleep out on porches. Little groups who thought they were intellectual used to call it the Athens of America. It wasn't that, but it wasn't a neon-lighted slum either.[77]

Like the snow shining on the peaks of the San Gabriels that you can still see from downtown Los Angeles in 1949, the city of the past is just out of reach. It is like the world frozen in some canvas by Poussin or Claude Lorrain, those painted pastorals that stretch the viewer's longing in two directions: longing for the eternal present of the foreground, where gods and goddesses mingle with imaginary shepherds in the fields and groves, longing for that distant unrealizable city that defines the limits of the fictional.

That far-off city is always there in Chandler's novels. It is a kind of unspoken, uninvoked presence, a second city under the city of the book you are reading. It is as if, through some witchery of language, we had set out for the distant city in the ideal past. The closer we got to it, the more apparent its falseness, its decay, became. In spite of the Claude Glasses we had perched on the ends of our noses like good eighteenth-century tourists, the blue distance we saw through the lenses turned out to be only smog, and the city turned out to be L.A. The longing was still there, but what we longed for was gone. And we no longer knew, exactly, what it was we had longed for in the first place, or what we had lost. As in those pastoral woods and glades forever fled, there was no time in this city; but it was not because this was some eternal land, some land in a myth. It was because there was no history here. The city had no past, or had forgotten it. Like the people who lived here, the city was inventing itself from scratch. It would be someplace that could only exist in the present, a present that gave the sense of constant, glittering change, but whose sparkle and newness turned out to be as phony as everything else. Those rooms in which time stops—or in which we see that it had never really been the moving, fluid thing it was supposed to be after all—are the haunting testimonies to our knowledge of the profound emptiness of this city of dreams.

It is significant that the invention of the modern detective novel roughly parallels the invention of photography. The streets and rooms in the Paris Edgar Allan Poe imagined are not so far different, after all, from Eugène

Atget's images of the actual Paris fifty years later, which have been compared to photographs of scenes of a crime.[78] It had taken some time for photography to separate itself from the pretensions of nineteenth-century painting and find its own way as an art form, but early on the files of Parisian and Italian and American police had been filled with photographs of criminals, their emulsified surfaces minutely interrogated by anthropologists to fill in the fictional lineaments of the ultimate perpetrator, the Criminal Type. Tellingly, Chandler's detective is closer to the petty criminals in those files in his poverty, his specialized knowledge, his occasional violence, his nights in jail, than to the world on the other side of the law. Like the crooks, the detective lives at the margins of power. His attributes—almost all of them—are the necessary ingredients Poe found in the makeup of the con man: minuteness, impertinence, perseverance, ingenuity, audacity, nonchalance, grin . . . Strike grin. The detective doesn't grin.[79]

We keep coming back to the haunting absences of Chandler's places, looking for that little piece of evidence we may have missed. While the eye lingers over these scenes, the factitious rush of the narrative pauses, gives us space to take in the minute descriptions of the dingy furniture, the desperately decorated flash interiors, cheap under the chrome and the mirrors, the telltale signs of everything that is poor and insufficient and false. What might have held these fragments together is the sensibility of the dwellers of these rooms; but they are gone now, absent themselves (even if they are standing there, waiting for the eye to return to them, the story to start up again). Their histories are absent, their desires, the lies they tell themselves and the world. It is as if the air has been sucked out of these rooms, leaving only the smell of reefer, cheap perfume, gin. The only human presence we sense is the photographer behind the lens, who is an absence himself.

That absence is named by his creator, Philip Marlowe.

Born in Santa Rosa. A couple of years of college at the University of Oregon or Oregon State. A nose broken trying to block a punt. He ended up in Los Angeles, Chandler said, because sooner or later everyone did. He'd worked as an investigator for an insurance company. He'd worked for the DA and been canned. No wife. No ex-wife. No children. His parents are dead. He has killed a man. He has read Flaubert. When we first see him he's thirty-eight years old.

He imagines what he might have been. He would have worked in the hardware store in Santa Rosa and married the boss's daughter and had five kids and read them the funny papers on Sunday morning and smacked their heads when they got out of line and squabbled about them with the wife. And he might even have gotten rich—small-town rich, and had an eight-room house, two cars in the garage, chicken every Sunday, the *Reader's Digest* on the living room table, the wife with a cast-iron permanent, and him with a brain like a sack of Portland cement.[80]

He chooses none of this: not the small-town pastoral, not the small-town history, not the children that connect the past to the future. He chooses the city: there he must invent himself moment by moment in the opportunities the city presents to test his integrity, to fix its haunted images on the surface of his sensibility.

City of Oblivion

The detective story is a form that finds something out so that another thing might remain hidden. Like the chessboard Marlowe keeps set up with a problem in his apartment, its solution is already there, hidden in the text. It remains only for the reader to fill up his empty hour trying to rediscover the meaningless, formal moves that will replicate it. The real story is elsewhere. Abandoned mother. Abandoned child. Chandler and his mother run to England, living off the charity of a smug and well-off grandmother and aunt. In his class photograph he is the only one not wearing the school uniform. He starts the tentative beginning of a literary career. Then he comes back to the United States. When the war breaks out he enlists in Canada. Another photograph shows him not quite convincing in the kilts of his regiment. In the trenches of the Lens-Aras sector he is knocked unconscious by the concussion of a German shell.

After the war he is in Los Angeles. Every five years the city reinvents itself. It peddles sunshine and bungalows and the quick fixes of the movies and quack religions. Already the orange groves are being plowed up for housing tracts. Chandler is working in the oil business. Derricks sprout in Santa Monica and Los Angeles like forests of iron trees. (In his first novel a murdered man lies buried under the sump of an oil well behind a millionaire's mansion.) He is drinking heavily. One place in Chandler's books is described with the starkest horror: the drunk tank in the county jail.

*In the drunk tank it is not so good. No bunk, no chair, no blankets,
no nothing. You lie on the concrete floor. You sit on the toilet and
vomit in your own lap. That is the depth of misery. I've seen it.*[81]

Like the alcoholic, what the city wishes for is not death, not the Big Sleep,
but oblivion.

There is one place that never appears in Chandler's writing. A bedroom covered with pink ruffles and the kind of furniture that at one time in Hollywood
was called French. This place is real and it is inhabited by Cissy Chandler.
Cissy Chandler is eighteen years older than her husband. She dyes her hair
blonde and wears clothes decades too young for herself. She rarely leaves her
house and the pink ruffled bedroom. It is unclear if Chandler ever knew just
exactly how old his wife really was.[82] Like the grifters and cons who inhabit
his novels, she is playing someone else.

Crooks

While Ernest Hemingway was shooting up Africa and Gertrude Stein was
chatting about literature with Dashiell Hammett in a Pasadena mansion,
Raymond Chandler was moving with Cissy from furnished apartment to
furnished apartment in Los Angeles and Riverside and La Jolla and Pacific
Palisades. He was forty-five, fired, broke, a dried-out alcoholic, unknown
except to readers of *Black Mask*. He was learning to write as you learn anything else, memorizing the formulas of the pulps, trying to write his way
back into the world. "I never slept in the park but I came damn close to it,"
he wrote. Once, he said, he went five days without eating anything but soup.
All the time the city is erasing one version of itself to create another that will
be forgotten as well. The wooden mansions of Bunker Hill give way to flea-
bag hotels and seedy crooks, Central Avenue becomes a black city within a
city. A History of Forgetting, Norman Klein calls Los Angeles's version of its
past. Myth succeeds myth. The Myth of the climate, the Myth of the freeway Metropolis, the Myth of a renewed Downtown.[83]

It is almost a joke, this city. It is like a master-character, the type of all the
criminals and liars and cons Philip Marlowe runs up against. The focus is
always tight and sharp. Lift up a corner of the city and what you find crawling around under it stands for everything else. Without substance, without
permanence, Chandler's LA is an endlessly shifting montage of shabby houses

and shabby people and empty, glittering facades. The stories of the Angelenos are as authentic as the sixteen-year-old virgins the call houses are pushing every spring. Everyone has some past life in the back of his interior closet, everyone has a scam. This is flip-side America. It is Thomas Jefferson's worst nightmare. A vision of the pustulating city mobs that Jefferson feared would destroy the institutions of a democracy founded on sturdy Anglo-Saxon tillers of the soil. But in Chandler's city, there is a sort of perfect democracy, after all: the millionaires, the gangsters, the car-park attendants, the would-be actresses—everyone is equally a crook.

Parentless, historyless, Marlowe is defined against the denizens of the city, who are parodies of themselves, mongrels.

> "You're not Mex?"
>
> "I'm part Chinese, part Hawaiian, part Filipino, and part nigger. You'd hate to be me."[84]

Tocqueville saw the arc of American democracy ending in a final solitude, in the lone man cut off from ancestors, from posterity, from his fellows.[85] The citizens of Chandler's Los Angeles end up in much the same place, and how perilously close to zero they are! For if self is created in the flux of social exchange, exchange here has become the economy of the scam; scammers scamming each other in an endless circulation of fictive identities.

If everyone is equally a crook, so is everyone equally a fake. The women especially are fakes. Actresses, all of them. Lovers of hoodlums, and both of them—hoods and women—lethal. With the unspoken horrors of that pink, faux French bedroom waiting for him, Chandler imagines his hero caught between these poisonous women and the deceptions of those women-pretending-to-be-men, the "pansy decorators," the pornographers with their boyfriends and their fake Chinese decor and their fake fu manchu mustaches. And everywhere are the fake shrinks and doctors who administer the fake cures and the very real drugs to the horrible needs of the people of the city. Thus Marlowe's integrity is bound up with his sexual purity in some strange way. He rips apart his bed when it has been desecrated by a woman he has succumbed to; he refuses to sleep with another woman in this same bed, which has become a shrine to some miraculously immaculate sexual coupling in the past. "I had a dream here once, a year and a half ago. There's still a shred of it left. I'd like it to stay in charge."[86] Marlowe's sexual purity

133

is expressed as a kind of poverty, like his rectitude as a detective who prefers the dinginess of his lonely office to the glitter of tainted money. There is a kind of special pleading for the aestheticized one-night stand.

> *"I don't love you," she said.*
>> *"Why would you? But let's not be cynical about it. There are sublime moments—even if they are only moments."*[87]

It is significant that Marlowe, who is remarkable for his self-control, administers one of his most vicious beatings—a beating that is entirely gratuitous—to a slender boy whose crime is to be in love with one of the queasy homosexuals that populate Chandler's city. And why not? "Everybody," Marlowe says, "is running away from something."[88]

The Theater of Mean Streets

Like all detective stories, Chandler's novels work by stripping away the false stories to get at the true story. But Marlowe himself remains an emptiness. It is as if Marlowe has had to vacate his private story so that the novel might tell its own. His story is barely sketched, his life pared down to nothing, a few twitches of character, a register of his likes and dislikes. He is, as I have said, a lacuna in the text, an emptiness around which the novel coagulates.

> *I didn't mind what she called me, what anybody called me. But this was the room I had to live in. It was all I had in the way of a home. In it was everything that was mine, that had any association for me, any past, anything that took the place of a family. Not much; a few books, pictures, radio, chessmen, old letters, stuff like that. Nothing. Such as they were they had all my memories.*[89]

But, of course, we don't get to read those letters, look at the pictures, learn his memories: Marlowe's integrity is bound up with his essential nullity. For he is nothing but that integrity, and without a real history, without a project, that integrity must be constantly tested.

As in Hemingway, that visceral fear of the homosexual in Chandler signals in its own way a certain attraction. The homosexuals in the novels are part of the world of the city of facades, pansy decorators who layer one form of cheap fakery over another, Chinese embroidery and yellow satin cushions in rooms with soft furniture and floor cushions and damask-covered divans in shadowy corners like casting couches, the kind of rooms "where people sit with their feet in their laps and sip absinthe through lumps of sugar and talk with high affected voices and sometime just squeak."[90] Perhaps the aversion and the attraction are one with another because the pansies and the queers and the queens of Marlowe's world are too close, in fact, to the detective himself. They too are on the margins. They too are part of the culture of fear that pervades the politics of the time, and that is a backdrop to the books, a secret brotherhood, with its own coded language and gestures, like the gangsters with their bought politicians and cops and like the communists who were being splashed across the Los Angeles papers.[91]

Roger Wade, the self-loathing alcoholic writer of bodice-rippers in *The Long Goodbye*, may be Chandler's attempt to distance himself from his private fears by creating a caricature of himself on the page. Wade lives in the purity of a "restricted" suburban enclave called Idle Valley.

> *"I had a male secretary once. Used to dictate to him. Let him go. He bothered me sitting there waiting for me to create. Mistake. Ought to have kept him. Word would have got around I was a homo. The clever boys that write book reviews because they can't write anything else would have caught on and started giving me the buildup. Have to take care of their own, you know. They're all queers, every damn one of them. The queer is the artistic arbiter of our age, chum. The pervert is the top guy now."*[92]

The homos are fakes, as Marlowe is not—fake men. But all that stands between him and them is his hold on some fragile authentic world, the solitude of his room and of his dreary office. With no ancestors and no progeny, all he has is his loneliness, a thin wall between him and the rootlessness and inauthenticity of these men who, as his author describes them, are not men, these pure facades. But the attraction and the fear finally may be less about sex than about its inescapable metaphors: a wish for, and fear of, being known, of being penetrated. The detective is a *private* eye. He is the eye that can see through everything, but cannot see itself. Like the cop friend who Marlowe suggests is sounding like a red, he wouldn't know what he is because he hasn't been investigated yet. 135

Here and there in this city of lies Marlowe runs into some version of himself, some lonely human outpost of integrity. Some tired cop doing his job as if it mattered to anyone. Some simply competent and decent citizen treading water in the slough. Taggart Wilde, the DA in *The Big Sleep*, is one of these versions.[93] His white frame house at Fourth and Lafayette Park sits in a couple of acres of rolling front lawn.

> *It was one of those solid old-fashioned houses which it used to be the thing to move bodily to new locations as the city grew westward. Wilde came of an old Los Angeles family and had probably been born in the house when it was on West Adams or Figueroa or St. James Park.*[94]

There are no foundations in Los Angeles, only unrooted human sites of integrity, that move, as Marlowe himself moves, from apartment to apartment, to rented houses with clean kitchens and broken woodpecker mailboxes; as Chandler moved from furnished apartment to furnished apartment with Cissy even after he had found himself as a writer.

"Down these mean streets a man must go," Chandler wrote famously. Could that man do anything else? Without the mean streets as his theater, the man would disappear, implode into his emptiness. The novels continue, one very like the next. Marlowe is cheated by his clients, is sucked into their filth, their secrets, and their crimes. He learns nothing he didn't know before. The artist, the detective, the blackmailer brokering other people's secrets for a buck—as it turns out, they aren't that much different from each other. The city grows, sprawling, centerless. Out in the Valley Dad is reading the sports page and thinking he's high-class because of his three-car garage and Mom is painting the bags out from under her eyes and Junior is talking pigeon English with high school girls who carry contraceptives in their makeup kits. California is the department-store state. The most of everything and the best of nothing.[95] The small-time bookmakers and gamblers are pushed out by other hoods: Puss Walgreen gives way to Eddie Mars and Eddie will give way to someone else. The succession of gangsters only mirrors the succession of bankers and movie executives and corporate condottierri who are taking over the daytime city.[96] It's a big town now, Eddie. Some very tough people have checked in here lately. The penalty of growth . . . The smog eats into the city more and more. By 1953 it has crept as far west as Beverly Hills.

And in the end, what is left? The detective becomes, like Chandler's pansy decorators, and lesbian dress designers, nothing but a style, a few insults, a few gestures across a desk. Wisecracks snapping in the dead space of the empty rooms. Even Marlowe can get tired of this world that seems to repeat some bad filmed version of itself.

> "What I like about this place is everything runs so true to type," I said. "The cop on the gate, the shine on the door, the cigarette and check girls, the fat greasy sensual Jew with the tall stately bored showgirl, the well-dressed, drunk and horribly rude director cursing the barman, the silent guy with the gun, the night club owner with the soft gray hair and the B-picture mannerisms, and now you—the tall dark torcher with the negligent sneer, the husky voice, the hard-boiled vocabulary."[97]

Marlowe is becoming a parody of himself, and he knows it. Like Hemingway (Marlowe nicknames a cop who speaks only in tough-guy repetitions Hemingway), he's running on empty. He's tired of the game. He's tired of the tired little gestures of his trade, the snotting back and forth across a desk, the pause to light a cigarette, all the rest. He's becoming a series of tics. Finally, he becomes merely a voice, a lyrical anti-poet of the city. A voice that contains nothing but the awful sense of loss that is all he has left to put up against the ugliness and violence and disappointment of life; a voice that haunts those dingy rooms and preternaturally illuminated scenes of emptiness, scenes of crimes that have been committed or that will be committed, in a perpetual elegy for a city that never was, except in the imagination.

Epilogue: Et in Arcadia Ego

Fame brought its own refined agonies to Chandler, and it brought Hollywood, and once more he started to drink. He left behind the manuscript of an unfinished novel. Marlowe is now middle-aged, tired, married to the beautiful heiress who gave him that one perfect sexual night. She has brought him to the disaster of that rented house in Palm Springs. "I always find what I want," she had said in that other book, "But when I find it, I don't want it any more." Now she's found Marlowe, and he's found her. *¿Quién es? ¿Quién es?*

Raymond Chandler drank himself to death in La Jolla in 1959. Three years later, mentally unstable, ruined with drink and pills, and finally hopeless, Ernest Hemingway killed himself at his Ketchum, Idaho, house with his favorite shotgun. Gertrude Stein had died in Paris in 1946.

Like Hemingway and Stein, Chandler aspired to a place without motion, a place with a stillness at its center, beyond history and history's pain. Suspended between memory and the need to forget, their words could not take them there.

Hans Namuth, *Jackson Pollock's Studio Floor* (1950), with paint residue from 1946–52, after which this surface was covered with pressed wood. Black-and-white photograph of Pollock's studio, fall 1950. © 1998, Hans Namuth Ltd. Courtesy Peter Namuth.

I saw a landscape the likes of which no human being could have seen.

Jackson Pollock

Five

Sublime America

THE ARTIST'S STUDIO

The artist in his studio: an old subject. You think of the huge paintings that turn their backs to us on their easels in Velásquez and Rembrandt, as if to insist on the obdurate materiality of canvas, stretcher bars, nails, and glue, like a kind of Calvary their artists must surmount. Insolent Courbet centers himself between an allegorized riffraff and the intelligentsia, pointing his terrible beard at a canvas on which he paints a landscape like a window in the studio wall, creating ex nihilo like *Le Bon Dieu*, while, unneeded, his model gazes on in adoration. How do you paint the insufficiency of art? Its inability to be anything more than an illusion of meaning made up of dabs of pigment and arbitrary boundaries of line, an embarrassed squeak in the great silence. And more urgently: how do you paint, without mediation, the world?

Eakins had often imagined this scene: the woodchips on the floor, the carved figures in the background, the plans for scrolls of ships—for William Rush had begun as a carver of ship's figureheads—and in the foreground,

Thomas Eakins, *William Rush and His Model* (1908). Oil on canvas. Honolulu Academy of Arts, gift of the Friends of the Academy, 1947 (548.1).

the model herself, her back toward us in the golden light, her hair up, holding on her shoulder a large book to stand for the water bird Rush will place there in his allegory of the Schuylkill River.[1]

To one side, in Eakins's painting, dressed in formal clothes, as if posing for history, slim-figured Rush drives a chisel into the wood with his mallet. At the other side, knitting, sits a chaperone. But it is the skin of the model that arrests us. Her bright petticoats, stockings, and bonnet lie tossed on a chair before her. If you could cross that line, if you could paint nature unencumbered by the codes of symbols and their fashions. If you could paint her naked . . .

Eakins returned to this subject thirty years later with a new understanding. When he painted his first version of this scene in 1877, he'd been thirty-three years old. The sculptor William Rush had been dead for half a century and was virtually forgotten in his native city of Philadelphia; the ornamental fountain with the water nymph that Eakins imagined him carving was slowly rotting under its paint. Eakins was now sixty-four. For thirty years he had struggled for an uncompromising realism. Beyond the patient drawings, the clay maquettes, the photographs, the perspectives and studies of light, beyond the stink of the dissecting table, beyond the scandals of the school, beyond money and reputation and disappointment, always this unspeakable ambition: to touch directly the hand of nature, to touch her in her primal nakedness. Embedded in the very conception of the 1907–8 version of William Rush and his model is the pathos of failure. The session has ended; there is no chaperone, there are no petticoats draped on a chair. We do not even see what the sculptor is carving. Except for the scroll of a ship's prow in the foreground, the studio is empty. It is unimportant. The model is not young. She faces us directly, the light touching her nose and breasts, her uncovered pubic triangle, one reddened knee. In shirtsleeves, his mallet still in one hand, the artist helps her descend from the platform. It is like some grave, courteous dance. The artist, whose face we do not see, has the sturdy form of Thomas Eakins. We remember the model's big feet. It's a dream, Eakins is telling us. To touch the hand of nature can only happen in the mind.

WILDERNESS

> *The question is not what you look at—but how you look &*
> *whether you see.*

> Henry David Thoreau, *Journal*, August 5, 1851

There was a preacher once, giving a cold sermon in a cold New England church. In the congregation that afternoon sat Emerson, and his eyes moved from the preacher to the window behind him. It was snowing. And Emerson, his mind drifting, thought that the snowstorm was real, but the preacher merely spectral. The words from the pulpit droned on. In back of the preacher was the beautiful meteor of the snow.[2]

Beyond words was Nature. Emerson longed to drink it in without the filter of language, although it is only in language that he could express himself. He imagined that he could be some great transparent eyeball, to be nothing, and see all. He imagined the currents of Universal Being circulating through him. That he could be a part or particle of God.[3]

But if Emerson tried to imagine a landscape somehow beyond the bounds of the human ego, the landscape itself kept falling away from a nation that was defining itself by material conquest. Early on there was implicit in the painted images of this country a profound sense of regret. Thomas Cole, the romantic who first staked out the landscapes of the Hudson River Valley as a site for painted meditation, was even in 1836 mourning their passing.

> *Yet I cannot but express my sorrow that the beauty of such land-*
> *scapes is quickly passing away—the ravages of the axe are daily*
> *increasing—the most noble scenes are made destitute, and often-*
> *times with a wantonness and barbarism scarcely credible in a civ-*
> *ilized nation. The wayside is becoming shadeless, and another*
> *generation will behold spots, now rife with beauty, desecrated by*
> *what is called improvement.*[4]

Four years later, Cole amplified his remarks to the Catskill Lyceum.

> *Among the inhabitants of this village, he must be dull indeed, who*
> *has not observed how, within the last ten years, the beauty of its*
> *environs has been shorn away; year by year the groves that adorned*
> *the banks of the Catskill wasted away; but in one year more fatal*
> *than the rest the whole of that noble grove by Van Vechten's mill,*
> *through which wound what is called the Snake Road, and at the*
> *same time the ancient grove of cedar, that shadowed the Indian*
> *burying-ground, were cut down.*[5]

Already Cole was painting a landscape that existed only in his mind.

"I can quite understand how, coming from a fresh, pure, and very ugly country like America," Ruskin wrote in a letter to Charles Eliot Norton in 1856, "there may be a kind of thirst upon you for ruins and shadows which nothing can easily assuage; that after the scraped cleanliness and business and fussiness of it (America), mildew and mould may be meat and drink to you. . . . You may wonder at my impertinence in calling America an ugly country," Ruskin continued, "but I have just been seeing a number of land-scapes by an American painter of some repute; and the ugliness of them is Wonderful. I see that they are true studies, and that the ugliness of the country must be Unfathomable."[6]

Our history as a nation was recent. What was ancient, the Indian mounds of the Ohio and Mississippi drainage, lay locked in profound silence. "He who stands on the mounds of the West," Cole wrote, "the most venerable remains of American antiquity, may experience the emotion of the sublime, but it is the sublimity of a shoreless ocean un-islanded by the recorded deeds of man."[7]

The land—that limitless expanse of land—which might have stored the spiritual values that in older countries lay in the treasure boxes of history, was only another kind of merchandise, bought in large quantities, and retailed in small lots.[8] "The Americans entered the wilderness as masters," the Austrian traveler Francis Grund wrote, "determined to subdue it; and not as children of nature nursed and brought up in its bosom. They could not at first love what was not their own; and when it became theirs, they had already changed its face."

> *The succession of changes was so rapid that scarcely one could leave a permanent impression on their minds. They treated nature as a conquered subject; not as a mother who gave them birth. They were the children of another world; who came thither to burn, ransack and destroy, and not to preserve what they had found. They burned the forests, dug up the bowels of the earth, diverted rivers from their course, or united them at their pleasure; and annihilated the distances which separated the North from the South, and the East from the West.*[9]

What was left after the forests were cleared, the rivers diverted, and all the lots were sold was a kind of historyless void that could be filled only by the grandiosity of the destinies manifest and shamelessly revealed that were to be penned by the national poet Whitman and Emerson called for, a poem whose unrolling democratic scroll would become itself some vast landscape. It was a vision of a kind of gigantism of the Word filled with vatic utterances, railroad tracks, grapeshot, and Great White Whales.

Bierstadt and Thomas Moran in the West, the Luminists in the East, would try to paint nature as if it were outside the frame of history, a nature devoid of man (if we except the solitary artist-viewer or the primitives in their skin tents at the base of some imaginary peak), but standing for his transcendental aspirations. But it was a nature that existed beyond the hoot of the railroad train that Thoreau could hear from his bean field at Walden Pond and the wind thrumming in the telegraph wires. The glaze of the painters was like that pane of glass separating Emerson from the snowstorm and confining him to the stove, the meeting house, the blizzard of words.

WHAT IS THE COLOR OF THE WORLD

> *Nature is a personality so vast and universal that we have never seen one of her features. . . . These farms which I have myself surveyed, these bounds which I have set up appear dimly still as through a mist; but they have no chemistry to fix them; they fade from the surface of the glass; and the picture which the painter painted stands out dimly from beneath. The world with which we are commonly acquainted leaves no trace, and it will have no anniversary.*

Henry David Thoreau, "Walking"

Sometime in 1850, Henry David Thoreau, surveyor, philosopher, loafer, and pencil maker, of Concord, Massachusetts, began the long daily walks that would be the center of his life. The walks were a kind of spiritual discipline, a method of achieving his great longing, his need not merely to observe nature but to merge with it. The journals he kept faithfully for twenty-four years—he was to die at forty-four—reconstruct the walks, note his moods and observations of nature, frame them with philosophical aphorisms. Walking became his occasion as an artist. Thoreau writes in his journal entry of February 27, 1851, "Obey the law which reveals and not the law revealed." The law which reveals is the law of nature, not the law of Sam the jailer and Congressman Hoar.[10] He wished his neighbors, the Concord farmers and merchants, the philosophers too, no doubt, were wilder. He wished for "a wildness whose glance no civilization could endure."

More than his published work, his walking became that "unroofed book" he longed to make. His journals are the records of those experiments beyond the chartered borders of things, at the margins of the printed word.

> *Now at 4 Pm I hear the Pewee in the woods & the Cuccoo reminds me of some silence among the birds I had not noticed—The vireo (red-eyed?) sings like a robin at even incessantly. for I have now turned into Conants woods. The oven bird helps fill some pauses.*

The poison sumack shows its green berries now unconscious of
guilt. The heart leaved loosestrife—Lysimachia Ciliata is seen in
low open woods—The breeze displays the white under sides of the
oak leaves & gives a fresh & flowing look to the woods. The river is
a dark blue winding stripe amid the green of the meadow What is
the color of the world.—Green mixed with yellowish & reddish for
hills & ripe grass—& darker green for trees & forests—blue spot-
ted with dark & white for sky & clouds—& dark blue for water.
Beyond the old house I hear the squirrel chirp in the wall like a
sparrow so Nature merges her creations into one.[11]

The entries are written as if in haste, the thoughts come in flashes of insight, grammar breaks down, commas—those servile commas Gertrude Stein so disliked—are replaced by dashes. The dashes show that a thought is not shaped by beginnings, middles, and ends, but is a process, as nature itself is a process, with no beginning, with no end, androgynous, borderless, present. The discoveries of walking were like the discoveries that Jackson Pollock would make as he worked on the great, wordless texts of his poured painting a hundred years later.

It was night, especially, that gave Thoreau what he was looking for. The boundaries of things dissolved, fields he had himself surveyed became strange, unpeopled. Often he walked until dawn. The journal entries he made in the day recorded his experiences. They were like the logbooks of some esoteric journey.

I now descend round the corner of the grain field—through the
pitch-pine wood in to a lower field, more inclosed by woods—&
find my self in a colder damp & misty atmosphere, with much dew
on the grass—I seem to be nearer to the origin of things.[12]

One night he saw the moon reflected in Walden Pond and realized that the sheaf of light that seemed to spring from where the viewer stood was the illusion of the viewer himself: if there were a myriad of eyes, the whole surface of the pond would seem to shimmer, its waves would turn up their mirrors to be covered with those bright flamelike reflections, and all would be dispersed into the atmosphere, flooding it with light.[13]

Snug in their beds the Transcendentalists slept. Emerson was asleep, and under the churchyard sod William Ellery Channing was asleep, and Margaret Fuller was asleep, asleep in the deep, and Bronson Alcott slept, stuffed with Orphic fudge (although perchance his long-suffering daughter Louisa was still up, sewing by lamplight); they all slept, warm in the envelope of the Oversoul, which ensured that nature, and sleep and death, had a meaning, and Thoreau, although perhaps he didn't know it, was journeying into another place, one beyond meanings. "The poet writes the history of his body," he said. It was his body, moving through woods and pastures, that was both instrument and record, recording on its subtle surface nature, taste, touch, sight, smell—smell especially—birdsong, and the chirking of the crickets. But even as he walked, he was taking notes, imagining some nature reconstituted on the page, as if it would not quite exist for him if he couldn't see its reflection in language. "I am conscious," he wrote, "of the presence and criticism of a part of me, which, as it were, is not a part of me, but a spectator, sharing no experience, but taking note of it."[14] A cold reflection, perhaps, like the light of the moon, which Reese's Cyclopedia said condensed in the best mirrors, produced no sensible heat upon the thermometer.[15] And once, toward dawn, he dropped his pencil and could not find it in the dark.[16]

LANDSCAPES OF THE MIND

From beyond the fields of East Hampton, the Atlantic opened to the curve of the horizon. A few miles out of the town was a straggling hamlet local people called the Springs. It was there that Jackson Pollock and his wife, Lee Krasner, moved in the fall of 1945. The two-story farmhouse they bought had five acres, a barn, and a view of Accabonac Harbor. The ocean reminded Pollock of the flat stretches of the West he'd grown up in, of land seen from the roof of a boxcar when he'd hoboed back to California in the thirties. The next June, Pollock moved the barn and began using it as a studio.

He had already begun laying his canvas flat on the floor. In the barn he could work with a canvas of great size, walk around it, see it from any angle. He had opened a large window high up in the north wall. He didn't want to see the harbor. He didn't want to be disturbed by the outside view when he was working. The landscape he had in mind was inside him.

148 Two years earlier, in 1943, he had painted a large canvas he called *Guardians of the Secret*. It began, Pollock's biographers Steven Naifeh and Gregory White

Jackson Pollock, *Guardians of the Secret* (1943). Oil on canvas, 48 3/8 in. x 75 3/8 in. San Francisco Museum of Modern Art, Albert M. Bender Collection, Albert M. Bender Bequest Fund purchase. © Pollock-Krasner Foundation / Artists Rights Society (ARS), New York.

Smith believe, as a portrait of Pollock's family around the dinner table. Beneath the table lies the family dog. Jackson Pollock himself is not in the picture, for the picture is in him.[17] As he worked on the painting, figures began to become more obscure: only the two guardians at either end of the table clearly remain, and the dog. (For Pollock, still working with semidigested theories of Freud and Jung, the dog was a father figure.) The table itself has become the lid of a sarcophagus or a cartouche, finally covered in untranslatable hieroglyphics. As with the box of furs in *Fur Traders Descending the Missouri*, we do not see inside.

William Rubin, Pollock's subtlest critic, says rightly that the table—whatever else it may be—is a painting within a painting.[18] But perhaps it isn't a painting at all, but some sort of occult and enigmatic description of what a painting would say if it could speak—and if we could understand the language in which it told its story. It lies in the frame of something not yet resolved in the artist. The secret was guarded well; to reproduce it, to hold it in the painting, became power itself, as if one could possess a riddle or magic charm that could be painted but not uttered. Pollock spoke of the enigmatic image of the painting called *The She-Wolf* of the same year. "Any attempt on my part to say something about it, to attempt the explanation of *the inexplicable* could only destroy it."[19] He was painting out of himself, his anguish and experience. But the power of the experience was in its very untranslatability. And finally, one might not even paint the image at all, but cover it with the runes of its secret. But by the winter of 1946, Pollock had turned this secret, and its untranslatable language, inside out.

In a beautiful passage in their biography of Pollock, Naifeh and Smith talk about the winter light that fell into that studio-shed.

> *On the coldest mornings, he would fix himself a mug of "hobo coffee," wrap himself in every piece of clothing he owned, and fight his way to the barn. Inside, condensation would coat the old boards with frost and little drifts of snow would build up in the open spaces between. But the light! According to Lee, on days when it snowed, "there was this incredible white light and Jackson would indulge in the experience of light then because of the luminescence of the snow."[20]*

In that freezing barn it was as if the winter light had become a many-dimensioned surface itself. Pollock was working in a new way, spinning filaments of paint from the ends of sticks and paint-stiffened brushes.

Pollock was not the first to paint this way.[21] But it was his complete immersion in the method that was significant. In getting rid of the brush as an extension of the artist's hand, he was taking a leap into the realms of a new kind of painting. Twisted, flipped from the end of a stick, the skeins of paint created a whole vocabulary of lines, threads, blotches, which Pollock insisted he could control. Air itself became a passage in the history of the paint. And space and air and time were let back into the hermetically sealed vacuum of the canvas. For the painting was now a kind of diptych: a painting, yes, a material product, a thing, and at the same time a ghostly adjunct of itself, a record of the events that transpired in the real time of its making, of chance and improvisation and gesture and response in the dance of the paint on the canvas.

The paintings were landscapes. Interior landscapes. Hans Hofmann had talked about a mythical perfect painting, as if, in some Platonic sphere beyond the mundane, there were some lost original that the artist was always trying to reproduce.[22] The failure to capture the perfect work was based on a kind of nostalgia for something that had never been there in the first place, a longing for some aesthetic homeland that could never be reclaimed. Looking, maybe, for company in his quest, Hofmann had once told Pollock that he should work from nature. Pollock's reply is famous: I *am* nature.[23]

The eye seeks the center of these poured paintings. No borders constrain it—it must go into the painting, be surrounded by it. We do not view the painting, but enter it. The world was no longer seen by the painter through a window or reflected through the optics of the camera obscura: the painting was a reconstructed now. An environment.[24] And Pollock could be *literally* in the painting, stepping inside the largest canvases to paint. He worked from all sides. There was no bottom or top here, or left or right, while he painted. He worked, he said, inside out, like nature. His concern was with the rhythms of nature, with the way the ocean moved.[25] But it is clear as well that he wanted to make some *object*, that his process was locked in the canvas, a retrospect.

Before Pollock had poured paint, he had sometimes used his fingers to push the medium. Now, he printed his paint-smeared hands themselves on the canvas, as if trying to embed his hands and the moment of making in the painting, a record, an evidence of his presence, like the cigarette butts and debris of everyday life that became locked in the dried paint. The canvases hung between the moment of their making and the hypothetical open-ended future; but the stuff of the now was swept up and into the rhythms of the work itself, like the garbage that flows in the current of the Gulf Stream in Hemingway's *Green Hills of Africa*.[26] Handprints might serve to measure the scale of Pollock's paintings, but in a sense the paintings were without scale, for they played havoc with the ideal depth from which they were to be viewed. They demanded distance to see their wholeness, yet they drew the viewer into the intimate details of the weaving, the individual lacings and loopings and poured lines. And some of Pollock's large canvases seemed to be depthless as well, creating a space that was neither that of Renaissance perspective, falling back from the frame in a long tunnel of light and shade, nor that of the shallow relief of high cubism. Skein on skein the painting was built up.

Although the flat sheen of aluminum paint, the clash of colors, might sometimes pull against it, the painting wanted to detach itself from the canvas. The paintings, like nature itself, existed both in and beyond the mind, and the mind looked at these webs of paint and imagined them extending infinitely beyond the edges of the canvas. They were working toward a kind of other-reality, paintings that wanted to have no front and no back.

With the young architect Peter Blake, Pollock imagined a gallery for his works—an ideal museum—whose glass walls opened out onto the scenes he loved, meadow and bay and curtain of sky; whose paintings themselves were on sheets of glass, through which that landscape could be seen, or abutted against mirrors that reflected them infinitely. Pollock mocked up some wire-and-plaster painted sculptures that were versions of his poured paintings in three-dimensional space. He propped up the painted sheet of glass he had made in the film Hans Namuth had done of him and gazed through it to the water beyond the studio.[27] Sitting there, trying to merge the drips and squiggles on the glass with the meadow and the water beyond, Pollock was looking for something that long before him had compelled his country's artists.

DANCER AND THE DANCE

How can we know the dancer from the dance?

William Butler Yeats, "Among School Children"

By lifting his brush from the canvas, Pollock had opened up new realms of possibility. In its chronicle of the loops of paint that had hovered in the air as Pollock worked, one could read the canvas not as an object, but as a record of that lost moment of creation, like a piece of improvised music captured in a printed score. He disliked naming his paintings. He disliked the finality of signing them. Sometimes he would invite friends to his studio to name his canvases before a show. (At a certain point he simply numbered them, but this was no solution either, and smelled of the ideological rigor of the critics.) His reluctance to name was a parallel to his reluctance to talk about his work, a kind of silence that, like the silence of his family dinner table, was a protection. And naming was also a way of foreclosing possibility. Of foreclosing wonder. The landscapes that he was now painting, the poured paintings of the late forties and early fifties, had their power in a decision not to name, not to map.[28] If Pollock can be seen as an explorer of a new aesthetic terrain, his method was to abandon the masculine posture of conquest and make himself, not the unmarked landscape, penetrable. That language of the swirls and signs that wanted to point back to no signifieds was like a child's attempts to mimic writing, not as a system of signs, but as a magic power in itself. The untranslatable runes that had the mystery of *Guardians of the Secret* locked inside them had become a free calligraphy. The veil that Pollock had once talked of putting over the image of an early poured painting was now the image itself. A membrane, a kind of placenta that wanted to communicate with Nature—the unconscious pulsing of the body, the unrecoverable depths of the mind, the movement of stars and tides—directly.[29]

But Pollock had come up to the limits of intelligibility. He had longed to move beyond the quotation marks of the frame, that comforting enclosure that announces that what is within can be translated into some language we know. His project had brought him to the edge of our willingness to believe that those dots and drips and loops of liquid enamel that danced from the ends of his stiffened brushes meant anything at all. He insisted that there was no chaos in his work, that he could control the paint; but the order underneath his painting's potentially infinite complexity lay beyond comprehension, like that of nature itself. Once he asked his wife, "Is this a painting?"

Out of his studio, named, signed, catalogued, the paintings entered the world of things. The allowance Peggy Guggenheim had given Pollock in his starving days had come from a family fortune coined out of the landscapes of Colorado and Chile and Mexico and Utah. With celebrity, Pollock's landscapes of the mind became part of the terrain of postwar Manhattan, with its galleries, its offices, its brokerages and banks—a terrain of money and power and vertical real estate. The dream was left like something you tried to remember after a troubled sleep.

In the gallery Pollock unrolls his canvases and mounts them for hanging. The paint bends around the stretcher bars, trying to suggest that borderless space he imagined. He pushed against those borders, but ultimately pulled back from the edges. How could he have gone beyond the great poured canvases? Kant thought nothing was more sublime than the inscription above the temple of Isis, the primitive Nature Mother: "I am all that is, that was, and that will be, and no mortal has lifted my veil."[30] Nor, finally, could Jackson

Pollock. When he found he had reached a limit imposed by the paint itself, he was forced to retreat. For the next step beyond those great poured landscapes might not be a painting at all.

BEYOND THE VEIL

> *Say what some poets will, Nature is not so much her own ever-sweet interpreter, as the mere supplier of that cunning alphabet, whereby selecting and combining as he pleases, each man reads his own peculiar lesson according to his own peculiar mind and mood.*

> Herman Melville, *Pierre, or The Ambiguities*

He could lose contact with his painting. This was different from the moments or days of meditation when he tried to understand what he had been doing and that were part of the rhythm of the work itself. Sometimes he could lose contact for an hour or two. Or for weeks. If the painting came out of him like some primal experience, like a body externalized into swirls and drips of paint, then he had to perform the complicated art of both remembering and forgetting who he was at once. For Kant, the road to the sublime had lain through culture: the sublime was a thing of the mind, it was the triumph of the mind over the infinite perspective of nature, over all that we experience as chaos, fear, the terror of annihilation. Beyond the sensible, Kant knew, lay the abyss of the infinite. "Thus any spectator who beholds massive mountains climbing skyward, deep gorges with raging streams in them, wastelands lying in deep shadow and inviting melancholy meditation, and so on is indeed seized by *amazement* bordering on terror, by horror and a sacred thrill."[31] But it was an aestheticized fear, a way of tickling the imagination, for the spectator knew he was safe.[32] Kant had seen a church steeple, pointing like a finger to the numinous world beyond the senses, but he had never seen a mountain. And perhaps, courageous heart that he was, he had never looked over the brink of the self.

For Pollock the drips and swirls of his filaments of paint were attempts to abolish the veils of culture through which his pictures were seen and to create meaning out of what without them was essentially meaningless: splashes of pigment on a length of canvas. His failure was implicit. For you never

154

really could forget. You never could communicate directly with the sublime. Walking in the woods and fields of Concord, Thoreau had seemed once to be nearing the origin of things. But that final lifting of the veil was forbidden. One must not look at nature directly; one must look with the side of the eye, through and beyond her: "To look at her is as fatal as to look at the head of Medusa."[33] Pollock's airborne, un-languaged calligraphy became only another order of hieroglyphics; the paint was, finally, only a symbol of a symbol. There was nothing beyond the veil but another veil, another version of the self, and all the pain and history that it contained.[34]

THE BLACK POURINGS

The web of black filaments, the ganglia of the great paintings, became thickened. There was only a dash of color now—sometimes not even that. The paintings were small, drawings on a page. Old imagery began to appear, the anguished forms of monstrous women. It was almost the negative of the great colored pourings, a dark presentment of whatever was locked in the chest of *Guardians of the Secret*. He made a picture he called *The Deep*. The skin of the painting opens to reveal the negative slash out of which the work comes. But he could not move the painting beyond the limits of its tautology. It couldn't be a painting and *horror vacui* at once. It was only an aesthetic statement—paint on a canvas. Courbet in his pigheaded sublimity had once painted something he called *The Origin of the World*, a dead-ahead view of the pubes of a model. But truncated by the perspective, it was a torso without limbs or head, and Jacques Lacan, who once owned it, wisely kept it covered: it was the sort of thing one couldn't look at without some logothete standing by to draw the curtain.[35] There was no curtain over *The Deep*, except, perhaps, the beauty of the color, the treatment of paint. Pollock's champion Clement Greenberg thought he had been close to something in the painting, but just missed it.[36]

Pollock returned to the easel, and the figure. Then once more to abstraction. There were some beautiful things left to paint still, but they were only paintings, and, in the last years, mired in alcoholism, he stopped painting completely.

The fame, the money, that his heroic paintings began to bring to Jackson Pollock in the last years of his life could not compensate for the failure of his project. He had come up against the limits of his painting and perhaps, in some sense, against the limits of all painting: the barrier he had tried to breach between nature and consciousness was consciousness itself. He had nowhere else to go. At the end there was only the long curve, that little whisper of panic when the wheel floats free.

After the death of Lee Krasner in 1984, the house and studio in the Springs became a museum. They pulled up the covering of the studio and revealed what had been the floor when Pollock had made the great poured paintings. The visitor looks at the chaotic splashes of paint on the dark floor. Gradually, there emerges amid the tangle of spatters and filaments a lighter rectangle where there is less paint, a kind of negative of some canvas that is no longer there. Is this absence the "perfect painting" Hofmann had imagined? The visitor keeps thinking of lines from Keats that he has managed at last to peel away from the cottony layers of greeting-card sentimentality through which he had always heard them. *A thing of beauty is a joy forever: Its loveliness increases; It will never pass into nothingness . . .* The brave lines lift and die. What lasts longest, after all, might be nothingness leaking out with a final hiss. The visitor talks to the curator about space in the paintings. "There is a depth," she says, "but not a perspective." The visitor says that he has seen *Lucifer* in San Francisco. "There it is," she says. And under his feet are the long threads of the pale green enamel of the painting, and the tangle of black, like ragged ends of a weaving that no longer exists. It is like seeing the ghostly trail of a particle left behind in a cloud chamber.

Dorothea Lange, *Drought Refugees—Equipage* (ca. 1935). Black-and-white photograph. © The Dorothea Lange Collection, Oakland Museum of California, City of Oakland. Gift of Paul S. Taylor.

You can get lonesome for a lot of things. People down around where I come from, they're lonesome for a job. Lonesome for some spending money. Lonesome for some drinking whiskey. Lonesome for good times, pretty gals, wine, women, and song like they see stuck up in their face by other people. Thinking maybe that you were down and out, disgusted, busted, and can't be trusted gives you a lonesome feeling. That somehow the world sorta turned against you or there's something about it you don't understand.

Woody Guthrie

Six

Lonesome America

SILENCE

When Alexis de Tocqueville entered the Michigan wilderness in 1831, it was, above all else, the silence that impressed itself on him. At night, and even at noon, the silence was so profound and the calm so complete that it created a sense of isolation and abandonment greater even than that he had felt in the mid-Atlantic.

> *Here not only man is missing, but even the voices of animals are not heard. The smallest of them have left these regions to go nearer human habitation, the larger to go farther away; those who remain keep hidden under shelter from the rays of the sun. Thus everything is still, everything in the woods is silent under the foliage; one would say that the Creator has for a moment turned his face away and that the forces of nature are paralysed.*[1]

Lost in this silence, the settler had learned to take delight in solitude. The traveler was greeted in the rough cabin of the settler with a hand held out according to custom, but the settler's face expressed neither benevolence nor joy. He spoke only in order to question, satisfying an intellectual, not an emotional or social, need, and as soon as he drew out the information he wanted he once more fell silent. For Tocqueville it was profoundly disturbing.

> *This unknown man is the representative of a race to which belongs the future of the new world: a restless, reasoning, adventurous race which does coldly what only the ardour of passion can explain; race cold and passionate, which traffics in everything, not excepting morality and religion; nation of conquerors who submit themselves to the savage life without ever allowing themselves to be seduced by it, who in civilization and enlightenment love only what is useful to well-being, and who shut themselves in the American solitudes with an axe and some newspapers. . . . It's this nomad people which the rivers and lakes do not stop, before which the forests fall and the prairies are covered with shade, and which, after having reached the Pacific ocean, will reverse its steps to trouble and destroy the societies which it will have formed behind it.[2]*

Always there was the feeling of the end of the wilderness, that one was seeing it for the last time. "It's this idea of destruction," Tocqueville wrote, "this conception of near and inevitable change which gives in our opinion so original a character and so touching a beauty to the solitudes of America. . . . One feels proud to be a man, and at the same time one experiences I know not what bitter regret at the power God has given us over nature. The soul is agitated by these ideas, these contrary sentiments. But all the impressions it receives are great and leave a deep mark."[3] Cut off from both ancestors and his rootless posterity, Tocqueville's democratic man is alone in a silence that becomes a kind of outward representation of his inner solitude.

Steamboating down the Ohio between Pittsburgh and Cincinnati in 1842, Charles Dickens did not attempt to analyze the settler's inner world, but like the Frenchman, saw only solitude, silence, despair.

> *For miles, and miles, and miles, these solitudes are unbroken by any sign of human life or trace of human footstep; nor is anything seen to move about them but the blue jay, whose colour is so bright, and yet so delicate, that it looks like a flying flower. At lengthened*

intervals a log cabin, with its little space of cleared land about it, nestles under a rising ground, and sends its thread of blue smoke curling up into the sky. It stands in the corner of the poor field of wheat, which is full of great unsightly stumps, like earthy butchers'-blocks. Sometimes the ground is only just now cleared: the felled trees lying yet upon the soil: and the log-house only this morning begun. As we pass this clearing, the settler leans upon his axe or hammer, and looks wistfully at the people from the world. The children creep out of the temporary hut, which is like a gipsy tent upon the ground, and clap their hands and shout. The dog only glances round at us, and then looks up into his master's face again, as if he were rendered uneasy by any suspension of the common business, and had nothing more to do with pleasurers.[4]

The steamboat rattles on. The cabin is lost in the distance. There are only the overgrown solitudes of the banks and a sense not of the green pulsation of life, but of decay.

That profound solitude that Tocqueville and Dickens experienced is interrupted by war and the sudden irruption of religious enthusiasms, scorching through the land like wildfire and leaving burnt stumps and ashes of souls behind.

In the late 1820s, the British visitor Fanny Trollope found herself at one of those camp meetings in the wilds of Indiana.

We reached the ground about an hour before midnight, and the approach to it was highly picturesque. The spot chosen was the verge of an unbroken forest, where a space of about twenty acres appeared to have been partially cleared for the purpose. Tents of different sizes were pitched very near together in a circle round the cleared space; behind them were ranged an exterior circle of carriages of every description, and at the back of each were fastened the horses which had drawn them thither. Through this triple circle of defence we distinguished numerous fires burning brightly within it; and still more numerous lights flickering from the trees that were left in the enclosure. The moon was in meridian splendour above our heads. . . .

At midnight a horn sounded through the camp, which, we

were told, was to call the people from private to public worship;
and we presently saw them flocking from all sides to the front of
the preachers' stand. . . .

One of the preachers began in a low nasal tone, and, like all
other Methodist preachers, assured us of the enormous depravity
of man as he comes from the hands of his Maker, and of his per-
fect sanctification after he had wrestled sufficiently with the Lord
to get hold of him, et cætera. The admiration of the crowd was
evinced by almost constant cries of "Amen! Amen!" "Jesus! Jesus!"
"Glory! Glory!" and the like. But this comparative tranquility did
not last long; the preacher told them that "this night was the time
fixed upon for anxious sinners to wrestle with the Lord;" and that
he and his brethren "were at hand to help them," and that such as
needed their help were to come forward into "the pen."[5]

The hymn singing gave way in those forest groves of America, along the
banks of the rivers, in the tents on the outskirts of the unpainted towns,
and the sinners were dragged to the mourners' bench shouting and raving.
Barking like dogs. Speaking in tongues. The Methodist circuit preacher Peter
Cartwright saw more than five hundred persons taken with what he called
the jerks at one time.

Most usually persons taken with the jerks, to obtain relief, as
they said, would rise up and dance. Some would run, but could
not get away. Some would resist: on such the jerks were general-
ly very severe.[6]

The limbs of the young girls tangled and their hair was wild, in a promiscu-
ous orgy of sin and repentance.

"Woe! Woe to the backsliders! hear it, hear it Jesus! when I was
fifteen my mother died, and I backslided, oh Jesus, I backslid-
ed! take me home to my mother, Jesus! take me home to her, for I
am weary! Oh John Mitchel! John Mitchel! . . . Shall I sit on the
sunny bank of salvation with my mother? my own dear mother?
oh Jesus, take me home, take me home!"[7]

Beyond the glare of the fires, there was the gang of frontier toughs, drinking, profane, mocking, crowing like cocks, sometimes bursting through the revival to break it up. That violent spirit of mockery and liquor-fueled profanation was an expression of the frontier soul as well. But sooner or later, more than one of the toughs would find himself being pulled to the mourners' bench, shouting and sobbing and praying to be saved from the Fire.

There would be music in those isolated cabins and in the clearings and later in the villages and towns that would spring up along the roads and at the landings of the rivers. Reels and jigs and always the hymns that came from the log churches and outdoor pulpits. But there would be a note of haunting sorrow under even some of the most joyous tunes.[8] On the moving edge of the white world, deep connections of class and family and home were constantly being overturned, replaced, forgotten. The old religious rituals of Europe had become stripped down to two jagged ecstasies alternating between themselves, the ecstasy of sin and the ecstasy of salvation: the savage to be tamed was not out there, in the forest, but in oneself. But even in the midst of the multitude of sinners and ecstasists, the American spirit was alone, and "in perfect solitude," in Harold Bloom's conception, "learns again its absolute isolation as a spark of God floating in a sea of space."[9]

DYING COWBOY

A cowboy lay dying. He was dying on the streets of Laredo, he was dying on the lone prairie where the coyotes howl and the wind blows free. But the cowboy was once a sailor. He was a sailor in a weeper called "Oh Bury Me Not on the Deep Blue Sea." Or the cowboy was an unfortunate rake in some Irish city, dying of syphilis. Or a Michigan lumberjack. Or he was a buffalo hunter, leaving old Crego's bones to bleach on the Texas plains.[10] In 1952 the cowboy was a hillbilly singer from Alabama named Hank Williams. Ralph Gleason, who was the *San Francisco Chronicle* jazz and pop editor at the time, went over to Oakland that June to interview Hank Williams in the Leamington Hotel. Williams came out of the bathroom, lean, slightly stooped, long-jawed. He was thin and pale, with deep-set eyes, and he might have been hung over. He caught up a handful of pills from the bureau and swallowed them one at a time. After he was finished, he threw the rest of the pills in his suitcase and went down to the hotel coffee shop with Gleason and gave an interview. He told the old stories. How his earliest memory was sitting next to his mother

163

on the organ stool in Mt. Olive when she played. How he'd learned the guitar from a black musician who played with a Montgomery street band. "I was shinin' shoes and sellin' newspapers and followin' this Nigrah around to get him to teach me to play the git-tar. I'd give him 15¢ or whatever I could get a hold of for a lesson. When I was about eight years old, I got my first git-tar. A second hand $3.50 git-tar my mother bought me."

He said that what he was writing was folk music. "Folk music is sincere. There ain't nuthin' phony about it. When a folk singer sings a sad song, he's sad. He means it. The tunes are simple and easy to remember and the singers, they're sincere about them." Johnny Ray was sincere too. And Roy Acuff. And forgotten singers like Bill Darnell. Hank Williams was twenty-nine years old, doing two hundred one-nighters a year and grossing what he said was over $400,000.

That night Gleason drove down San Pablo Avenue through El Cerrito and Richmond to a one-story white building set in a muddy parking lot called San Pablo Hall to hear Hank Williams sing.

Wally Elliott, the local DJ who had set up Williams, had changed from the business suit that made him look like a Ford salesman into a Stetson and handmade boots. The band, Gleason remembered, was terrible. It was called the Driftin' Cowboys, but Gleason suspected the only Driftin' Cowboy was Hank Williams himself. Then Williams came on and started to sing. He had a guitar and a Western hat and looked shorter somehow than he had in the coffee shop. Sometimes he seemed to squeeze himself to get the notes out.

> And he had that thing. He made them scream when he sang and that audience was shipped right up from Enid or Wichita Falls intact. . . . There were lots of those blondes you see at C&W affairs, the kind of hair that mother never had and nature never grew and the tight skirts that won't quit and the guys looking barbershop neat but still with a touch of dust on them. "Shit-kicker dances" the outside world called them then but some great people came through to play for them and this time it was Hank Williams and the Driftin' Cowboys.

Gleason didn't remember Williams singing any of the religious songs, the songs he put out under the name of Luke the Drifter, or "I Saw the Light," but he remembered hearing all the others, the big hits. "Jambalaya" and

"Lovesick Blues" and "Move It On Over" and "Hey Good Lookin'" and the Heart Songs—"Cold Cold Heart" and "Your Cheatin' Heart."

At intermission Gleason tried to talk to Williams, but Williams was a little out of it and didn't remember their conversation earlier that day. The people at the dance were drinking whiskey, and things were starting to get a little rough. Gleason looked around awhile and left. Six months later Hank Williams was dead.[11]

COWBOYS, HILLBILLIES, AND HOBOES

Of course, real cowboys had come from somewhere, too. It had all happened so fast—the roundups and the bronc riding and the horseplay, a flash of bright neckerchiefs and spurs—then it was gone. Teddy Blue Abbott and his friends rode off to the 1884 fall roundup out of Miles City, Montana, with a pair of whore's bloomers for a banner, singing, "Cowboy Annie was her name / And the N Bar outfit was her game / And when the beef is four years old / We'll fill her pillow slips with gold."[12] But up on the Musselshell, Harry Rutter got sore one day and tore down the bloomers Teddy Blue had hung on the wall of their cabin and threw them in the stove. He said it wasn't decent, and Teddy had to agree. The Wild West had always been, after all, the Genteel West too.

The cowboys were poor boys. Some of the Texas punchers were so poor and their ordinary chuck was so bad that canned tomatoes and peaches and flapjacks and hot bread were the food of paradise. "Jesus Christ," one of them said to cowboys on the Montana range. "Do you fellows have white bread three times a day?" Another Texas boy turned down the sugar tin, saying he didn't take salt in his coffee: the only sweetening he'd ever seen was sorghum syrup.[13]

The songs these poor boys composed, copied, rewrote, remembered from minstrel shows[14] and Methodist hymnbooks, remade from the parlor poetry columns of the newspapers, were scraps of something to hang onto. A whoop of high spirits and brag, a shred of memory from the genteel world. There were a few songs that might have grown out of their life itself, haunting trail songs and bunkhouse doggerel like the endless, often obscene couplets of "The Old Chisholm Trail," but the sentiments and the stories in the songs most often came from the East, and before that from the broadsides and the folksongs and rural lore of the old country.[15] The great days of the open range were over almost as soon as they began. The railroads at the end of the cattle trails had made the cowboys possible and the owners of the Chicago packing plants rich, but as far as those horseback drovers went, for all their dash and bravado they were balanced on the edge of bare existence.

In March of 1889, a New Mexico cowboy named Jack Thorp, with an East Coast prep school education and blue blood connections (Teddy Roosevelt had been a member of his Polo Club), was trailing after a couple of stray horses from the Bar W Ranch in Carrizozo, New Mexico, when darkness caught him on the open prairie. Looking for a place to spend the night, he saw a campfire and heard the sound of a banjo plinking and someone singing. He decided to go over and have some company. The camp turned out to be that of Nigger Add, the range boss for the LFD. Add was famous in that part of the world and his crews were usually black cowboys from south Texas.[16] Thorp hobbled his horses, got a plate and cup from the chuckwagon, and helped himself to the coffee and the stew. After he'd eaten, he asked who'd been singing when he'd ridden up, and heads nodded to a young black cowboy named 'Lasses. Thorp asked the cowboy if he'd sing the song again, and the boy sang the two verses he knew. Then Thorp sang a song, and somebody knew a couple of verses of "Sam Bass," and then the boys from Add's crew started singing cotton-picking songs. Before he spread his tarp and rolled himself up in his soogan Thorp copied into his notebook the two verses of "Dodgin' Joe" that 'Lasses had sung.[17]

That night at Nigger Add's camp was the beginning of a year-long, fifteen-hundred-mile journey through New Mexico and Texas and back again, Thorp breaking horses if he needed money and hunting for songs. It was a vocation Thorp continued for much of his life and had led, in 1908, to a little red paper–covered book that was the first published collection of cowboy songs.

Two years after Thorp's little book came out, in the summer of 1910, ex-Dakota rancher, ex-president, ex–Rough Rider Theodore Roosevelt sat down in a hotel room in Cheyenne, Wyoming, and wrote a paragraph or two for a Texas professor's own book of cowboy songs. The name of the young professor was John Lomax. Unlike Thorp, who'd gone west when his father lost his money, Lomax had grown up on a Texas farm, but his project was backed by the best the East had to offer, a Harvard fellowship and the blessings of George Lyman Kittredge.

Getting Roosevelt to write his thoughts on cowboy oral literature was no doubt a coup for Lomax, but it moved his book from the realm of scholarship to that of ideological romance. For Roosevelt, the world of the cowboy songs was essentially the world that had produced the English ballad, and Jesse James was merely a newer version of Robin Hood. The cowboys' crude, homespun ballads were unfortunately being pushed out of circulation on the range by what Roosevelt's friend Owen Wister called the "ill-smelling saloon cleverness" of the music hall. Roosevelt and his fellow patricians Wister and Frederic Remington had given to the world a cowboy who was a contemporary freelance knight, an Anglo-Saxon aristocrat in the rough, and who, with his manhood and independence, would become the symbolic front for imperialist adventure and a ruthless Social Darwinism. (Missing, for the most part, from their books and pictures were the Mexicans who'd invented the cowboy's trade and given names to his tools, the Indian and mixed-blood buckaroos, and the hundreds of black cowboys like Nigger Add.) Though he might have had second thoughts, Lomax himself was caught up by the Arthurian imagery, and in the preface to his 1910 collection he drew the cowboy as a last, romantic figure of conquest, always "on the skirmish line of civilization."

Jack Thorp had dedicated his little volume "as a reminder of the trail days and roundups of the past."[18] And Lomax had seen his cowboy Galahad with "his face turned steadily down the long, long road, 'the road that the sun goes down.'"[19] The old–time cowboy, Wister said (and his friend Theodore Roosevelt agreed), was gone. The wind had blown away the ashes of his campfires, and the empty sardine tin, the sign of his passage, lay rusting on the western earth.[20]

The original cowboy had served his purpose, and now, but for the remnants loitering in saloons and railroad depots, coughing up blood in TB sanitariums, stoved-up, and always broke, was done for. But almost from the first, posing for a photographer in Miles City in his chaps and spurs or looking at his reflection in a whorehouse mirror, the cowboy was posing for an image of himself.[21] The image had been created by dime novels and Wild West shows and the dreams of little boys. If the mirrors in which he saw himself had been tunnels to the future, the cowboy might have seen, looking back at him from the file of be-Stetsoned movie stars and radio crooners, the faces of poor white southern boys who were creating an indigenous music of loneliness and irremediable loss. It was precisely because the wilderness was gone that we needed the cowboy.

In 1916 an English choral director and folklorist named Cecil Sharp found himself song hunting in the Appalachians. The voice he found or thought he found in the hills of North Carolina and Virginia and West Virginia and Kentucky was not the rough croak of Thorp or Lomax's cowboys (he characterized Lomax's book as a volume that contained "nothing but the dregs of literature and the garbage of musical phrase") but the voice of an eighteenth-century English peasant singing songs that went back to the Elizabethans. And it came as much of a surprise to Sharp as to anyone that it still existed in America. He'd given an interview to a Chicago paper in 1915 whose writer summed up his ideas.

> *By Mr Sharp's definition a new folk music is impossible without a complete reversion to a feudal state. This is true, because folk music is the product of an unselfconscious peasantry; a peasantry which refuses to transmit the eccentricities of any individual; which simply omits and forgets what does not belong to the spirit of the people. . . . But this is a doleful theory to propound to Americans who feel the urge of nationality. How can we have any folk music? We are in the clutches of compulsory education. The farest backwoods farmer has a phonograph with records of Rubinstein's melody of F and Mischa Elman's richly sentimental reading of Dvorak's humoresque. . . . Thus Mr Sharp leaves us to a barren fate, not possessing a folk music and not able to get one.*[22]

Kittredge had thought in 1882 that almost nothing remained to be recovered of the English and Scottish ballads that Francis Child had compiled from ancient books and manuscripts in oral tradition in this country or Europe.[23] But here, a little more than a day by train from Boston, Sharp and his secretary, Maud Karpeles, found themselves surrounded by Carolina voices singing dozens of Child's songs, and they heard "Barbara Allen" and "The False Knight upon the Road" and "Earl Brand" and "Lamkin" and "Lord Randal" and "Young Hunting." Even the gapped modal scales were, Sharp thought, the old music that had ceased to be sung in England.

In all, he and Maud Karpeles made three collecting trips to Appalachia, in the spring, summer, and fall months of 1916–18.[24] By foot and by springless jolt-wagon and by rattling mail hack and (it seemed incredible to them) by Ford car, shuttling from town to town on creeping local trains that detoured around washed-out bridges and climbed up into the most beautiful scenery they had ever seen, laurel and dogwood and magnolia, small purple iris and violets and ferns and wildflowers they couldn't begin to name, they went, their two suitcases and Miss Karpeles's typewriter slung across the back of a mule. They were terrified of the footbridges that crossed the torrents and that were often only a single log. The settlements they visited, along the sides of mountain creeks and rivers and where the fields were so steep a man could stand erect to hoe his corn patch, had names like Possum Trot, Owl's Nest, Dish Rag, Kingdom Come, Hell for Sartin, Devil's Fork—which the missionaries renamed Sweet Water—Shooting Creek, and that fabled paradise called the Meadows of Dan. Often Sharp was sick: hayfever, asthma, unknown fevers. Maud Karpeles would sometimes make a bed next to his cot on the floor to tend to him. The food, what there was of it, was, for the palates of these unfortunate vegetarians, atrocious, even the stewed apples swimming in hog fat. Invited to a meal at a settlement house, Sharp asked, plaintively, if one was permitted to bring one's own tea. The heat was intense, and always there were flies and stinging insects.

Barefoot, impoverished by any standards but their own, the mountaineers lived as Sharp saw it, in islands surrounded by a rising ocean of industrialism and ugliness.

Sharp didn't inquire after the black songs, the blues, and work songs. Nor after the mining songs, some of which had come from the old country itself, and which thrust the industrial world, and with it history, into Fairy Land. For history may have led those runaway indentured servants plucked from the slums of London and Glasgow, landless English farmers, starved out Highlanders and Ulster men, to the mountains, but history would not forget them. They had conquered the forest and the Indians and had come out of the hills to join Washington's army with scalp-knives and tomahawks in their belts. They had fought beside Jackson at New Orleans and with Grant and Lee and Stonewall Jackson in the killing fields of the Civil War. And here was history again bearing down on them. The mountaineers volunteered for the army and were sent to camps in New Jersey and then to France, the bands played at the railroad depots, and prices spiked in the country towns and crossroads. Sharp himself couldn't keep the war at bay: in early September 1916 he received word that three of his English Morris dancers had been killed in the Battle of the Somme. Then in October he learned that his son Charlie had been seriously wounded. Even among the mountain folk who remained where it seemed they had always been, time refused to stand still. At the Meadows of Dan, which Sharp and Maud Karpeles reached by a road so perilous they often had to get out of the Ford and walk, they discovered a "thoroughly respectable, church-going, school-attending population" making money hand over fist because of the rise of food prices, living in frame houses instead of log cabins, and sporting their own motorcars. When they finally got to Shooting Creek, Sharp found that the missionaries had got there first and moonshining had left the folk rolling in money. The women showed up to the preaching dressed in low-necked dresses and with powdered faces. Everywhere were Holy Rollers who were killing the singing of love songs, and missionaries and do-gooders trying to get the people to put on shoes and wash.[25] And everywhere, following them like a stray dog, was a parlor tearjerker called "The Rosewood Casket."[26] After three seasons of intense collecting Sharp was sorry to leave the mountains but finally was ready to go. What he wanted more then anything else was quiet, no children, no Victrolas, no strumming of ragtime, no Rosewood Caskets.[27]

Sitting in train depots in cheap suits and straw boaters, their mail-order banjos and fiddles in their laps, traveling from town to town in flivvers or by "side-door Pullman," were exactly the sort of musicians Sharp had so studiously avoided. They were not English yeomen, plinking away in pristine, historyless purity: they were, like the singers Sharp had listened to and whose songs he and Maud Karpeles had meticulously transcribed, Hillbillies. The Hillbillies had taken the dubious place of the half-breeds before them in the national consciousness. They were the mongrelized, degraded folk that respectable America somehow needed to demarcate the borders of its civilization. They were, to the outside world, a subspecies of humanity.[28] But even hillbillies might have fifty cents or a dollar in their pockets and it was only a few years after the war that representatives from Okeh and the Victor Talking Machine Company would be blanketing the South with recording equipment. In hotel rooms and hired halls the hillbilly singers listened to their thin and crackling voices singing back to them from the brittle phono-graph disks, and it must have been an endorsement of themselves and that home they had imagined they had come from; that place, like Cecil Sharp's fairy land, that had never quite existed except in the longing for it.

The country singers and fiddlers let the name hillbilly stick to them, degrad-ing, insulting even, and turned their songs and their stage presences into a sort of humorous put-on of the New York record labels that were selling their music to other hillbillies. Or they bore the name with self-mockery or defiance, like the hayseed overalls and brogans that soon would largely give way to the flashy western shirts and the hand-tooled boots adopted from the singing cowboys.[29] They were singing Old-Time Tunes, but whose old time? The echoes and revenants of the songs from across the water were mixed up in the heads of the hillbilly musicians with brush arbor hymns, revival ser-mons smelling of the pit, comic turns from tent shows and medicine shows, blackface minstrel routines, the reconstructed yodels of Swiss vaudevillians, Victorian tearjerkers, songs of coal mines and weave rooms, Tin Pan Alley hits, the twang of Hawaiian guitar players, and their own versions of the blues and shouts of the black men and women they lived among and mostly despised. Wedged between ads for such elixirs as Crazy Water Crystals and Hamlin's Wizard Oil,[30] goat gland, transplants, and Bible tracts on the radi-os that now played in any home that had a wire into it, and on battery sets in those that didn't, A. P. Carter was the American Theocritus, summoning up from his Clinch Mountain Home an American Arcadia, with bubbling fountains and birds whose speech he could miraculously understand, but like the Arcadia invented in the libraries of Alexandria, it was a world with-out sleet and shit and backbreaking toil, a world that Hesiod, that farmer-singer of an earlier day, would hardly have recognized. There were fields and hollows still, the smell of woodsmoke and the tastes of the old foods, corn and molasses and liquor from the still, and there were brush arbor revivals, river baptisms, and the orgies and raptures of damnation and salvation. But there were cities at the terminals of the railroads, there were automobiles and telephone lines, and the tipples of coal mines and brick mills looming above the shacks where the workers lived and died.

> *To go into the town on Saturday afternoon and night, to stroll with*
> *the throng, to gape at the well-dressed and the big automobiles, to*

bathe in the holiday cacophony; in the case of the women, to crowd happily along counters and finger the goods they could not buy; in the case of the males, maybe only to stand with the courthouse habitués and talk and spit tobacco juice, or in the press about a radio loud-speaker blaring a baseball or football game from the front of a store and let off steam with the old hunting yell; maybe to have a drink, maybe to get drunk, to laugh with passing girls, to pick them up if you had a car, or to go swaggering or hesitating into the hotels with their corridors saturated with the smell of bichloride of mercury, or the secret, steamy bawdy houses; maybe to have a fight, maybe with knives or guns, maybe against the cops; maybe to end whooping and singing, maybe bloody and goddamning, in the jailhouse—it was more and more in the dream and reality of such excursions that the old romantic-hedonistic impulses found egress, and that men and women were gratefully emptied of their irritations and repressions, and left to return to their daily tasks stolid, unlonely, and tame again.[31]

It's 1928 and from phonographs in the row houses of the mill towns, in shacks on logged-off hillsides, in working-class districts in Cincinnati and Washington DC, you can hear Jimmie Rodgers's disembodied voice singing about hoboes waiting for a train, dying old pals, and peach-picking time in Georgia; yodeling those blue yodels and playing the bluesy tunes he learned from black men on the rail lines he'd ridden as a brakeman.[32] That perpetual rootlessness had become, in Jimmie Rodgers, an end in itself, a jaunty hobo existentialism. A celebration of trains and women and rough and rowdy ways.

Now Jimmie's in the jailhouse in his straw boater and sharp suit, singing about a St. Louis prostitute who'd killed her ragtime-piano-playing pimp. The colors of the protagonists have been bleached white but when Frankie takes her forty-four out of her kimono and shoots Johnnie through the door of that cheap hotel, it's a real gun, even if it does go rooty-toot-toot.[33] And now Jimmie's hearing that train whistle, taking him away from the warm kitchen and the Danville girl, away from the prospect of home, away from churches and parlors and front porches, away from everything into a state of perpetual hoboing.

The South of Jimmie Rodgers had been so violated by the upheavals of history and racism and a rapacious new industrial system that there was only a hole where that limitless prospect that Emerson had envisioned for the Young American had been, and in the vacuum left by its absence there grew in the songs of Rodgers and hillbillies like him a music that had traded the past for nostalgia and looked toward a future that could promise nothing but endless wandering. The train whistle that haunted the farthest American valleys would become a symbol of the rootlessness embedded in our culture. There was always another train to hop, another town to light in. Jimmie the Kid cocks his skimmer over one eye. The TB is killing him. Spit 'er up, Jimmie, and sing some more.[34] Hey Hey Hey. It won't be long now.

LONESOME WHISTLE

The midnight train is whining low
I'm so lonesome I could cry.

Hank Williams

In 1934 an eleven-year-old boy named Hiram Williams was sitting under the house in Georgiana, Alabama, on an old car seat, picking out chords on a pawnshop guitar. Skinny kid, steel-rimmed glasses, suffering from spina bifida occulta and carrying around in him the hookworm endemic to the rural South. He was named for Hiram of Tyre, from the First Book of Kings. Hiram, the widow's son, the artist who adorned the pillars of Solomon's Temple with lilies and pomegranates of brass. Lon Williams, the boy's father, had been shipped off to France in the First World War and before he'd seen any action had been badly beaten by another soldier in a fight over a woman.[35] He was in and out of the VA hospital, and finally he just didn't come home. Hiram was hard to get close to. Trying to fathom him, people who had known him then turned to a formula: they remembered him as a boy who seemed to always have something on his mind.[36] His first memories were of a boxcar house in the timber camp where his father had driven a log train. He heard the sounds of gospel music from a black church a mile away and told a friend that some day he was going to write songs like that.

By 1937, Lillie Williams had moved the family to Montgomery and was running a boardinghouse. Hank Williams won the Empire Theater's amateur night with a song he wrote called the "WPA Blues."

I got a home in Montgomery
A place I like to stay,
But I have to work for the WPA,
And I'm dissatisfied—I'm dissatisfied.[37]

The dissatisfaction articulated in the "WPA Blues" never got much further than that. In the images that would follow, it would be diffused under a haze of longing and honky-tonking, the consolations of the other world, and the old southern fatalism.

There's a ferocious, determined mother scraping for nickels and dimes, running boardinghouses, running her son. Sometimes they'd fight, fight like men would fight. Hank's been drinking since he was eleven. And always there's the pain in his back that needs constant muffling. He'd gone out to work in the shipyards of Mobile and as far as Portland, Oregon, during the war. He is eighteen or nineteen and he doesn't want to live.[38] Coming home from playing a dance at Fort Deposit with the band, Hank is sleeping off a drunk in the backseat of the car. Lillie is driving. There's a beacon light at Dannelly Field Airport and she knows it always takes a while to get her son awake when he's been drinking: "Hank, wake up, we're nearly home. I just saw the light."

Just like a blind man, I wandered alone
Worries and fears I claimed for my own
Then like the blind man that God gave back his sight
Praise the Lord, I saw the light.

I saw the light, I saw the light
No more darkness, no more night . . . [39]

The soul of an American like Hank Williams is like a logged-out forest, a place where only the stumps and refuse of the past still remain, a territory made out of the failed war of rebellion, the failed earth, poverty, flight. It is tinder dry, waiting for conflagration. Waiting for that Pentecostal fire that descends and consumes the dry soul, that speaks in every language, that knows every wound and sin. And if the fire doesn't descend, there's only a sense of waiting, a sense of something missing at last, and a return to a world that is insufficient, that can offer neither nourishment nor fire. The skinny boy with the guitar is heir to all that, trying to catch on, trying to make something out of who he is and where he comes from.

It's 1948. Williams is playing in juke joints and schoolhouses and at dance marathons and in bars so rough they have chicken wire in front of the bandstand to keep the bottles from hitting the band.[40] He's constructed his stage presence out of three fictions, the Hillbilly, the Singing Cowboy, and the Rambling Man, and souped up his music with the rhythms of the pop songs and Texas swing bands he's hearing on the jukeboxes. He gets on the local radio, and pretty soon he's cutting his first side for MGM, a novelty tune about being in the doghouse called "Move It On Over."

The jitterbug bounce of that tune would increasingly give way to the mournful reprises of the Heart Songs and the songs of restless wandering and trains going somewhere—always with their promise of finding that unnamable thing he was looking for. And under the sadness and the restlessness was a kind of silence, a suppressed half of the experience of being Hank Williams.

Caught in the Depression-era photographs of the Farm Security Administration, the southern towns of Hank Williams's youth have the kind of silent pathos about them that is, perhaps, under all photographs, but that is palpable here, as present as the heat that you know is rising from the highway or that rebounds from the brick fronts of the stores of Main Street. Pulled up in front of the low line of shops are dusty automobiles and wagons with their mules bowing under the heat. It is a ferocious silence, the silence of a place caught in some kind of emotional correlative of stalled time. Coming down into the Black Belt in the Jim Crow car thirty years earlier, W. E. B. Du Bois had looked at the great cotton country, its soil black and fertile or sometimes thin and gray, at the fruit trees, the dilapidated buildings, the small towns, and had seen beyond the landscape and into the human wreckage war and slavery and reconstruction had left behind. He called it "that strange land of shadows." The shadows for Du Bois were both black and white, two peoples who had become so inextricably bound in their fates and their psychologies through the cruelties that had attempted to separate them that they had become phantoms of each other.[41]

The great fact of this land, Du Bois learned, was debt. The insuperable, constant burden of an economic cycle that left the great mass of sharecroppers, white and black, always indebted for seed and fertilizer and the meal and poor clothes—the "furnish"—that had been advanced against their share of the crop; but the debt went beyond that. For held out to the impoverished white sharecroppers—and to white loggers and miners and factory hands—beyond any humiliation and degradation there was a compensatory wage, the "public and psychological wage" of white privilege. It was a wage that could only be maintained by enforcing the borders of that white privilege—if necessary through violence: when the black street musician Rufus Payne told the skinny, fatherless boy who followed him around the streets of Greenville and whom he called "Little White boss" that the white folks wouldn't like to see him taking so much care of him, he was worried not so much about the sensibilities of white Alabama as about his survival: propped up in the windows of the drugstores and barbershops of the South there were still found photographs of black bodies hanging from trees and telephone poles, sometimes burned and horribly mutilated. There had been three lynchings of black men between the turn of the century and 1920 in Butler County.[42]

Yet for the whites the consciousness of racial superiority was based on negation. It was a shameful and unearned potency, and under it lay a sense of envy and psychic debt. Envy for a sexuality seen as more generous, a religion less punishing, a body closer to nature, a life less freighted with the burden of white privilege.[43] In his great book *The Wages of Whiteness*, David Roediger enumerated the contents of the inner world of the nineteenth-century white worker in relation to this imagined black community and saw a "complex mixture of hate, sadness and longing."[44] If Hank Williams shared that inner world with white southern boys of his generation, or, if he did, to what extent, we cannot finally know, but there is something analogous in his music, and Roediger might well have been describing its emotional terrain and that sense of something unvoiced and incomplete that often made it seem Williams's songs had come out of spiritual nowhere, as if they were floating in some rootless inner space without a pin to stick them on the map of the soul.

In 1949 Hank Williams had his first hit. The song was called "Lovesick Blues." Williams had learned it from a phonograph record cut by a white singer and comedian named Emmett Miller who did blackface routines on the vaudeville circuit. The song was a blue yodel with music by a white vaudevillian and sometime test pilot and lyrics by a Tin Pan Alley journeyman whose parents were immigrant Jews from the Ukraine.

There is something in the twisting trail of that song that is worth thinking about. The black men and women of the South, whose daily presence was so much a part of its life, were almost unspoken in the words of Hank Williams's songs, or indeed in those of any of the white country boys who had grown up around him. But that darker half of the South existed in the music itself, infusing the old English or Scottish or Irish tunes with its African language of syncopation and blue notes, stop-time rhythms and melismas. Singing "Lovesick Blues," Hank Williams was recapitulating a trail of music that led from the slave block to the nineteenth-century minstrel show to vaudeville, where it picked up the yodel from itinerant Swiss, to Tin Pan Alley and back once more to the South. But for Hank Williams, the boy who had tagged along after Tee-Tot Payne and listened to the singing coming from a black church, that darker world represented some longing that was deeper and more complex than the pedigree of a musical style. He had a feeling called the blues, all right, and no matter how the song had gotten to him, he made it his own, he knew how to sing it. *You pull that last sigh out . . . Sigh-eye.*

In those days Williams was learning to make an emotional connection with his audience, to strike that plangent note that answered something mute and alone inside them. It was an inner country of humiliation and longing and injured pride he shared with the poor white boys and girls of his generation, an emotional space that had only to be suggested to be found beyond the maudlin and the banal and the sentimental in his songs. When Hank was singing "Lovesick Blues," though the song might have come out of Tin Pan Alley, he was creating a felt connection with his people that went further than the simple words to the song and its tune. Listening to that music, they became a kind of emotional nation, a people.

You had to know the singers were still your own. You had to know they were the sons and daughters of coal miners and sharecroppers and mill workers and they would never change. Kitty Wells had dropped out of school in the Depression to iron shirts in a factory for nine dollars a week. Roy Acuff had traveled with a small-time medicine show. Rose Maddox had gone to California with her family in a boxcar. Ernest Tubb had dug ditches for the WPA. The people who were buying his records felt that Hank Williams was like that, that he was one of them. Like the minstrel's burnt cork, the three-hundred-dollar cowboy suit wasn't intended to hide the poor white boy inside it, or to separate him from his audience. It was part of an act they all conspired in, a fantasy of money and glamour that was always recognized as just that—a fantasy. "To sing like a hillbilly, you had to have lived like a hillbilly," Williams said. "You had to have smelt a lot of mule manure."[45] Between him and his audience was a bond that was instant and nearly inarticulate. It had something to do with a shared sense of history and with the isolation they felt in him and in themselves.

Often the songs were about women, women who were gone, women you couldn't hold on to because you needed them too much or who needed you too much, or who had just left on some train going somewhere and who weren't coming back. The bathos of the country lyrics that were coming out of lives like Hank Williams's verged away from the irony and the emotional realism of the blues and toward a kind of abject fatalism, as if the woman in the song could only be seen against some final unsatisfiable longing, as if she took form only when she was gone. Listening to the songs, we are surprised at how many couple their hopeless words with jaunty tunes. But the familiar hoedown music, like the self-pity, was a way of containing what might otherwise turn violent, might cut too deep.[46] It was the same with all of the sentimentalized themes, the home places and heaven places and the rosewood coffins; the silver-haired daddies and Bible-reading old mothers. The gospel music in the churches and on the radio had ingrained in it a real resentment against the proud and the powerful, who would kneel at the Judgment Seat alongside the poor and the plain (and it may be that even hope is a form of resentment), but the resentment tended to become smoothed over, drowned in a maudlin soup of sentiment in the music Hank Williams and the poor white southerners like him had begun to make. Still, if you listen hard to those songs, you hear, under their facile attempts to divert the rage of living into tears and sighs, something else, something that really does verge on the tragic, and that is the sense of the insufficiency of the tropes of loneliness or lostness or tears to answer to the real pain under the tears, to the humiliation and rage—a rage so great, it may be, and a lostness so profound that they could not be spoken. That very insufficiency makes the songs redouble their effects, makes them sound sometimes as if they are deliberately parodying themselves. And perhaps in some sense they are.[47]

In Nashville, Williams would find out that when he was on the air he couldn't give a name to the stuff that was leaking out of the hole in his bucket. The defiance in that bluesy style Jimmie Rodgers had learned from the black singers he had known, with its concentrated poetry and its erotic force and the sting of its ironic humor, was being channeled, modulated, censored by the economic pressures of phonograph record sales and radio promotion. By what the money men imagined were the moral sensibilities of an audience of hicks. "Mr. Peer made us famous," Maybelle and Sara Carter used to say of the pioneer producer of black and country music, "and we made him rich." As for Ralph Peer himself, he could be openly contemptuous of what he called "the hillbilly and nigger stuff" and none too exacting in its execution in his rush to press records.[48] Before long, Hank Williams (or his co-writer) would be publishing advice for other singers: *Don't write any song which might offend a certain class of people. You should avoid especially the offending of any religious groups or races . . . Avoid writing songs that have or could have double meanings or could be interpreted in any indecent manner.*[49] All that history and lore and regional dialect were being squeezed out in favor of some sort of radio gruel, a tamed and homogenized music whose very silences and euphemisms expressed the contradictions they tried to obliterate.[50] (It would be years before country singers could try to reclaim their originality as Outlaws or articulate their resentment of this naked exploitation in songs like Hank Williams's grandson's "Trashville.") But for Hank Williams the terrible need to succeed was wrapped up in a world of dollars and the fine print of contracts he could scarcely read. For all the money and the fame, for all the honky-tonking and the bragging, it was as if the rage and love and joy of Saturday night had nowhere to go, and only that nameless, lonely cheated feeling was left.

The people who were closest to Williams, his women, his collaborators, the men who played the guitars and the fiddles behind him, claimed you could never reach him. He made up a novelty song about a cigar store Indian who falls in love with an Indian maid in an antique store across the street. Locked in the silence of his frozen persona, the Indian can't give a sign, because—the rhyme is inspired—his heart is made of knotty pine. Kaw-Liga, the wooden Indian, was Williams's version of himself. The extravagant sorrow of his music, the sighs and the soulful yodels that went beyond words, were ways of concealing him from himself and from the world. Minnie Pearl, the hillbilly comic by way of a Nashville girls' school, said Williams had a woods-animal distrust of anyone who might have more learning than he had.[51] On

179

stage he was someone else, his lanky leg swinging to the beat, cool, full of humor: he could only really live on stage.[52]

Hillbilly Hits the Jackpot
After Lean Years in Youth[53]

What could you do if you were a hillbilly? You could get drunk and fight. You could get drafted into the army. You could move into town or go to Detroit or the West Coast and get a job in a plant. You could disappear from Middle America's consciousness as the endless stream of black sharecroppers and factory workers and Mexican crop pickers had, become a shadow. You could hit the jackpot.

Everything is speeding now. Hank is wearing a Nudie Cohen cowboy suit and singing on the Grand Ole Opry and sucking the insides out of Benzedrine inhalers in the back of his Packard driving from date to date wedged in with the band he calls the Drifting Cowboys. He has two kids and a wife, his son would later say, with a shape that could melt the wax off a Dixie cup at fifty feet.[54] He's writing songs on envelopes, the backs of bills, anything he can find.

There's a photograph of Hank in front of his new house in Nashville in '49. A skinny guy in a white Stetson leaning on a new Caddy convertible. It's a brick ranch house like suburbs everywhere were filling up with.

The good-looking wife is another one of those relentless females he had to have around him. She's already tried to divorce him once. On jobs in little towns and in cities he'll look for a woman he can take to his room, ask a cop maybe, "Know any goin' women around here?"[55] Bang her in a motel while the band waits in the car.

He's binge drinking now. He's hitting Audrey hard.

If your Mama's cross and she won't treat you right
Beat her every morning and love her every night.[56]

He creates an alter ego, someone he calls Luke the Drifter, to record maudlin recitations—tearjerkers about poor little Colored Children's funerals and Too Many Parties—and he's singing those mournful songs: "Ain't that the awfulest morbidest song you ever heard in your life?" he told one journalist.[57] But at the same time he's writing about honky-tonks and Long Gone Daddies and all the rest. It was the old pattern of the exorbitant seesawing of sin and salvation. The Preacher and the Artist, Luke the Drifter and Hiram the widow's son—the two halves never come together; they bounce off each other with those violent alternations of emotion that are perhaps the real drug Hank Williams is hooked on. The gift of the spirit could fill a soul with light in a log church or a revival tent at the edge of a mill town, but it could just as suddenly be withdrawn, be gone like the friends who would ditch you when you drank too much or needed them too much, or like those cold-hearted women who might never have been there at all. Like the Sunday morning hangover after the Saturday night drunk, there was nothing more terrible and lonely than that.

The songs keep coming. Driving between shows he's pounding the rhythms out on the dashboard of the car. Somebody takes a shirt cardboard or something and scratches down the lyrics while he works them out aloud. He has a wallet bulging with songs, good-time songs about jambalaya and honky-tonks and that place he knows right over the hill. Songs about those women he needs and hates and all the rage is dissipated into drinking, self-pity, and that little yodeling sob. The words are all wrong, but the sadness is right.

> *Hear that lonesome whippoorwill*
> *He sounds too blue to fly*
> *The midnight train is whining low*
> *I'm so lonesome I could cry.*

Beneath the self-pity and pain there was a silence that was deeper than the words.

> *I've never seen a night so long*
> *When time goes crawling by . . .*

And under the hyperinflated American ego he carried with him like the satchel that held his dope and his spare shirts and his gun, there was something about him that wanted to die, something that could not resist the downward pull of isolation. He wanted to forget, and so did his audience, and the way to forget was to dissolve everything into a solution of sorrow and lostness, as if that process could dissolve the past and the present too. But the sorrow and lostness doubled back upon themselves, became something like the contempt the world had for white trash like him. There wasn't a pill in the world that could cure what Hank had.

Joke going around in 2002:

What happens when you play a country western song backwards?

You get the truck back, you get the house back, you get the kids back . . .

Hank is in California, divorced, looking at a part in a Jane Powell and Farley Granger pic. In San Diego he is drinking before a show he's in with Ernest Tubb and Minnie Pearl. "Minnie, I can't work. I can't work, Minnie. Tell 'em." But they put him on the stage and it's bad. Minnie Pearl and the promoter's wife and someone else Minnie couldn't remember got him into a car and drove around trying to keep him from getting drunker before the next show. They started singing. Hank was hunched down, looking out the window. He started singing "I Saw the Light," and then he stopped and looked at Minnie and his face broke up and he said, "Minnie, I don't see no light. There ain't no light."[58] It's the spring of 1952. Hank is not yet twenty-nine.

December 31, 1952. Hank Williams is dying. Birmingham, Gadsden, Fort Payne, heading north for shows in Charleston, West Virginia, and Canton, Ohio. For a while Hank had sat up front in the limousine, singing "Jambalaya" and Red Foley's hit "Midnight" to his driver. He's the number one country singer, with two hits on the charts, and he's doing shows with pick-up bands and waking up soaked in his own piss.

END OF THE DREAM

Somewhere in the burnt fields of Texas or Oklahoma in the 1930s, Jefferson's pastoral ideal reached its end. There were no more Indian lands worth stealing, and the exhausted soil couldn't resist drought or boll weevils or foreclosure by the bank. The farmers had sunk into tenancy and their independence had given way to control by political bosses and the illusions of a crude populism. Pushed off the land like some routed army, the Arkies and Okies and Panhandle Texans learned in the pea fields and cotton fields of California's Central Valley what their pride, which was almost all they had left, was worth. On the scale of life white ranchers and small-town businessmen held up to them, they were lower, even, than the black and Mexican crop workers and something less than human. "We ain't people," a displaced Okie kid told his teacher in a valley town, "we are sharecroppers."[59]

Dorothea Lange photographed these Okies and Arkies and Texans in labor camps and broken down and stranded on the road in the thirties. A few years later she was in Oakland and Richmond photographing these same refugees and a new wave of emigrants from the South and Midwest. The war has brought them prosperity. They walk in their hard hats looking through plate-glass windows at the things they can now afford to buy, their cars fill the lots at the Richmond shipyards, they sit in bars and gather to hear Dude Martin sing, and they bring their storefront churches with them.[60] They have the same country faces Hank Williams was playing to.

They'd drifted over America from little towns in the South and Midwest following defense work in the plants, or following the housing boom or the oil rigs, or had just gotten washed up in the Depression and stranded somewhere. Hank Williams was part of that spiritual migration and final homelessness.

Sitting in a clapboard house with one wire attached to the single light and the other to the radio, a part-Indian Okie girl named Roxanne Dunbar sat listening to those country songs during the Second World War. They "allowed us to know we were a part of, and one with, our kind of people in a faraway place in the old homeland of Tennessee," she would later write. And she would quote from Jeremiah to figure the emotional world of her struggling parents:[61]

> *I have forsaken mine house, I have left mine heritage. . . . Mine heritage is unto me as a lion in the forest; it crieth out against me: therefore have I hated it. Mine heritage is unto me as a speckled bird, the birds round about are against her.*

As she listened to Roy Acuff sing the Church of God anthem "The Great Speckled Bird," Jeremiah's cry of outrage became for Roxie Dunbar an earnest of the final triumph of the hillbillies and Okies and rednecks of the world:

> *This music was delivered to us, drowning us in song and belief, helping keep us docile. . . . It helped keep us women religious while it comforted and encouraged our men, who boozed it up and slugged it out in taverns over cheating hearts.*
>
> *We poor rural whites were no longer foot-soldier Indian Fighters, and were not easy to silence if we got mad. What we had was oral history, a powerful memory, so the music, a part of that history as well as how we told it, absolutely seduced us.*[62]

If the pastoral ideal had died as a living thing, it held on as a pure vision in the music that had articulated it. The old homeplace was still there, but farther and farther away from the factories and the vast industrialized fields of cotton and wheat and tomatoes; and under everything, in poverty and in prosperity, was the embittered populism that came out in the songs, in their sorrows, in their constant reiteration of erotic failure, beer-joint despair, and resignation, as if failure itself had become a badge of honor and a form of resistance to the dehumanizing power of the postwar American Dream. Great battles had been fought—and mostly lost—in southeastern textile mills, in the coal fields of Kentucky and West Virginia, and in the cotton fields of California's central valley. And there were songs—sometimes great songs—that attempted to lift up those southern mill workers and coal miners in their bitter strikes, old gospel songs with powerful new words like "Which Side Are You On?" and "We Shall Not Be Moved." But the protest for the most part had a way of unraveling into personal lament in the music, the anger dissipating into barroom machismo or some final, ultimately inarticulate sorrow.[63]

In 1946, while Hank Williams was still driving from bar to bar around the south with the Drifting Cowboys, trying to catch a break, a Capitol A&R man asked a singer and virtuoso guitar picker from the Kentucky coal country named Merle Travis to put together a folk song album. Out of that Capitol album came two great coal mining songs, "Sixteen Tons" and "Dark as a Dungeon." The come-all-ye beginning of "Dark as a Dungeon" was as much as Cecil Sharp or anyone with an ear for a folk song could ask. As Travis sings he opens up beneath the beautiful green hills of Appalachia a negative land of darkness, damp, and coal. In Marx's account of the harsh logic of industrial production, a hatmaker becomes a hat; in Travis's song, a miner becomes the coal itself. Only death can release him: he looks down from his place in heaven and pities the miner digging his bones. When he recorded his powerful song, Merle Travis had given it a short introduction that ended with a little embarrassed chuckle. It was as if he had to apologize to the America of 1946 for that drop of pity he had left in the song.[64] That little chuckle was the other side of the anger in "Dark as a Dungeon" and the throb at the center of Hank Williams's voice. And it might have been their final emotional truth—that and the sense of being finally and profoundly alone.

184

For years after he died Hank Williams's mournful ghost was still drifting over the cigarette smoke and the talk and the thin undercurrent of violence in the bars of Cold War America where ex-cowboys and would-be cowboys and hillbillies and truck drivers and construction workers would stop after work downing beers and listening to the wanging pedal steel. You could stop in a bar like that with maybe Kitty Wells on the jukebox telling you it wasn't God who made honky-tonk angels, and have a beer and think about dancing with the barmaid, holding her tight and knowing all the time she was going to cheat on you or you were going to cheat on her. The music in those bars, with all its self-conscious honky-tonking, self-pity, and doleful religiosity, was on its way to becoming the voice of the American white working class, of blue-collar workers with Polish and Italian names in Philadelphia and Chicago, as well as of the hillbillies and cowboys who had created it.[65] Hank Williams had spoken to them and for them. Their pride in their independence and toughness, their sense of moral rectitude still showed through, assimilated now to a maudlin patriotism that would turn truculent in the '60s. They listened to Hank sing, a voice that was compounded as much of silence as of words.

In grade schools kids were ducking and covering, and fallout from Nevada was blowing downwind like invisible snow. White southern boys as poor as Hiram Williams had been were assimilating the rhythms of the juke joints and bars of black America and soon one of them named Elvis Presley would be traveling the country circuit. When the singer Ira Louvin called him a "white nigger" playing "nigger trash"[66] it was clear some cultural line had been crossed, but it remained to be seen if the Elvises and Buddys and Jerry Lees had brought a racial and erotic revolution to their world or were simply adding their mite to that postwar creation of tics and needs, the American teenager. Korea was scattering a blizzard of white crosses over the landscape of America. Just around the corner, off the coast of Cuba, the United States and the Soviet Union would soon push themselves to the brink of nuclear war and around the corner from that was Vietnam.

Still, on jukeboxes and record players Hank was dishing out that jambalaya and carrying on about some coldhearted woman. He was still driving off in that hot rod Ford to that place that was always right over the hill. Or the next hill. Or the next. And we were going with him to that place, the place where everything would be all right. Where everything would be easy and good. But somehow we never got there. It was shit-kicker music.

The wilderness still lived in the best of our songs, but it was no longer a wilderness of trees and prairies and great rivers, but that internal wilderness whose silence and sense of loss had been there even from the first. The utopian future, the empty slate in the imaginations of generations of pioneers, was gone like the lands of the Indians: the place right over the hill was in fact a place in a mythical past, a nostalgia for somewhere that had never been. By 1979 country singer Larry Gatlin was telling a new generation of Okies and Arkies and Alabama boys who might have been dreaming of the big move west that all the gold in California was locked up in a Beverly Hills vault in somebody else's name.[67]

We still sang of those trains taking us off to the lands of eternal sunshine, the Wabash Cannonball, the Orange Blossom Special, the City of New Orleans, just as Hank Williams had sung of the Pan American and the California Zephyr, but in fact those mythical trains had become the bearers of something we were leaving, not some promise we were going toward, and if we were going home it was to someplace that would be changed by the very knowledge of what we had seen and that in leaving we would never be able to see again.

It was snowing in Chattanooga. Hank Williams tried to get a plane in Knoxville but the airport was fogged in. He had somehow found a bottle and was starting to drink. His back was killing him and he got a shot of morphine and vitamin B12 and he was hiccupping. And then they were driving on to Canton in a baby blue Cadillac and Hank was dying in the back seat, full of chloral hydrate and liquor and morphine, wrapped in a blanket, in his white cowboy boots, white Stetson, and blue serge suit with a pearl-handled pistol in his pocket or in his grip and a scrap of a song about busted love called "Then Came that Fatal Day" floating on the floor, driving to a New Year's Day show he will never make.

Acknowledgments

I have accrued many debts in writing and thinking about this book. Those to
a pair of classics of American cultural history are foremost: Leo Marx's *The
Machine in the Garden* and Henry Nash Smith's *Virgin Land*. Several works
by Alan Trachtenberg have also been most important to me, and I've profited
especially by his view of the World's Columbian Exposition of 1893 presented in
The Incorporation of America and of Timothy O'Sullivan's survey photographs
in *Reading American Photographs*. I hope I've differed from Trachtenberg's
approach to the exposition and O'Sullivan sufficiently to make my work on
those subjects interesting. It was in Trachtenberg's *Brooklyn Bridge: Fact and
Symbol* that I came across the remarkable view of the American attitude to
the wilderness expressed by the traveler Francis Grund. The standard biog-
raphies of Henry Adams and Clarence King by Ernest Samuels and Thurman
Wilkins have been indispensable. The work of William H. Gass and Richard
Bridgman on Gertrude Stein helped me make whatever sense I've been able

to make of that complicated figure. Central to my understanding of the sin-salvation dichotomy that pervades Hank Williams's music, and that of country music in general, is Wilbur Cash's *The Mind of the South*. Bill Malone's wonderful *Don't Get Above Your Raisin'* gave me an enriched sense of the cultural and historical context of the makers of this indigenous music. James N. Gregory's *American Exodus: The Dust Bowl Migration and Okie Culture in California* taught me much about the 1930s diaspora of white southerners and of the culture they brought with them to California. Martha Sandweiss's excellent *Print the Legend: Photography and the American West* introduced me to Emerson's provocative statement that America has no past—and I would never have stumbled upon it by myself, since it appears in Emerson's original speech as it was printed in *The Dial* but not in his reworded standard version. Another significant text was put in my hand by my daughter Eleni, who lent me Matt Wray and Annalee Newitz's *White Trash: Race and Class in America*, with essays by Roxanne Dunbar and Barbara Ching that proved important to me. My son Tony led me to the music of Hank Williams III and to lyrics I found significant. I would like to note the kindness of Helen A. Harrison, director of the Pollock-Krasner House and Study Center in East Hampton, who opened the doors to me on a beautiful fall day and spent an hour talking of Jackson Pollock and his work. Irving Feldman and Frank Bergon are two friends who read through many pages of this book in manuscript and worked diligently to save me from my own confusions and the bogs of academic fashion. Do not blame them: they did their best.

Dorothea Lange, *The Road West—U.S. 54 in New Mexico* (1938). Black-and-white photograph. © The Dorothea Lange Collection, Oakland Museum of California, City of Oakland. Gift of Paul S. Taylor.

Notes

OVERTURE: THE UNPAINTABLE WEST

1. The painting itself might have been inspired by the sort of vignette incorporated in the panoramas popular in Bingham's era, such as John Banvard's "three mile long moving panorama" of a journey down the Missouri and Mississippi rivers to the Gulf. See Angela Miller, "The Mechanisms of the Market and the Invention of Western Regionalism: The Example of George Caleb Bingham," in *American Iconology: New Approaches to Nineteenth-Century Art and Literature*, ed. David C. Miller (New Haven CT: Yale University Press, 1993), p. 116.

2. Clark's last entry in his journals is "Friday (25th) of September 1806. a fine morning   we commenced wrighting &c." It was in fact September 26. Gary E. Moulton, ed., *The Definitive Journals of Lewis and Clark*, 13 vols., vol. 8, *Over the Rockies to St. Louis* (Lincoln: University of Nebraska Press, 1983–2001), p. 372.

3. Moulton, *Definitive Journals*, 4:292–94.

4. Moulton, *Definitive Journals*, 4:285. The "Thompson" to whom Lewis refers is the Scottish poet James Thomson (1700–1748), author of *The Seasons* and *The Castle of Indolence*. In the description of the painting galleries of the latter appear these lines, interesting in this connection: "Whate'er *Lorrain* light-touch'd with softening Hue / Or savage *Rosa* dash'd or learned *Poussin* drew" (canto 38).

5. Moulton, *Definitive Journals*, 4:332.

6. Moulton, *Definitive Journals*, 4:290. Lewis's mentor, Jefferson, had described Virginia's natural bridge in terms of the sublime and the beautiful in his *Notes on*

the State of Virginia (1785). He included "Burke on the sublime and beautiful" in a list of essential books in a letter to Robert Skipwith in 1771. See Thomas Jefferson, *Writings*, ed. Merrill D. Peterson, (New York: Library of America, distributed by Penguin Books, 1984), p. 148 for *Notes* and p. 744 for the reference to Burke.

7. Edmund Burke, *A Philosophical Enquiry into the Origin of our Ideas of the Sublime and Beautiful*, ed. James T. Boulton (1757, 1759; Notre Dame IN: University of Notre Dame Press, 1968), p. 115.

8. "But love approaches much nearer to contempt than is commonly imagined," Burke, *Philosophical Enquiry*, p. 67.

9. Moulton, *Definitive Journals*, 5:347.

10. Moulton, *Definitive Journals*, 6:75.

11. Moulton, *Definitive Journals*, 6:187, 205.

12. Clark, quoting Lewis, in Moulton, *Definitive Journals*, 6:32, 34 n. 6.

13. Donald Jackson, ed., *Letters of the Lewis and Clark Expedition with Related Documents, 1783–1854* (Urbana: University of Illinois Press, 1962), p. 74.

14. Jefferson to Governor William Henry Harrison, February 27, 1803, in Jefferson, *Writings*, pp. 1118–19.

15. Moulton, *Definitive Journals*, 6:79.

16. Moulton, *Definitive Journals*, 6:126.

17. James P. Ronda, *Lewis and Clark among the Indians* (Lincoln: University of Nebraska Press, 1984), pp. 191, 202–4.

18. Moulton, *Definitive Journals*, 6:84.

19. Jefferson, *Writings*, pp. 961–63. Moulton, *Definitive Journals*, 6:183. Clark was able to buy some of the blubber from the Indians.

20. Moulton, *Definitive Journals*, 8:302–3.

21. Jackson, *Letters of the Lewis and Clark Expedition*, pp. 315–16.

22. Jefferson had instructed Lewis to attempt to find young Indians who might be brought back with the expedition and instructed in the arts of civilization. See Ronda, *Lewis and Clark among the Indians*, p. 6.

23. Henry M. Brackenridge, *Journal of a Voyage up the Missouri River in 1811*, qtd. in Larry E. Morris, *The Fate of the Corps: What Became of the Lewis and Clark Explorers after the Expedition* (New Haven CT: Yale University Press, 2004), p. 107.

24. Journal of John C. Luttig, qtd. in Morris, *Fate of the Corps*, p. 115. Clark took on the care of the girl, whose name was Lisette.

25. Reuben Holmes, "The Five Scalps," in Missouri Historical Society, *Glimpses of the Past* 5, nos. 1–3 (January–March 1938): 19–24.

26. L. R. Hafen, in L. R. Hafen, ed., *The Mountain Men and the Fur Trade of the Far West*, vol. 9 (Glendale CA: A. H. Clark Co., 1972), p. 61.

27. Albert Furtwangler, *Sacagawea's Son* (Portland: Oregon Historical Society Press, 2004).

28. The year 1845 also saw the death of Andrew Jackson, who as president had promoted a policy of massive removal of the Indians of the South.

29. Qtd. in Bernard W. Sheehan, *Seeds of Extinction: Jeffersonian Philanthropy and the American Indian* (Chapel Hill: University of North Carolina Press, 1973), p. 229.

30. George Catlin, *Letters and Notes on the Manners, Customs, and Conditions of the North American Indians*, 2 vols. (1844; New York: Dover Publications, 1973), 1:256.

31. See Dawn Glanz, *How the West Was Drawn: American Art and the Settling of the Frontier* (Ann Arbor MI: UMI Research Press, 1982), p. 44.

32. *Song of Myself*, from *Leaves of Grass* (1855). Punctuation from the 1891–92 edition: *Walt Whitman: Complete Poetry and Collected Prose*, ed. Justin Kaplan (New York: Library of America, distributed by Viking Press, 1982), pp. 196–97.

33. To get a hint of what Bingham left unexpressed, you need only examine the painting by Bingham's contemporary Charles Deas, *The Voyageurs*, completed the same year as *Fur Traders Descending the Missouri*, and perhaps its source. Under the grotesque comedy of the frontier family who inhabits the chaos of pots and pans and robes of an overladen canoe—the trapper with his battered stovepipe hat, his Indian wife, and their heterogeneous brats—is a desperate fear. They are paddling furiously, not toward the new civilization of racial amalgamation Jefferson and others had wished for them, but backward, to a despoiled wilderness upstream. See Angela Miller, "Mechanisms of the Market," pp. 119–20. See also Nancy Rash, *The Painting and Politics of George Caleb Bingham* (New Haven CT: Yale University Press, 1991), pp. 50–51.

34. Alexis de Tocqueville, *Democracy in America*, trans. Henry Reeve, rev. Francis Bowen (1839, 1840), ed. Phillips Bradley, 2 vols. (New York: Alfred A. Knopf, 1945), 1:342.

35. Tocqueville, *Democracy in America*, 1:345–46 n.

36. Ezra 10:2. There is intriguing, but inconclusive, evidence that William Clark may have himself fathered a mixed-blood son when among the Nez Perce during the Lewis and Clark expedition. See Ronda, *Lewis and Clark among the Indians*, p. 233.

37. Robert S. Tilton, in *Pocahontas: The Evolution of an American Narrative* (Cambridge: Cambridge University Press, 1994), p. 64, quotes Natty Bumppo in Cooper's *The Prairie*: "The half-and-halfs that one meets in these distant districts are altogether more barbarous than the real savage."

38. Washington Irving, *Astoria*, qtd. in G. Edward White, *The Eastern Establishment and the Western Experience: The West of Frederic Remington, Theodore Roosevelt, and Owen Wister* (1968; Austin: University of Texas Press, 1959), p. 37.

39. Alexis de Tocqueville, "A Fortnight in the Wilderness," trans. George Wilson Pierson, in *Tocqueville in America* (1938; Baltimore: Johns Hopkins University Press, 1996), p. 274.

40. Ralph Waldo Emerson, "The Young American," *The Dial* 4, no. 4 (April 1844): 492.

41. Bernard De Voto, *The Year of Decision: 1846* (Boston: Little, Brown & Co., 1943), pp. 134–36.

42. Bret Harte, "How I Went to the Mines," in *The Writings of Bret Harte*, vol. 18, *A Treasure of the Redwoods and Other Tales* (Boston: Houghton Mifflin Co., 1903), p. 254.

43. Patrick Gass to John H. Eaton, in Jackson, *Letters of the Lewis and Clark Expedition*, p. 647.

44. Information on Patrick Gass's life comes from J. G. Jacob, *The Life and Times of Patrick Gass, Now Sole Survivor of the Overland Expedition to the Pacific, Under Lewis and Clark, in 1804–5–6* (Wellsburg VA: Jacob & Smith, 1859) and James Kendall Hosmer's introduction to the 1904 reprint of the 1811 edition of Gass's journal of the Lewis and Clark expedition (Chicago: A. C. McClurg & Co., 1904). See also Morris, *Fate of the Corps*, pp. 181–85. On Gass's racism see the letter from his daughter to Eva Emery Dye, MSS 1089, Eva Emery Dye Papers, Oregon Historical Society.

45. Kris Lackey, *RoadFrames: The American Highway Narrative* (Lincoln: University of Nebraska Press, 1997), p. 1. For a biographical notice of Patrick Gass, see Charles G. Clarke, *The Men of the Lewis and Clark Expedition* (Lincoln: University of Nebraska Press, 1970), pp. 39–40. Though he said he only learned to read and "cipher" after he came of age, Gass himself kept a journal of the Lewis and Clark expedition, whose original is lost. The extant version of Gass's journal is volume 10 of the University of Nebraska edition of the journals of Lewis and Clark.

46. Whitman, *Song of Myself*, from *Leaves of Grass* (1891–92), in Whitman, *Complete Poetry*, p. 211.

47. Tocqueville, *Democracy in America*, 2:99.

48. Mary Vardoulakis, *Gold in the Streets* (New York: Dodd, Mead & Co., 1945), p. 117.

1. THE INNER GEOLOGY OF CLARENCE KING

1. Asbury Harpending, *The Great Diamond Hoax and Other Stirring Incidents in the Life of Asbury Harpending*, ed. James H. Wilson (1915; Norman: University of Oklahoma Press, 1958), pp. 156–57.

2. Harpending, *Great Diamond Hoax*, p. 157.

3. "The Diamond Discovery of 1872," corrected typescript, Samuel F. Emmons Papers, Library of Congress Manuscript Division, Container No. 27.

4. Bruce A. Woodward, whose *Diamonds in the Salt* (Boulder CO: Pruett Press, 1967) is the only book-length study of the Great Diamond Hoax, quotes a letter of July 16, 1872, from King's future friend John Hay to Samuel L. M. Barlow, a prominent New York attorney representing the diamond interests, that might stand for the level of enthusiasm for the enterprise. "I had a very pleasant talk with Mr. Janin, which convinced me I ought to sell my shirt and pawn my Bible for stock. But your words of profound wisdom yesterday have impressed me deeply. Therefore, I will

take 100 shares @ $4,000. If I lose it all, I will be grateful to you. If I make $6,000, I will sue you for the other $9,000" (p. 46).

5. Harpending, *Great Diamond Hoax*, p. 143.

6. The house at the corner of Church and High streets belonged to King's aunt Caroline King. It is described by King's secretary and one-time business partner Edgar Beecher Bronson in *Reminiscences of a Ranchman* (1908, rev. 1910; Lincoln: University of Nebraska Press, 1962), p. 5. I am extrapolating from Bronson. The figures on the chests and fabrics are imagined.

7. From King's review of *Sketches of Creation* by Alexander Winchell, *Overland Monthly* 5 (December 1870): 582, qtd. in Thurman Wilkins, *Clarence King: A Biography*, rev. and enlarged ed. (1958; Albuquerque: University of New Mexico Press, 1988), pp. 16–17. Where not noted, incidents from King's life are taken from Wilkins's book.

8. Wilkins, *Clarence King*, pp. 15–18; Bronson, *Reminiscences*, p. 338.

9. Francis P. Farquhar, "The Whitney Survey of Mount Shasta, 1862: A Letter from William H. Brewer to Professor Brush," *California Historical Society Quarterly* 7, no. 2 (June 1928): 129.

10. Descriptions of Bear Valley and the Mariposa are from Frederick Law Olmsted, *The Papers of Frederick Law Olmsted*, vol. 5, *The California Frontier, 1863–1865*, ed. Victoria Post Ranney (Baltimore MD: Johns Hopkins University Press, 1990), pp. 98–173.

11. Clarence King, *Mountaineering in the Sierra Nevada* (1872; Lincoln: University of Nebraska Press, 1970), p. 179.

12. King, *Mountaineering*, pp. 33–34.

13. King named the peak after John Tyndall, his predecessor as a scientist and literary mountaineer.

14. King, *Mountaineering*, pp. 54–55.

15. William H. Brewer, *Up and Down California in 1860–64: The Journal of William H. Brewer, Professor of Agriculture in the Sheffield Scientific School from 1864 to 1903*, ed. Francis P. Farquhar (New Haven CT: Yale University Press, 1930), p. 525.

16. King, *Mountaineering*, p. 93.

17. Information on Timothy O'Sullivan, and an interpretation of his photographs, have been largely derived from Joel Snyder, *American Frontiers: The Photographs of Timothy H. O'Sullivan, 1867–1874* (Millerton NY: Aperture, 1981). See page 45: "At times, O'Sullivan denies the viewer a fixed position in the scene, often providing no foreground upon which the viewer may imaginatively stand and enter the picture to move through the represented space."

18. Joel Snyder, in *American Frontiers*, compares King's catastrophic view of geology to O'Sullivan's battlefield photography: "The human counterpart of explosive, natural action is war. As a photographer of a holy war in which a nation tore itself apart and was told to 'change or die'—a photographer of the aftermath or traces of war, of mangled corpses and fields that imply, but do not show, the fleeting presence

of the terrible force of destruction—Timothy O'Sullivan seems not merely appropriate, but inescapably fitting for the job of King's photographer" (p. 19).

19. Wilkins, *Clarence King*, p. 102.

20. Qtd. in Wilkins, *Clarence King*, p. 101.

21. Brewer's recollection of the Shasta climb in a speech of 1886, qtd. by Farquhar in "Whitney Survey on Mount Shasta, 1862," p. 128 n.

22. Alan Trachtenberg, *Reading American Photographs: Images as History; Mathew Brady to Walker Evans* (New York: Hill & Wang, 1989), p. 149.

23. Henry Adams, *The Education of Henry Adams*, in Henry Adams, *Novels, Mont Saint Michel, The Education, Poems*, ed. Ernest Samuels and Jayne N. Samuels (New York: Library of America, distributed by Viking Press, 1983), p. 1004. Hereafter referred to as *Education*.

24. Adams, *Education*, p. 1005.

25. King, *Mountaineering*, p. 292.

26. Clarence King, "Catastrophism and Evolution," *American Naturalist* (August 1877): 470, 450.

27. King, *Mountaineering*, pp. 190–91.

28. Wilkins, *Clarence King*, p. 325.

29. She also refused King's sister her permission to marry.

30. The notebook is found in the Clarence King Papers, Huntington Library, San Marino, California.

31. The description of Copples's hotel is from chapter 10, "Cut-off Copples's," in King, *Mountaineering*, pp. 215–18.

32. Wilkins, *Clarence King*, p. 359.

33. Wilkins, *Clarence King*, p. 354.

34. From King's review of Bancroft's *Native Races of the Pacific States* in the *Atlantic Monthly*, February 1875, p. 172.

35. A paraphrase of King's description of night in the tropics, from the review noted above, p. 172.

36. *New York Daily Mirror*, November 22, 1933.

37. Clarence King Papers, Huntington Library, San Marino, California.

38. James Pope-Hennessy, *Monckton Milnes: The Flight of Youth, 1851–1885* (London: Constable, 1951), p. 134.

39. Bronson, *Reminiscences*, p. 356.

40. *New York Daily Mirror*, November 22, 1933.

41. John La Farge, in *Clarence King Memoirs* (New York: G. P. Putnam's Sons, 1904), p. 190.

42. Wilkins, *Clarence King*, p. 389 n.

43. Clarence King to John Hay, May 16, 1894, qtd. in Patricia O'Toole, *The Five of Hearts: An Intimate Portrait of Henry Adams and His Friends, 1880–1918* (New York: Clarkson N. Potter, 1990), pp. 275–76.

44. La Farge, *Clarence King Memoirs*, pp. 192–94.

45. *New York Daily Mirror*, November 22, 1933.

46. King, *Mountaineering*, p. 242.

47. The story of King's secret marriage to Ada Todd became public in 1933, when Ada sued the descendants of James Terry Gardiner for the principal of a trust she believed King had left for her and had entrusted to Gardiner's keeping. See *King v. Peabody et al.*, File No. 26821-1931, Records of the New York Supreme Court, New York County Clerk's Office. King's surviving letters to Ada are quoted in the trial records and in the newspaper accounts of the trial proceedings quoted above.

2. HENRY ADAMS AT THE FAIR

1. Henry Adams, *The Letters of Henry Adams*, ed. J. C. Levenson, Ernest Samuels, Charles Vandersee, and Viola Hopkins Winner, with the assistance of Jayne N. Samuels and Eleanor Pearre Abbot (Cambridge MA: Harvard University Press, Belknap Press), 4:98–99. Hereafter referred to as *Letters*.

2. Adams, *Letters*, 4:99–101.

3. Reid Badger, *The Great American Fair: The World's Columbian Exposition and American Culture* (Chicago: Nelson Hall, 1979), p. 68.

4. David F. Burg, *Chicago's White City of 1893* (Lexington: University Press of Kentucky, 1976), p. 232.

5. Adams, *Letters*, 4:102–3.

6. Adams, *Letters*, 4:108.

7. Adams, *Letters*, 4:112.

8. Adams, *Letters*, 4:127.

9. Adams, *Letters*, 4:125.

10. Adams, *Letters*, 4:126.

11. Burg, *Chicago's White City*, p. 45.

12. Adams, *Letters*, 4:133.

13. Adams, *Education*, p. 932.

14. Clover Adams to Ellen (Hooper) Gurney, qtd. in Eugenia Kaledin, *The Education of Mrs. Henry Adams* (Philadelphia: Temple University Press, 1981), pp. 105–6.

15. *Journals of Ralph Waldo Emerson, 1864–1876*, ed. Edward Waldo Emerson and Waldo Emerson Forbes (Boston: Houghton Mifflin Co., 1914), pp. 405–8. My view of Adams's Nile journey is based largely on Otto Friedrich, *Clover* (New York: Simon & Schuster, 1979).

16. Ward Thoron, ed., *The Letters of Mrs. Henry Adams, 1865–1883* (Boston: Little, Brown & Co., 1937), pp. 60–79.

17. Friedrich, *Clover*, pp. 164–66.

18. Henry James, "Pandora" (1884), in Henry James, *Complete Stories, 1874–1884* (New York: Library of America, distributed by Penguin Putnam, 1999), p. 838.

197

19. Thoron, *Letters of Mrs. Henry Adams*, pp. 266–67, 272.

20. "One consequence of having no children," Adams wrote to Charles Milnes Gaskell, "is that husband and wife become very dependent on each other and live very much together. This is my case" (Friedrich, *Clover*, p. 214).

21. O'Toole, *Five of Hearts*, p. 103.

22. Qtd. in Friedrich, *Clover*, p. 133.

23. Adams, *Letters*, 4:134–35.

24. In the *Aeneid*, having seen a vision of Rome's future glory in the underworld, Aeneas returns to earth not through the gates of horn, from whence issue true dreams, but from the gates of ivory, from which come the false.

25. Adams, *Education*, p. 1031.

26. *Chicago Tribune*, October 8, 1893.

27. Burg, *Chicago's White City*, p. 69.

28. Burg, *Chicago's White City*, pp. 105–6.

29. Friedrich, *Clover*, p. 316.

30. Adams, *Education*, p. 1031.

31. Descriptions of Chicago Day at the Exposition are found in the *Chicago Tribune* of October 9 and 10, 1893.

32. Stanley Appelbaum, *The Chicago World's Fair of 1893: A Photographic Record* (New York: Dover Publications, 1980), p. 102.

33. Adams, *Letters*, 4:133–34.

34. Ernest Samuels, *Henry Adams* (Cambridge MA: Harvard University Press, 1989), pp. 292–93.

35. Adams, *Letters*, 4:131–34.

36. Adams, *Education*, pp. 1031–32.

37. Adams, *Education*, p. 1033.

38. The description of the August 30 demonstration comes from the *Chicago Tribune*, August 31, 1893.

39. Brooks Adams, introduction to Henry Adams, *The Degradation of the Democratic Dogma* (New York: Macmillan Co., 1920), pp. 94–95.

40. Adams, *Education*, p. 1029.

41. Brooks Adams, introduction to Adams, *Degradation*, p. 96.

42. Brooks Adams, introduction to Adams, *Degradation*, pp. 34–35.

43. Henry Adams, *History of the United States during the Second Administration of James Madison, 1813–1817* (New York: Library of America, 1986), pp. 1332–33.

44. "Unbroken Evolution under uniform conditions pleased every one—except curates and bishops;—it was the very best substitute for religion; a safe, conservative, practical, thoroughly Common-law deity" (Adams, *Education*, p. 926).

45. Frank Joslyn Baum and Russell P. MacFall, *To Please a Child: A Biography of L. Frank Baum, Royal Historian of Oz* (Chicago: Reilly & Lee Co., 1961), pp. 80–81.

46. Hubert Howe Bancroft, *The Book of the Fair*, 5 vols. (Chicago: Bancroft Co., 1893), 5:878.

47. Bancroft, *Book of the Fair*, 5:940.

48. Adams, *Education*, p. 1033.

49. Adams, *Letters*, 4:105.

50. Scott Joplin, *Complete Piano Works*, ed. Vera Brodsky Lawrence (New York: New York Public Library, 1981). From the introduction by Rudi Blesh, p. xxxv.

51. Norman Bolotin and Christine Laing, *The Chicago World's Fair of 1893: The World's Columbian Exposition* (Washington DC: Preservation Press), pp. 20, 157.

52. *Chicago Tribune*, July 6, 1894; Frederic Remington, "Chicago under the Mob," *Harpers Weekly*, July 7, 1894, in *The Collected Writings of Frederic Remington*, ed. Peggy and Harold Samuels (Garden City NY: Doubleday & Co., 1979), p. 192.

53. The account of the fire is a pastiche of reports from the *Chicago Tribune*, July 6, 1894.

54. Adams, *Education*, p. 1138.

55. Henry Adams, "The Tendency of History," in Adams, *Degradation*, pp. 130–33.

56. "Style and the Monument" (unsigned), *North American Review* 141 (November 1885): 443–53.

57. *New York World*, October 31, 1893; *New York Daily Tribune*, November 4, 1893.

58. Henry Adams, "King," in *Clarence King Memoirs*, pp. 183–85.

59. John Carlos Rowe, in "Henry Adams's *Education* in the Age of Imperialism," in *New Essays on The Education of Henry Adams* (Cambridge: Cambridge University Press, 1996), pp. 87–114, argues that Adams's public silence masked an active participation through his association with John Hay.

60. Adams, *Education*, p. 723.

61. Qtd. in Friedrich, *Clover*, p. 341.

62. In his *Education*, Adams quotes Pascal: "I have often said that all the troubles of man come from his not knowing how to sit still. . . . We combat obstacles in order to get repose, and, when got, the repose is insupportable; for we think either of the troubles we have, or of those that threaten us; and even if we felt safe on every side, *ennui* would of its own accord spring up from the depths of the heart where it is rooted by nature, and would fill the mind with its venom" (p. 1110).

3. THE CRUELTY OF SEEING

1. Qtd. in Oliver W. Larkin, *Art and Life in America* (New York: Holt, Rinehardt & Winston, 1960), p. 181.

2. Kate Chopin, *The Awakening* (1899; New York: W. W. Norton & Co., 1976), p. 53.

3. Nell Kimball, *Nell Kimball, Her Life as an American Madam by Herself* (New York: Macmillan, 1970), p. 26.

4. King, "Style and the Monument," 445–46.

5. Kimball, *Her Life*, p. 223.

6. Kimball, *Her Life*, pp. 4–5.

7. Kimball, *Her Life*, p. 233.

8. Kimball, *Her Life*, pp. 8–9.

9. Kimball, *Her Life*, p. 9.

10. Kimball, *Her Life*, p. 5.

11. E. J. Bellocq, *Storyville Portraits: Photographs from the New Orleans Red-Light District, Circa* 1912, reproduced from prints made by Lee Friedlander, preface by Lee Friedlander, ed. John Szarkowski (New York: Museum of Modern Art, 1970; distributed by New York Graphic Society, Greenwich CT).

12. Bellocq, *Storyville Portraits*, pp. 8–9.

13. Rex Rose, "The Last Days of Ernest J. Bellocq," in *The Exquisite Corpse: A Journal of Letters and Life*, ed. Andrei Codrescu, http://www.corpse.org/issue_10/gallery/bellocq (accessed April 28, 2003), p. 9.

14. Donatien-Alphonse-François Comte de Sade, *Justine*, in *The Complete Justine, Philosophy in the Bedroom and Other Writings*, trans. Richard Seaver and Austryn Wainhouse (New York: Grove Press, Inc., 1965), p. 606.

15. Rose, "Last Days of Ernest J. Bellocq," pp. 8–9.

16. A point made in a letter by Joseph L. Ruby, in *New York Review of Books*, March 6, 1997.

17. Kimball, *Her Life*, p. 210.

18. Kimball, *Her Life*, p. 279.

19. Kimball, *Her Life*, pp. 282, 115, 286.

20. Kimball, *Her Life*, p. 115.

4. SOME VERSIONS OF THE PASTORAL

1. Paraphrased from a letter by Gertrude Stein quoted in James R. Mellow, *Charmed Circle: Gertrude Stein and Company* (New York: Praeger, 1974), p. 396.

2. Gertrude Stein, *The Geographical History of America, or The Relation of Human Nature to the Human Mind* (1936), in *Gertrude Stein: Writings, 1932–1946*, selected and edited by Catharine R. Stimpson and Harriet Chessman (New York: Library of America, distributed by Penguin Putnam, 1998), p. 387. Hereafter cited as *Geographical History*.

3. See William H. Gass's excellent introduction to the Vintage edition of *The Geographical History of America* (New York: Vintage Books, 1973), p. 11: "I do not believe she had any knowledge of Frederick Jackson Turner's frontier hypothesis, but her understanding of American history was based on something very like it: 'In the United States there is more space where nobody is than where anybody is.' There is

no question that she, like Turner, thought human behavior was in great part a function of the amount of free land available. On the frontier, Turner believed, civilization was regularly being reborn. When westward the course of empire no longer took its way, Americans moved 'in' and went east to Paris in order to go west within the mind—a land like their own without time. . . . The human mind went on like the prairie, on and on without limit."

4. John Hyde Preston, "A Conversation with Gertrude Stein," in Brewster Ghiselin, *The Creative Process: A Symposium* (1956; Berkeley and Los Angeles: University of California Press, 1985), p. 166.

5. Stein discounts her sketch "Blood on the Dining-Room Floor": "Although I did it, I did not really do it." Gertrude Stein, *Everybody's Autobiography* (1937; New York: Random House, 1937), p. 85.

6. Stein, *Everybody's Autobiography*, p. 85.

7. Stein, *Everybody's Autobiography*, p. 175.

8. Paraphrased from Stein, *Geographical History*, p. 376.

9. Gertrude Stein, *Wars I Have Seen* (New York: Random House, 1945), p. 12.

10. Stein, *Everybody's Autobiography*, p. 115.

11. Stein, *Everybody's Autobiography*, p. 134.

12. Stein, *Wars I Have Seen*, p. 9.

13. Paraphrased from Stein, *Wars I Have Seen*, pp. 22, 24.

14. Stein, *Wars I Have Seen*, p. 21.

15. Gertrude Stein, *The Making of Americans: Being a History of a Family's Progress* (1925; Normal IL: Dalkey Archive Press, 1995), p. 47.

16. Stein, *Everybody's Autobiography*, p. 150.

17. Stein, *Everybody's Autobiography*, p. 133.

18. Stein, *Everybody's Autobiography*, p. 75.

19. Qtd. from Stein, *Wars I Have Seen*, p. 31.

20. Qtd. from Stein, *Wars I Have Seen*, p. 27.

21. Paraphrased from Stein, *Wars I Have Seen*, p. 25.

22. Stein, *Geographical History*, p. 452.

23. See Michael J. Hoffman, "Gertrude Stein in the Psychology Laboratory," *American Quarterly* 17, no. 1 (Spring 1965): 127–32, for a very clear description of Stein's early experiments and their relation to her work.

24. Stein, *Geographical History*, p. 452.

25. Stein, *Everybody's Autobiography*, p. 86.

26. Stein, *Everybody's Autobiography*, p. 70.

27. John Malcolm Brinnin, *The Third Rose: Gertrude Stein and Her World* (1959; New York: Grove Press, 1961), p. 19.

28. William James, *The Principles of Psychology*, 2 vols. (1890; New York: Henry Holt Co., 1950), 1:630, 635.

29. Stein, *Lectures in America*, in *Writings, 1932–1946*, pp. 293–94 (hereafter cited

as *Lectures in America*). "By a continuously moving picture of any one [in the cinema], there is no memory of any other thing and there is that thing existing, it is in a way if you like one portrait of anything not a number of them."

30. For the best description of her thinking on this side of her method, see her lecture "Portraits and Repetition," in *Lectures*.

31. See note 3 in this chapter.

32. Stein, *Everybody's Autobiography*, p. 223.

33. "As I can read any number of soothing novels in fact nothing else soothes me I found it not a thing that it was interesting to do" (Stein, *Lectures*, p. 297).

34. Stein, *Geographical History*, p. 424. This is stated less amusingly in her *Making of Americans*, pp. 440–41: "It is queer that words that meant something in our thinking and our feeling can later come to have in them in us not at all any meaning. . . . Often then I have to lose words I have once been using, now I commence again with words that have meaning."

35. Stein, *Making of Americans*, p. 33.

36. Qtd. in Richard Bridgman, *Gertrude Stein in Pieces* (New York: Oxford University Press, 1970), pp. 111–12.

37. Excerpt from "Gertrude Stein Talking—A Transatlantic Interview," UCLAN *Review*, Summer 1962, Spring 1963, Winter 1964, reprinted in Robert Bartlett Haas, ed., *A Primer for the Gradual Understanding of Gertrude Stein* (Santa Barbara CA: Black Sparrow Press, 1976), p. 30.

38. William Lundell, radio interview with Gertrude Stein, November 12, 1934, transcript printed in *Paris Review* 116 (Fall 1990): 95.

39. Paraphrased from Stein, *Everybody's Autobiography*, p. 280.

40. Stein, *Everybody's Autobiography*, pp. 5, 110.

41. Stein, "Portraits and Repetition," in *Lectures*, p. 306.

42. Stein, *Everybody's Autobiography*, pp. 282–83.

43. Excerpt from "Gertrude Stein Talking," in Haas, *Primer*, p. 31. Her answer: "Begin with a small audience. If that small audience really believes, they make a big noise, and a big audience does not make a noise at all."

44. Stein, *Everybody's Autobiography*, p. 284.

45. Stein, *Everybody's Autobiography*, p. 286.

46. Stein, *Everybody's Autobiography*, p. 286–87.

47. Stein, *Everybody's Autobiography*, p. 288.

48. *San Francisco Chronicle*, April 10, 1935.

49. Mellow, *Charmed Circle*, pp. 476–77.

50. Stein, *Everybody's Autobiography*, p. 281.

51. Stein, *Everybody's Autobiography*, p. 291.

52. Preston, "Conversation with Gertrude Stein," p. 166.

53. Stein, *Everybody's Autobiography*, p. 289.

54. Preston, "Conversation with Gertrude Stein," pp. 166–67.

55. Stein, *Everybody's Autobiography*, p. 298.

56. Stein, *Everybody's Autobiography*, pp. 297, 308.

57. For new information on Gertrude Stein in Vichy, and especially her relationship with the collaborator Bernard Faÿ, see Janet Malcolm, "Gertrude Stein's War," *New Yorker*, June 2, 2003.

58. Gertrude Stein, *Four Saints in Three Acts*, in *Gertrude Stein: Writings, 1903–1932*, selected and edited by Catharine R. Stimpson and Harriet Chessman (New York: Library of America, distributed by Penguin Putnam, 1998), p. 613.

59. Gertrude Stein, "Reflection on the Atomic Bomb," in *Writings, 1932–1946*, p. 823.

60. Mabel Dodge Luhan, *Intimate Memories*, 4 vols., vol. 2, *European Experiences* (New York: Harcourt, Brace & Co., 1935), p. 324.

61. "I had to find out what it was inside any one, and by any one I mean every one I had to find out inside every one what was in them that was intrinsically exciting and I had to find out not by what they said not by what they did not by how much or how little they resembled any other one but I had t find it out by the intensity of movement that there was inside in any one them." Gertrude Stein, "Portraits and Repetitions," qtd. in Renate Stendhal, ed., *Gertrude Stein in Words and Pictures* (Chapel Hill: University of North Carolina Press, 1994), p. 76.

62. Ernest Hemingway, "Indian Camp," in Ernest Hemingway, *The Nick Adams Stories* (New York: Charles Scribner's Sons, 1972), pp. 20–21.

63. Ernest Hemingway, "The Doctor and the Doctor's Wife," in *Nick Adams Stories*, p. 25.

64. Ernest Hemingway, "Fathers and Sons," in *Nick Adams Stories*, p. 266.

65. Prudence Boulton was the model for Trudy in "Fathers and Sons," and for the Indian girl who first breaks Nick Adams's heart in "Ten Indians."

66. Hemingway, "Fathers and Sons," pp. 266–67.

67. Ernest Hemingway, "The Last Good Country," in *Nick Adams Stories*, p. 119.

68. Ernest Hemingway, *True at First Light*, ed. with introduction by Patrick Hemingway (New York: Simon & Schuster, 1999), p. 25.

69. Ernest Hemingway, *Green Hills of Africa* (New York: Charles Scribner's Sons, 1935), p. 72.

70. Hemingway, *Green Hills of Africa*, p. 72.

71. Hemingway, *True at First Light*, p. 191.

72. Hemingway, *True at First Light*, p. 189.

73. Raymond Chandler, *Playback* (1958), in *Later Novels and Other Writings* (New York: Library of America, distributed by Penguin Books, 1995), p. 759.

74. Paraphrased from Raymond Chandler, *The Big Sleep* (1939), in *Stories and Early Novels* (New York: Library of America, distributed by Penguin Books, 1995), pp. 717–18.

75. Paraphrased from Chandler, *Playback*, pp. 834–36.

76. Paraphrased from Chandler's unfinished "Poodle Springs Story," in *Raymond*

Chandler Speaking, ed. Dorothy Gardiner and Kathrine Sorley Walker (London: Allison & Busby, 1984), p. 255.

77. Raymond Chandler, *The Little Sister*, in *Later Novels*, p. 357.

78. The detective story, as far back as Oedipus, is preeminently a city genre. See the description of the "haggard" office in which Colt shot Adams in Melville's great story of the city, "Bartleby, the Scrivener" (1853), for a room similar in its atmosphere to Chandler's and Atget's rooms.

79. "Diddling Considered as One of the Exact Sciences" (1843), in Stuart and Susan Levine, eds., *The Short Fiction of Edgar Allan Poe* (Urbana: University of Illinois Press, 1976), p. 523.

80. Paraphrased from Raymond Chandler, *The Long Goodbye*, in *Later Novels*, p. 625.

81. Chandler, *Long Goodbye*, p. 459.

82. Frank MacShane, *The Life of Raymond Chandler* (New York: E. P. Dutton & Co., 1978), pp. 37–38.

83. Norman M. Klein, *The History of Forgetting: Los Angeles and the Erasure of Memory* (London: Verso, 1997), p. 1: "And yet the clues are still there. Two tunnels exit from downtown, but there is no hill above them, as if a large bird has flown away with it. Numerous lots west along Sunset Boulevard have steps on to what clearly used to be a house. Creaky Victorian cottages are stranded along streets just south of Sunset, cut short by a roaring freeway."

84. Chandler, *Playback*, p. 820.

85. Tocqueville, *Democracy in America*, 2:99.

86. Chandler, *Playback*, p. 797.

87. Chandler, *Playback*, p. 799.

88. Chandler, *Long Goodbye*, p. 563.

89. Chandler, *Big Sleep*, p. 708.

90. Chandler, *Farewell, My Lovely*, p. 801.

91. This conflation of communists and homosexuals in Los Angeles is the subject of an excellent paper by Daniel Hurewitz, "Pink, Red, and Long-Haired Enemies: Politicized Sexual Morality in 1930s Los Angeles," given at the October 2000 meeting of the Western History Association in San Antonio, Texas. See Daniel Hurewitz, *Bohemian Los Angeles and the Making of Modern Politics* (Berkeley and Los Angeles: University of California Press, 2007).

92. Chandler, *Long Goodbye*, pp. 625–26.

93. The last name, given Chandler's homophobia, is interesting: the Wilde with whom the English schoolboy with literary aspirations would have been most familiar would have been, of course, the queer and aesthete Oscar Fingal O'Flahertie Wills Wilde.

94. Chandler, *Big Sleep*, p. 667.

95. Chandler, *Little Sister*, pp. 357–58, 268.

96. See Mike Davis, *City of Quartz* (1990; New York: Vintage Books / Random House, 1992) pp. 104–5.

97. Chandler, *The High Window*, in *Stories and Early Novels*, p. 1093.

5. SUBLIME AMERICA

Epigraph: "The only time I heard him use the word 'landscape' in connection with his own work was one morning before going to the studio, when he said 'I saw a landscape the likes of which no human being could have seen.'" Lee Krasner, in *Jackson Pollock: Interviews, Articles, and Reviews*, ed. Pepe Karmel (New York: Museum of Modern Art / Harry N. Abrams, 1999), p. 37.

1. It would be interesting to see Eakins's choice of this subject as his attempt to correct the lubricities of his teacher the academician Gérôme's versions of the myth of Pygmalion.

2. Ralph Waldo Emerson, "An Address to the Senior Class in Divinity College, Cambridge, July 15, 1838," in Ralph Waldo Emerson, *Essays and Lectures* (New York: Library of America, distributed by Penguin Putnam, 1983), p. 84.

3. Ralph Waldo Emerson, "Nature," in *Essays and Lectures*, p. 10.

4. Thomas Cole, "Essay on American Scenery," *American Monthly Magazine* 1 (January 1836): 1–12. Reprinted in Thomas Cole, *The Collected Essays and Prose Sketches*, ed. Marshall Tymn, John Colet Archive of American Literature, 1620–1920, no. 7 (St. Paul MN: John Colet Press, 1980), p. 17.

5. "Lecture on American Scenery: Delivered before the Catskill Lyceum, April 1, 1841," originally published in *Northern Light* 1 (May 1841): 25–26. Reprinted in Cole, *Collected Essays*, p. 211.

6. Ruskin to Charles Eliot Norton, December 28, 1856, in *The Works of John Ruskin*, ed. E. T. Cook and Alexander Wedderburn, D.O., vol. 36, *The Letters of John Ruskin, 1827–1869* (London: G. Allen, 1909), 1:251.

7. Thomas Cole, "Essay on American Scenery," in Cole, *Collected Essays*, p. 16.

8. Francis J. Grund, *The Americans in their Moral, Social, and Political Relations*, 2 vols. (London, 1837), 2:65.

9. Grund, *Americans*, 1:266.

10. Henry David Thoreau, *A Year in Thoreau's Journal: 1851*, ed. H. Daniel Peck (New York: Penguin Books, 1993), p. 25. Samuel Staples arrested Thoreau in 1846 for not paying his poll tax as a protest against the Mexican War and what he saw as Massachusetts's complicity in slavery. Samuel Hoar was a U.S. congressman and Concord's leading citizen. On September 6 Thoreau was surprised to see the congressman walking on the short stretch of railroad between the depot and the back road. "He could do nothing that was not sanctioned by the longest use of men—and as men had voted in all their assemblies from the first to travel on the Public way—

he would confine himself to that—It would no doubt seem to him very improper—
not to say undignified to walk on the railroad—& then is it not forbidden by the
Rail-road corporations?" (*Thoreau's Journal:* 1851, p. 202).

11. Entry for July 16, 1851, *Thoreau's Journal,* p. 110.

12. Entry for June 11, 1851, *Thoreau's Journal,* p. 65.

13. Entry for June 13, 1851, *Thoreau's Journal,* p. 75.

14. Robert D. Richardson Jr., *Henry Thoreau: A Life of the Mind* (Berkeley and Los
Angeles: University of California Press, 1986), p. 279.

15. Entry for September 21, 1851, *Thoreau's Journal,* p. 229.

16. Entry for September 9, 1851, *Thoreau's Journal,* p. 214.

17. Steven Naifeh and Gregory White Smith, *Jackson Pollock: An American Saga*
(1989; New York: Harper Perennial, 1991), p. 456.

18. William Rubin, "Pollock as Jungian Illustrator: The Limits of Psychological
Criticism," *Art in America* (November and December 1979); reprinted in *Jackson
Pollock: Interviews, Articles, and Reviews,* p. 256. "The much-discussed central rectangle [of *Guardians of the Secret*]—though perhaps alluding to a casket, bed, altar,
table, or treasury, as different critics (myself included) have suggested—is without
question *a picture-within-a-picture*. We might title it with Pollock's own words: *The
Unconscious As The Source Of Art.*"

19. Qtd. by Rubin in "Pollock as Jungian Illustrator," p. 237.

20. Naifeh and Smith, *Jackson Pollock,* p. 532.

21. Siqueiros, with whom Pollock had worked, had indulged in such experiments,
as had Hans Hofmann and some of the Surrealists with whose work Pollock was
familiar before his first poured paintings. And, of course, critics and artists have
suggested other names.

22. Naifeh and Smith, *Jackson Pollock,* p. 385.

23. There are a number of versions of this incident. See, for example, Naifeh and
Smith, *Jackson Pollock,* p. 486. In their retelling, Hofmann responds, "Ah, but if you
work from inside you will repeat yourself." But why there is any more danger of
repeating yourself by working from inside than from "outside" in Hofmann's view
is unstated. Also see Jeffrey Potter, *To a Violent Grave: An Oral Biography of Jackson
Pollock* (New York: G. P. Putnam's Sons, 1985), p. 77.

24. Describing the effect of some of these paintings hung for a show at Betty
Parsons's gallery in 1950, Lee Krasner says, "It was more than an exhibition, it was
an environment" (qtd. in Naifeh and Smith, *Jackson Pollock,* p. 654).

25. Claude Cernuschi, *Jackson Pollock: Meaning and Significance* (New York:
HarperCollins, 1992), p. 135.

26. Hemingway, *Green Hills of Africa,* pp. 149–50.

27. It is interesting how Pollock, the least verbally analytical of all painters, comes
by different routes to solutions arrived at by the cerebral Duchamp, who had left
his "large glass" *The Bride Stripped Bare by Her Bachelors, Even* definitively unfin-

ished in 1923. These two artists, so very different in temperament and approach, are almost Doppelgängers.

28. Thoreau, qtd. in Richardson, *Henry Thoreau*, p. 380: "We can never begin to see anything as it is so long as we remember the scientific term which always our ignorance has imposed on us. Natural objects and phenomena are in this sense forever wild and unnamed by us."

29. Pollock: "My painting is direct . . . I want to express my feelings rather than illustrate them." From the narration by Pollock for the 1951 film *Jackson Pollock* by Hans Namuth. Reproduced in Herschel B. Chipp, with Peter Selz and Joshua C. Taylor, *Theories of Modern Art: A Source Book by Artists and Critics* (Berkeley and Los Angeles: University of California Press, 1968), p. 548.

30. Immanuel Kant, *Critique of Judgment* (1790), trans. Werner S. Pluhar (Indianapolis: Hackett Publishing Co., 1987), p. 185 n.

31. Kant, *Critique of Judgment*, p. 129.

32. Longinus (if the author of the fragments published under his name was Longinus), who is the first recorded critic to study the Sublime, saw his subject as in a large part an issue of rhetoric.

33. Qtd. in Richard J. Schneider, *Henry David Thoreau* (Boston: Twayne Publishers, 1987), p. 112.

34. "Whether he wakes or sleeps, whether he runs or walks, whether he uses a microscope or a telescope, or his naked eye, a man never discovers anything or leaves anything behind, but himself. Whatever he does or says he merely reports himself" (Thoreau, qtd. in Richardson, *Henry Thoreau*, p. 382).

35. It is interesting to speculate on whether it was this picture, by an artist whose "retinal" painting gave him the shudders, that Duchamp is parodying and playing philosophical variations on in his peepshow *Étant donnés*.

36. Naifeh and Smith, *Jackson Pollock*, p. 731.

6. LONESOME AMERICA

Epigraph: Woody Guthrie, qtd. in Mark Zwonitzer, with Charles Hirshberg, *Will You Miss Me When I'm Gone? The Carter Family and Their Legacy in American Music* (New York: Simon & Schuster, 2002), p. 137.

1. From Tocqueville's manuscript "Quinze jours au désert," reprinted and translated by George Wilson Pierson in his *Tocqueville in America* (1938; Baltimore: Johns Hopkins University Press, 1996), p. 264.

2. Pierson, *Tocqueville in America*, p. 244.

3. Pierson, *Tocquville in America*, pp. 278–79.

4. Charles Dickens, *American Notes for General Circulation* (1842; London: Penguin Group, 1985), pp. 204–5.

5. Fanny Trollope, *The Domestic Manners of the Americans*, ed. with an introduction and notes by Pamela Neville-Sington (1832; London: Penguin Group, 1997), pp. 126-29.

6. Peter Cartwright, *Autobiography of Peter Cartwright* (1856; Nashville: Abingdon Press, 1956), p. 45.

7. Trollope, *Domestic Manners of the Americans*, p. 131.

8. See for example *Traditional Fiddle Music of Kentucky, vol. 1: Up the Ohio and Licking Rivers*, Rounder CD 0376 (Cambridge MA: Rounder Records Corp., 1997).

9. Harold Bloom, *The American Religion: The Emergence of the Post-Christian Nation* (New York: Simon & Schuster, 1992), p. 32.

10. For the derivative nature of cowboy songs see Douglas J. McReynolds, "European Legends and American Cowboy Ballads," *Colorado Magazine* 56, nos. 3–4 (Summer–Fall 1979).

11. Ralph J. Gleason, "Perspectives: Hank Williams, Roy Acuff and Then God," *Rolling Stone*, June 28, 1969, p. 32.

12. E. C. "Teddy Blue" Abbott and Helena Huntington Smith, *We Pointed Them North: Recollections of a Cowpuncher* (1939; Norman: University of Oklahoma Press, 1955), pp. 111–13.

13. Abbott and Smith, *We Pointed Them North*, pp. 136–37.

14. The Virginian sings what is obviously one of these minstrel-show songs about a "Carolina Nigger," presumably amusing to Wister's audience in 1902.

15. McReynolds, "European Legends and American Cowboy Ballads," pp. 196–208. McReynolds claims that "not more than perhaps a dozen of the 153 ballads in John A. Lomax's 1910 *Cowboy Songs* could possibly be the result of spontaneous, communal composition" (p. 200).

16. Add's popularity is attested by the following story. When late in life Add decided to get married, word got out to the surrounding ranches in the Pecos Valley. But since the ranches were far apart, and communications difficult, no one knew what anyone else was sending as a wedding gift. On their wedding day, Add and his wife went to the Roswell, New Mexico, freight depot, where they'd been told their gifts were waiting for them. When they got there, they found *nineteen* cookstoves. N. Howard (Jack) Thorp, in collaboration with Neil M. Clark, *Pardner of the Wind* (Caldwell ID: Caxton Printers, 1945), p. 285n. Thorp made Add the hero of his song "Whose Old Cow?"

17. Thorp, *Pardner of the Wind*, pp. 21–24. A slightly abbreviated version of the chapter from which this incident is taken appeared as "Banjo in the Cow Camps," *Atlantic Monthly*, August 1940, pp. 195–203. This article is reprinted in N. Howard "Jack" Thorp, *Songs of the Cowboys*, with variants, commentary, notes, and lexicon by Austin E. and Alta S. Fife (1908; New York: Clarkson N. Potter, 1966).

18. Thorp, *Songs of the Cowboys*, preface, unpaged. Reproduced in the Fife edition.

19. John A. Lomax, *Cowboy Songs and Other Frontier Ballads* (New York: Sturgis & Walton Co., 1910), pp. xxii–xxiii. In his autobiography, Lomax shows that cowboys too could imagine themselves as knights, and gives an account of horseback "toonaments" where cowboys given sobriquets such as "The Knight of the Lost Cause" or "The Knight of the Slim Chance," riding full-tilt, speared rings with lances before admiring fellow cowboys, farmers, and the girl chosen as the Queen of the Jousts. John A. Lomax, *Adventures of a Ballad Hunter* (New York: Macmillan Co., 1947), pp. 15–17. See also Richard Hutson, "Ecce Cowboy: E. C. Abbott's *We Pointed Them North,*" *Western American Literature* 37, no. 2 (Summer 2002): 258. Hutson sees Abbott parodying "certain Victorian pretensions, such as the medievalism of chivalry" in the episode of Cattle Annie's bloomers.

20. Owen Wister, *The Virginian: A Horseman of the Plains* (1902; Lincoln: University of Nebraska Press, 1992), p. 37.

21. So embedded in myth was the cowboy that in one of those strange oddities of chronology, Stephen Crane could parody the Virginian's showdown with the arch-villain Trampas on the streets of Medicine Bow five years before Owen Wister's novel containing it appeared. Someone asked an old-time puncher if the cowboys actually talked the way Owen Wister said they did. "Well, maybe we didn't talk that way before Mr. Wister wrote his book, but we sure all talked that way after the book was published." Don Russell, *The Lives and Legends of Buffalo Bill* (Norman: University of Oklahoma Press, 1960), p. 256.

22. *Chicago Tribune*, April 18, 1915. Qtd. in Michael Yates, "Cecil Sharp in America: Collecting in the Appalachians," *Musical Traditions*, http://www.mustrad.org.uk/articles/sharp.htm, Article MT052.

23. Kittredge's note on Francis James Child in vol. 1 of Child's monumental *The English and Scottish Popular Ballads, in Five Volumes* (1882; New York: Dover Publications, 1965), 1:xxviii.

24. Incidents in Cecil Sharp's folk song–collecting trips in Appalachia are drawn from Yates, "Cecil Sharp in America," and chapters 12 and 13 in A. H. Fox Strangways, in collaboration with Maud Karpeles, *Cecil Sharp* (London: Oxford University Press, 1933), pp. 142–77. These chapters were written by Maud Karpeles.

25. Sharp found it a truism that dirt and good music were the usual bedfellows. "The fact is, philanthropy and art have nothing in common, and to unite them spells disaster" (Strangways, *Cecil Sharp*, p. 92).

26. D. K. Wilgus, *Anglo-American Folksong Scholarship since 1898* (New Brunswick NJ: Rutgers University Press, 1959), p. 171.

27. Yates, "Cecil Sharp in America."

28. Anthony Harkins, *Hillbilly: A Cultural History of an American Icon* (New York: Oxford University Press, 2004), pp. 4–5, 13.

29. See Archie Green, "Hillbilly Music: Source and Symbol," *Journal of American Folklore* 78, no. 309 (July–September 1965): 213–14. On the adoption of the ersatz cow-

boy uniform see D. K. Wilgus, "Country-Western Music and the Urban Hillbilly," in Américo Paredes and Ellen J. Stekert, eds., *The Urban Experience and Folk Tradition* (Austin: University of Texas Press, 1971), p. 146.

30. D. K. Wilgus, "An Introduction to the Study of Hillbilly Music," *Journal of American Folklore* 78, no. 309 (July–September 1965): 197.

31. W. J. Cash, *The Mind of the South* (1941; New York: Vintage Books, 1991), p. 289.

32. Nolan Porterfield, *Jimmie Rodgers: The Life and Times of America's Blue Yodeler* (Urbana: University of Illinois Press, 1979), p. 141.

33. For "Frankie and Johnny" AKA "Frankie and Albert," see Cecil Brown, "We Did Them Wrong: The Ballad of Frankie and Albert," in Sean Wilentz and Greil Marcus, eds., *The Rose and The Briar: Death, Love and Liberty in the American Ballad* (New York: W. W. Norton, 2005).

34. Porterfield, *Jimmie Rodgers*, p. 279.

35. Colin Escott, with George Merritt and William MacEwen, *Hank Williams: The Biography* (Boston: Little, Brown & Co., 1994), p. 4.

36. Bill Koon, *Hank Williams, So Lonesome* (1983; Jackson: University of Mississippi Press, 2001), p. 9.

37. Koon, *So Lonesome*, p. 16.

38. Escott and Florita, quoting an interview of Audrey Williams by Dorothy Horstman in 1973. Colin Escott and Kira Florita, *Hank Williams: Snapshots from the Lost Highways* (Cambridge MA: DaCapo Press, 2001), p. 46.

39. Escott, *Biography*, pp. 62–63.

40. Escott, *Biography*, p. 55.

41. W. E. B. Du Bois, *The Souls of Black Folk* (1903), in W. E. B. Du Bois, *Writings* (New York: Library of America, 1986; distributed by Viking Press), pp. 439–41, 457–58, 488, 490, 501–5. David R. Roediger, in *The Wages of Whiteness: Race and the Making of the American Working Class*, rev. ed. (London: Verso, 1999), p. 12, quotes from Du Bois's *Black Reconstruction in the United States, 1860–1880*: even when white workers "received a low wage [they were] compensated in part by a . . . public and psychological wage." That compensation, racial privilege, is the theme of Roediger's book.

42. Roger M. Williams, *Sing a Sad Song: The Life of Hank Williams*, 2nd ed. (Urbana: University of Illinois Press, 1981), pp. 4, 29.

43. John Dollard, *Caste and Class in a Southern Town* (New Haven CT: Yale University Press, 1937). The town Dollard studied was Indianola, Mississippi. His language of racial loss and gain parallels Du Bois.

44. Roediger, *Wages of Whiteness*, p. 5. The workers he was describing were males, as Roediger pointed out in his afterword to the revised edition.

45. Bill C. Malone, *Don't Get Above Your Raisin': Country Music and the Southern Working Class* (Urbana: University of Illinois Press, 2002), p. 15.

46. One might profitably compare Greek *rembetika*, Argentine tango, and country

western music for this strange blend of abject lyrics and mixed musical message. For the tango, see Fernando D. Astigueta, "Tango and Its Meaning for a Culture," *Journal of the American Academy of Psychoanalysis* 28, no. 3 (Fall 2000): 483–500.

47. "The most flamboyant country music . . . often functions as a sly, even campy, announcement of the fact that it is a *performance* rather than a spontaneous expression of some pure emotion or state of being. In other words, country music is capable of performing the rural role in such a way as to underline its construction and social purpose rather than its presumed natural essence, innocence, and/or bad taste." Barbara Ching, "Acting Naturally: Cultural Distinction and Critiques of Pure Country," in Matt Wray and Annalee Newitz, eds., *White Trash: Race and Class in America* (New York: Routledge, 1997), p. 233.

48. Zwonitzer and Hirshberg, *Will You Miss Me When I'm Gone?* pp. 83–84, 176, 183.

49. From *How to Write Folk and Western Music to Sell* by Hank Williams and Jimmy Rule, qtd. in Roger M. Williams, *Sing a Sad Song*, p. 113.

50. See D. K. Wilgus, "Country Western Music and the Urban Hillbilly," p. 142, on the smoothing out of regional styles by record companies hoping to maximize sales. The impulse toward repression may have been there from the start. When he looked at the American versions of those powerful ballads Francis Child had collected, the scholar Stanley Edgar Hyman found only "inadequate narrative, aborted drama, happy-ending tragedy, corrupt and meaningless verbiage and bad poetry in general." Perhaps it was the degeneration of the ballads over time, in their transmission. But for Hyman some of it, certainly, was the effect of the American ethos itself, with its "denial of death, its resistance to the tragic experience, its deep repression of sexuality, its overriding pieties, and its frantic emphasis on the rationalistic, the inconsequential, and the optimistic." It almost seemed that they—the American ballad texts—"are bad precisely to the degree that they have become successfully American." Stanley Edgar Hyman, "The Child Ballad in America: Some Aesthetic Criteria," *Journal of American Folklore* 70, no. 277 (July–September 1957): 239. Hyman, of course, was thinking of a white American ethos and was not examining the unrepressed expressions of love and death and the tragic in black ballads and blues.

51. Minnie Pearl, qtd. in Escott, *Biography*, p. 181.

52. Ralph Gleason interviewed Hank Williams for the *San Francisco Chronicle* in April 1952 (article published June 1, 1952, p. 29). In 1969 he remembered the interview and going out to see Williams play. See note 11 in this chapter.

53. Unidentified newspaper headline reproduced in Escott and Florita, *Snapshots*, p. 89.

54. Hank Williams Jr., describing his mother as she was when she met his father (Koon, *So Lonesome*, p. 21).

55. Roger M. Williams, *Sing a Sad Song*, p. 164.

56. Escott and Florita, *Snapshots*, p. 123. Photo of MS titled "It Works One Way

or the Other." The lines are used in "You're Gonna Change (or I'm Gonna Leave)" where the happy woman is bawled out at night.

57. Escott, *Biography*, p. 141.

58. Escott, *Biography*, p. 193.

59. James N. Gregory, *American Exodus: The Dust Bowl Migration and Okie Culture in California* (New York: Oxford University Press, 1989), p. 132.

60. Dorothea Lange, *Photographing the Second Gold Rush: Dorothea Lange and the East Bay at War,* 1941–1945, introduction by Charles Wollenberg (Berkeley: Heyday Books, 1995).

61. Roxanne Dunbar-Ortiz, *Red Dirt: Growing Up Okie* (London: Verso, 1997), pp. 71–72.

62. Dunbar-Ortiz, Red Dirt, p. 72.

63. Bill C. Malone, *Country Music, U.S.A.*, rev. ed. (Austin: University of Texas Press, 1985), pp. 129–35. The exception to the sporadic quality of country music protest is, of course, Woody Guthrie, but if Guthrie started from boomtown Oklahoma and musical hillbilly roots, he ended up moving with the urban left, and his songs today, with the exception of a few largely sanitized classics that have made their way into public school songfests, are largely kept alive by left-wing college students and unionists. When Alessandro Portelli went into Harlan County, Kentucky, whose bitter strikes were still remembered and sung about, he found that the same injustices that had solidified Italian industrial workers and impelled their militancy were seen by American coal miners as sources of personal humiliation and shame. See Alessandro Portelli, *The Death of Luigi Trastulli and Other Stories: Form and Meaning in Oral History* (Albany: SUNY Press, 1991), p. 202.

64. *Songs from the Hills* was a flop, but ten years later, in 1956, Tennessee Ernie Ford disguised the wry anger of the album's other great coal camp song with a novelty bounce and pushed "Sixteen Tons" up to the Hit Parade. Ralph Gleason noted that a year or two earlier, Tennessee Ernie's version probably wouldn't have gotten enough airplay to make it a hit: Senator Joe McCarthy, he said, "might not appreciate the general tenor of the song." As one of Merle Travis's friends remarked, we all owed most of our money to some sort of company store (Green, *Only a Miner*, p. 306–7).

65. Gregory, *American Exodus*, p. 241.

66. Zwonitzer and Hirshberg, *Will You Miss Me When I'm Gone?* p. 308.

67. Larry Gatlin, "All the Gold in California," 1979.

Index

215

immigrants, 72
Indian mounds, 145
Indians: Hemingway and, 116–19, 121–23; Jefferson and, 6–7; and Mexicans, 167; Tocqueville's views on, 13–15; and Turner, 69–70; and Worlds Columbian Exposition, 71–72. *See also specific tribes*
Irving, Washington, 14
"I Saw the Light" (Williams), 182
isolation, 178–81. *See also* solitude

Jackson, Andrew, 69, 192n28
Jackson Park, Chicago, 65, 66, 90
"Jambalaya" (Williams), 182
James, Henry, 44, 48, 49, 58–59, 86
James, William, 20, 104–7, 117
Janey. *See* Sacagawea
Janin, Henry, 27, 29, 30, 194n4
Jefferson, Thomas: history of administration of, 58, 70; letter to Cherokees from, 8; during Mexican war, 16; prediction of war by, 18; and Virginia's natural bridge, 191n6; vision of America of, 5–7, 133, 182
"the jerks," 162
Jews, 80–82, 115
Johnson, Emma, 87
Joyce, James, 109

kaïmos, 22
Kant, Immanuel, 153, 154
Karpeles, Maud, 168–70
Kaweah (King's horse), 46
"Kaw-Liga" (Williams), 179
Kettle Hill, Cuba, 80
Kilimanjaro, Mt., 124–25
Kimball, Nell, 87–90, 94–95
Kinetoscope, 65, 102
King, Clarence: on Adams, 40–41, 44, 46–49, 63–64, 78–79; arrest of, 78; background of, 27–28; childhood of, 31–33, 44; and Church St. house, 31, 45, 195n6; death of, 79, 82; effect on others by, 48–49; financial crisis of, 54–55; inner geology of, 41–51; marriage of, 47–48, 50, 197n47; at Mount Bullion, 34–35; at Mount Tyndall, 36–37; on "neo-Pullmanic" décor, 88; prospecting of, 28–31, 59; and relationships with women, 40, 44–48, 50, 59; sense of loss and failure of, 20, 21; travels of, 33–34,

38–39, 78–79; and view of geology, 195n18; voice of, 18, 19; at Worlds Columbian Exposition, 78
King, James, 32
King, Leroy, 47
Kings River gorge, 35
Kittredge, George Lyman, 166, 168–70
Klein, Norman, 132
Krasner, Lee, 149, 156, 206n24
Krebs (character in "Soldier's Home"), 120
Krupps Pavilion, 72, 75

Lacan, Jacques, 155
La Farge, John, 50, 60, 63
La Garde, ——, surgeon, 73
Lamar, Sen. Lucius Q.C., 59
Lamothe, Ferdinand. *See* Morton, Jelly Roll
landscape: American, 143–46; feminine, 15; gold rush and, 42; mourning of passing, 144; Pollock on, 149–53, 205n; Stein on, 99–100; vastness of, 37–41
Lange, Dorothea, 158, 182–83, 189
language, 107–10, 113, 118, 153
Lassen's Butte, 33
'Lasses (cowboy), 166
Lee, Robert E., 36
Lewis, Meriwether, 2–9, 11
Littless (Hemingway character), 122–23
Locksley Hall (Tennyson), 46
Lomax, John, 166–68, 208n15, 209n19
loneliness, 178–81. *See also* solitude
The Long Goodbye (Chandler), 135
Longinus, 207n32
Lorrain, Claude, 15
Los Angeles, 129–33, 136–37
loss, 19–22, 137, 144. *See also* absence
Louvin, Ira, 185
"Lovesick Blues" (Friend and Mills), 176–77
Luke the Drifter, 180
Lundy's Lane, battle of, 17
Lyell Sir Charles, 55

Maddox, Rose, 177
Madison, James, 58, 70
The Making of Americans (Stein), 105–8
Mandan Indians, 2, 11–12
Manet, Edouard, 63
Manila Bay, 80
Marlowe, Philip (character), 130–38
Mars, Eddie (character), 136

217

Lightning Source UK Ltd.
Milton Keynes UK
UKHW011428061022
410021UK00007B/227/J